EVERY WOMAN'S SEXUAL PROFILE IS DIFFERENT. WHICH ONE ARE YOU? FINDING OUT IS THE FIRST STEP IN AN EXPLOSIVE EROTIC ODYSSEY.

Early Bloomer

You're interested in sex at an early age, and probably easily orgasmic. What makes you different from other women?

Wildflower

You act out sexually, from psychological, rather than physical, need. Why do you have sexual experiences that usually don't give you pleasure?

Perfect Bud

You fit the "tight bud" theory of slowly developing female sexuality, and are orgasmic by your early twenties. Why are you considered the norm?

Late Bloomer

You won't experience orgasm until your late twenties or later. Why has it taken you so long to discover pleasure?

*St. Martin's Paperbacks Titles
by Susan Crain Bakos*

WHAT MEN REALLY WANT
SEXUAL PLEASURES

Sexual

PLEASURES

*What Women
Really Want,
What Women
Really Need*

SUSAN CRAIN BAKOS

ST. MARTIN'S PAPERBACKS

SEXUAL PLEASURES: WHAT WOMEN REALLY WANT, WHAT WOMEN REALLY NEED

Copyright © 1992 by Susan Crain Bakos.

Cover photograph by Herman Estevez.

Library of Congress Catalog Card Number: 91-36182

ISBN: 0-312-92847-5

Printed in the United States of America

St. Martin's Press hardcover edition/February 1992
St. Martin's Paperbacks edition/September 1992

10 9 8 7 6 5 4 3 2 1

For the Kaplan family—
Alex, Marilyn, Robert, Linda, Jack, Carol, Mel Pine.
And, in memory of Fanny Pine.

Acknowledgments

Thanks to the following people for their contributions:

—My agent, Nancy Love;

—My editors, Toni Lopopolo, Michael Sagalyn, and Ed Stackler;

—My ever-reliable and resourceful research assistants, Richard Bakos and Tamm Koerkenmeier—with special thanks to Tamm, who also conducted in-depth interviews of her twenty something-generation peers;

—Mel Pine and Al Freedman, who read and critiqued the initial draft;

—All my friends who now know more about women's orgasms than they were never afraid to ask—especially, Jack Heidenry, who is always there for me.

—The women who participated in my survey, especially those who consented to personal interviews.

Contents

Part 5: Women Who Have Lost Pleasure— And How They Regained It

Part 6: Reclaiming Pleasure

Preface: The Tyranny of the "Ifs"

ALMOST TWO YEARS ago I was listening to a group of my women friends talk about sex during lunch. These women were comparing the size and stamina of men they had known. (Yes, we're talking penis size and duration of erection, subjects men secretly fear we discuss. We do.) And, they were exchanging "most embarrassing sex stories," for example, the time one woman's period started during the initial encounter with a married lover in an expensive hotel room. Afterward, she told us, he pulled away from her, each of them streaked, smeared, and splotched with her menstrual blood, surveyed the damage to sheets, spread, and pillows, and said, "It looks like we've been sacrificing small animals in here," whereupon she began stripping the bed in preparation for soaking everything in a tubful of cold water to spare the maid the sight.

Can you imagine the man involved ever sharing *that* story with a group of his men friends over lunch?

Women talk more openly about sex to each other than men do, but there is still much we rarely share. I could tell you whose lover within that group has the biggest penis (assuming, of course, the data shared is reliable), or how many times a week each woman typically has sexual relations or when, where, and how each lost her virginity—but, I don't know how long it takes them to reach orgasm or if, like the majority of women, they need oral or manual stimulation to do so, or if in fact they often have trouble reaching orgasm or maybe never do. The subject of endless discussion, written and verbal, the *orgasm* still remains shrouded in secrecy. Modern women may brag about having multiple orgasms—which perhaps they have never even had but claim to have experienced because their competitive machisma side demands the boast—yet be too embarrassed to admit they need to stroke the clitoris during intercourse to come at all.

The wall of silence we build around certain essential sexual truths exacerbates our vulnerability to the myths about how a woman "should" behave sexually. The less we know about the reality of female sexuality—other women's and our own—the more readily we accept fantasy as a form of sexual theology. I call a group of those myths under which we have lived too much of our lives the "ifs." The ifs are found in the clause following, "It's okay to enjoy sex *if* . . ." and they include: . . . he loves me; he might marry me; he's a suitable partner in the eyes of the world; we're going to make a baby. But the primary *if*, which cuts across all lines is, *if I'm swept away by romantic feeling.*

That big *if* excuses us from accepting full responsibility for our own sexual behavior, which is exactly why it appeals to us. We don't have to admit to choosing sex, if by choosing we violate the teachings of church and mother or ignore the social prohibitions against certain kinds of sexual behavior. Like a romance novel heroine, we can claim we were carried beyond our boundaries by a force we couldn't control—an acceptable explanation for female passion, which, too many of us still believe, *shouldn't* be under our control.

Unfortunately, those who do not choose wait to be chosen—and wait to have their needs acknowledged and magically met by the ones who do choose. Men.

I wanted to write this book to carry the sexual conversation women have with each other deeper and further than it ever goes inside the padded booths of restaurants. Also, on a personal level, I wanted to make sense of my own sexual past, to put into perspective a history that has never quite been in sync with the behavioral "norms" of the day. And, I wanted to reach truth, not only my truth, but your truth and every woman's truth, the bedrock of sexual reality where what actually happens is more beautiful than the fantasy of what seldom, if ever, does. In finding that truth, we can help dispel the ifs, the prettily wrapped package of romantic nonsense that has led us all, men and women, to put too much pressure on the penis and on "love." These pressures keep intercourse from working for women as it does for men: as the primary method of achieving orgasm.

I started with the idea of tracing woman's sexual evolution, through the histories of many women, to find a pattern that would help all of us understand our own sexual cycle. When I began talking to women about their sex lives, I envisioned writing a book that was a version of *Passages*, as applied to female sexuality. I thought the stages of a woman's sexual evolution would follow a predictable pattern, roughly corresponding to the decades of her life, from the sexual awakening of her late teens through the post-menopause years. I also thought younger women in their twenties would be sexually freer than their mothers had been at their ages.

The 871 women I surveyed left me with a different picture of that evolution—and certainly of the reality behind the so-called sexual liberation of women.

Yes, there are stages. But, many women don't experience all of them. One woman may never evolve past stage one, while another may have run the gamut by age thirty. For men, becoming sexually active and reaching orgasm are virtually always synonymous, but not for women. A woman may have sexual relations with one or many men for five, ten, twenty, or more years without ever reaching orgasm—leaving her rooted in stage one, no matter her age or number of partners.

I found the women in this book by placing ads in city magazines nationwide, through friends who distributed questionnaires among their friends and professional associates, and within the International Women's Writing Guild, of which I am a member. Therefore my survey respondents, while they represent all parts of the country and also include some women from Canada and American expatriates living in Europe and South America, are:

- *More likely to live in major metropolitan areas than in small towns or rural areas*—57 percent are urbanites—particularly in the cities of the Northeast (31 percent).

- *More affluent and better educated* than the general populace—70 percent have personal or family incomes in excess of $25,000 and 62 percent are college graduates.

- *More likely than not to have white collar jobs* when employed—slightly over two-thirds hold management level positions or are members of professions such as law; medicine, including nursing; or teaching. There are also more writers, journalists, editors, and other communications specialists (a total of 19 percent) than the respondents of purely random surveys (which, by the way, are such cost-prohibitive undertakings that even the Kinsey Institute can't afford to do them anymore).

- *Predominantly thirtysomething:* While the ages of survey respondents ranged from eighteen to eighty-nine, the majority were in their twenties (26.6 percent), thirties (39.6 percent), or forties (19.3 percent).

- *More familiar with the married state than not*: 34.2 percent married, 18.9 percent divorced, 32.5 percent single, and 14.4 percent living with a man.

The survey results included many surprises. For example, while there have been enormous social changes affecting female sexual behavior in the past thirty years, young women are perhaps no more free sexually than were their mothers. The language of constraint may be different, but the message is the same: Hold out for love.

On the other hand, the participants reported a wide range of sexual behaviors and, in many cases, a great variety of partners, with the numbers ranging from one to four thousand. More than one third have experienced anal sex, bondage, or S&M activities. And, while the women identified themselves as predominantly heterosexual, 31.3 percent have had at least one lesbian encounter.

Through the women's responses to my five-page survey (see the appendix, page 261) about their sexual behavior and attitudes, I hoped to gather information that would:

- *Give women a vehicle for sexual self-discovery*—and a means of identifying themselves by sexual behavior characteristics.

- *Show women where they are on a scale of pleasure evolution*— and give them encouragement and support for moving forward.

- *Help them understand their own sexual pattern*—and learn how to change it, as other women have done, if they so desire.

- *And, especially help them* fully *claim their own sexual pleasure from within themselves.*

We, as women, do claim our sexual pleasure from inside ourselves.

It doesn't come from the outside. Female sexuality, fully realized and freely enjoyed, is not a gift bestowed by men. Nor is it something a woman may have only when Mother, church, female peers, or men decide she may. Some women have never claimed pleasure. Others, like some victims of rape, have claimed and lost it, and then perhaps somehow reclaimed it, often against great odds.

The overwhelming majority of the women who participated in my research have claimed, or reclaimed, pleasure.

But, that is no surprise. It is the nature of such studies that people who are for the most part comfortable and positive about sex fill out lengthy questionnaires and consent to talk about their sex lives for publication; those who are unhappy or uncomfortable tend not to be so open. Therefore the women represented here probably have richer and more varied sex lives than any 871 women assembled at random. And, that's good news for the reader.

They have shared their secrets; and their secrets can set you free.

PART 1

Who Are You?

CHAPTER 1

A Way of Classifying Sexual Identity

"Most men desire and experience sexual intercourse within a caring relationship. Most women, however enjoy sexual intercourse only when there is a greater level of commitment within the relationship."

—from "Desired and Experienced Levels of Premarital Affection and Sexual Intercourse During Dating," published by *The Journal of Sex Research*, Vol. 23, February 1987

*T*HE YOUNG WOMAN, who is or appears to be no older than twenty-five, is the American media's epitome of the sexually desirable woman. In spite of the attention paid to supermodels over thirty, hers is the face still gracing most magazine covers. And, hers is the body most avidly sought by men of all ages. Her sexual attitude is actually a large part of the alluring package. Sexually, she is orgasmic or soon will be, but she isn't knowing, experienced, *demanding*. Her desire to please is the strongest it will ever be. Love is more important to her than sex; or, if it isn't, she pretends it is. A man can look at her and see a sexual potential he fantasizes he alone can help her realize.

Some women remain in this state of suspended sexual animation no matter their chronological age. A woman friend, age thirty-eight, recently told me with pride that a man, of the kind we now describe as a Casanova, had been drawn to her in a crowded room because of her "innocent mouth." That the word "innocent" is unseemly when applied to a woman of her age and sexual experience never occurred to her. That by "innocent" he surely meant "naive and likely to play into his game" also eluded her until after she'd lost another round.

What we think we know about women and sex is really what we know about this idealized woman who is young or at least young in sexual attitude, the sexual ingenue. She is the woman about whom you are reading when a research study on sexual behavior or attitudes says "*women*" do, feel, experience, think, or whatever. The majority of the studies—nearly 85 percent of the studies on women reported in the past two years in the respected *The Journal of Sex Research*—are conducted by psychologists, psychiatrists, or sociologists on faculty at colleges and universities and are based on questionnaires distributed to the most readily available population: students between the ages of eighteen and twenty-two. The gist of these studies is: Women can't separate love and sex.

Their results are extrapolated and applied to the female population at large. The product of the analysis of limited data is a pseudoscientific profile of woman as sexual being that corresponds to the model of female sexual behavior found socially acceptable in most areas of society. Either she behaves as Mom, peers, and church think she should, or she doesn't and feels guilty and/or otherwise suffers for breaking the big rule linking sex and love. Though the woman of twenty is not expected to speak for women of thirty, forty, fifty, and beyond on any other subject, she is our sexual spokesperson.

Women, we are told, either can't or won't have sex without love.

But, what if *you* are different? Many of the women in my survey differ in this and in many other ways from the stereotypical sexual behavior profile of woman. In the personal sexual histories of the 871 women in my survey, I identified five stages of female sexual evolution and many different categories of respondents, defined by shared sexual behavior characteristics. No narrow study of college women purporting to speak for "women" could really speak for all of them.

The four major categories representing female sexual identities, determined primarily by the point in her sexual evolution when a woman becomes orgasmic, are:

Early Bloomers: 34.4 percent of the survey. Women who first masturbated before age twelve and were orgasmic with partners by age nineteen. They are comfortable with masturbation and touching themselves during intercourse—and report the fewest problems with reaching orgasm. While social prohibitions against sexual behaviors don't stop them from getting their needs met, they do often feel guilty, uncomfortable, or ashamed about their sexuality.

Perfect Buds: 23.3 percent of the survey. They have masturbated by age sixteen and have had their first orgasms, usually via masturbation, by age twenty-one. These women appear to develop according to the prevailing theory of female sexuality. Their high degree of satisfaction with their relationships may be due in part to their ease in conforming to the norm. As young women, many of us envy them.

Late Bloomers: 23.2 percent of the survey. They masturbate after age twenty-one, if at all; and they are not orgasmic until their late twenties or beyond. This group reported more problems reaching orgasm than did the others. They also seem to make poor partner choices more often. But, when late bloomers overcome the obstacles in their paths, they can experience deep sexual joy.

Wildflowers: 19.1 percent of the survey. They report greater participation in sexual variations and more partners—but not necessarily more pleasure. Some of them "act out" via sex and make bad partner choices. (Other women, the Sexual Explorers, who will be discussed in Chapter 22, exuberantly embrace their sexuality. Sexual explorers are covered more fully in a later chapter because women from all four major categories can become explorers in later life.)

The stages of female sexual evolution are:

Discovering Pleasure: The discovery phase is largely about becoming orgasmic, both alone and with a partner.

Denying Pleasure: The denial phase is marked by a conscious choice to put something else, usually "the relationship," ahead of the pursuit of deeper sexual pleasure. Women in this phase use sex to get a man, hold a man, force a commitment, or they are focused on conception rather than pleasure.

Claiming Pleasure: Women who truly claim pleasure—in a fuller sense than they had it in the discovery phase—have learned to be assertive about their sexual needs and desires. They actively seek, rather than passively wait for, pleasure. Some women never get to this stage, while others never lose it.

Losing Pleasure: Women who have lost the capacity for sexual pleasure include victims of rape, incest, and other forms of sexual abuse; victims of sexually transmitted diseases (STDs), particularly herpes; women who have suffered repeated pregnancies, miscarriages, difficult births; wives who have been sexually discarded by husbands; wives and lovers who have suffered long-term sexual repression by their partners.

Reclaiming Pleasure: It is difficult, but certainly possible, for women who have lost it to rediscover their capacity for pleasure. Many women have, and their stories offer encouragement for all women.

While the stages can be clearly identified, they aren't as inevitable as birthdays. A woman's sexual development is simply not as easily charted by her age as I initially believed it would be. When she "bloomed" is far more relevant in charting her future course than is her chronological age. A late bloomer, for example, seems to have a more difficult time overcoming the religious, family, social, and other pressures negatively affecting her sex life than other women do—but that doesn't mean she can't and won't, overcome them.

I also discovered that women who have claimed pleasure, at whatever age they did so, share certain behaviors. One of the most surprising is their ability to fantasize a love relationship while making love, yet let go of that fantasy when the sex is over. This is the way many women are able to have sex without love. We use these love fantasies in the same way many men use erotica—as arousal aides.

These sexual categories are meant to help women understand their sexual histories, not to trap them in yet one more bubble of modern psychobabble. Sometimes the categories overlap. Some women fit neatly into one or several, while other women seem to have the proverbial foot in two camps. Identifying yourself in these categories will help you see where you are and perhaps why you're at that point—and what other women in the same place are doing, or have done, to change or enhance their sex lives.

Not surprisingly given our societal attitudes about women, love, and sex, a woman's discovery of pleasure through sex is often conducted as a side trip on her real journey, the quest for love. She is bombarded with messages guiding her on the love quest and warning her off expressing too much interest in pleasure not directly tied into a relationship. This book is less concerned with relationships than sexual pleasure, but it is my belief, supported by the survey findings, that women who have claimed pleasure do have better relationships with men.

In the traditional view of female sexuality, all young women are buds, tightly closed, slow to open. Some actually are, but others burst open. You are going to find yourself in one of the four major categories above; and no one of them is the "right" place to be. Together, they create the gorgeous bouquet of female sexuality, in which every bloom is a beautiful one.

CHAPTER 2

Early Bloomers

"I started thinking about it, sex, at an early age. I can't remember not thinking about it."

—a twenty-nine-year-old from Georgia

I WAS IN high school, sometime in the early Sixties, and I was doing homework at the desk tucked into a corner of my bedroom," writes a forty-three-year-old journalist. "It was late autumn. The window was open a crack, enough to let in the scent of burning leaves. My mind wandered from trigonometry to thoughts of a certain boy kissing the tops of my breasts, which swelled attractively over my white cotton bra while the silly pointed tips of it remained empty. In my fantasies, I always cropped the pictures either above or below the wrinkled tips of my bras.

"He moved his hands under the bra, down my body, inside the lining of my panties. We stretched out full length and fully clothed on the sofa and rubbed against each other until we came. When it was over, he held me close and said, 'I love you.'

"Of course, he said, 'I love you!'

"I dressed him in the psychological clothing of a prince; and the prince wouldn't have touched the princess without loving her," she continues. "As always, the aura of romance permeated my sexual fantasies, making them acceptable to me."

In her mind, they were *love* fantasies. His whispered "I love you" was the benediction blessing her heated state. The difference between her and another girl—aside from the obvious one of precocious sexual development—was her ability to let the fantasy go when it had served its purpose.

"I didn't write this boy's name a hundred times in my notebook or contrive to bump into him in the hall between classes the next day or believe my life would be wonderful if only he'd give me his class ring.

"No. I went back to my work, still so warm that, minutes later, when I pulled up a bra strap that had slipped off my shoulder, the movement of the fabric against my breast made my nipples hard again, made me shiver. Almost thirty years later, I can recall the shiver."

She was an early bloomer; and so was I. Being among the first buds in the garden of female sexuality to burst open was uncomfortable in the early Sixties, when America was on the cusp of the sexual revolution; and I suspect it is still uncomfortable for girls today. Like boys who suddenly had erections they could not control, we were embarrassed by the heat and force of our unbidden sexual responses.

I had my first orgasm at age thirteen shimmying down an oak tree after I'd been reading a sexy novel in my treehouse, and perhaps touching myself. I don't remember if I did or did not touch. Perhaps, I've blanked the touching part out, because it wasn't acceptable while love fantasies were. I do remember the fantasies of sex and love and especially the feeling of being bombarded by desires that seemed to come from nowhere, from the heavens, like tiny bullets of frozen rain hitting my hot skin with sizzling ferocity. I can't believe my male contemporaries were any more tormented by their lusts than I was.

My own experience, like that of my sister journalist, was contradictory to the "opening bud" theory of female sexuality, which holds that all adolescent girls are tight little buds, whose appetite for sex will develop gradually over time. We weren't the only bursting buds. But we early bloomers were apparently in the minority.

The first time I reached orgasm while rubbing against a boy, he said, "Oh, wow, you were ready! Were you ready!" His eyes were filled with excitement, awe, and the absolute shock of discovery. I'm sure he'd never been with a girl who reached orgasm. Afterward, I felt so humiliated by my body, I didn't want to see him again. I had let myself go, lost control, exposed too much, put myself in a compromising position. You know the clichés. Like the whispered judgments of nuns, they taunted me. I cried myself to sleep that long-ago night, about two decades before the term "easily orgasmic" would have a positive connotation.

With hormones prematurely raging, it was difficult to be a "good" girl, one who didn't "go all the way" and didn't pet with the wrong kind of boys, i.e., greasers. My friend Carole and I were both early bloomers, the only two in our clique of a half-dozen girls. We knew, however, that we couldn't be "caught" pregnant in our teens, in the days before abortion was legal and the alternatives were early marriage or six months out of town "visiting a relative." That was also long before women carried condoms in their purses. By sheer luck or good choices in boyfriends, we remained in control of the sexual action designed to bring us, and our partners, to orgasm without penetration—not that either of us could have ever put the plan of action we followed into words—until we were high school seniors and dated college boys who did carry condoms in their wallets.

Condoms are easier to come by today for the average young woman, but, protecting oneself from pregnancy and disease is only part of it. Peers are still hostile to those who violate the behavioral code, as the experiences of younger women who participated in my research made clear. And, it is never easy to be the first within a peer group to experience any new physical state from developing breasts to sexual responsiveness.

Who Are They?

Of the total group, 34.4 percent were early bloomers, women who:

- *First masturbated before age twelve.*
- *Experienced first orgasm during masturbation and first intercourse by age sixteen.*

• *Became orgasmic with a partner by age nineteen.*

I expected their family backgrounds—especially those of the early bloomers under thirty—to be more liberal than the average participant's. After all, I reasoned, women over thirty have had more time to develop independent sexual attitudes on their own and may very well have believed when they were younger that sex and love should be strongly connected. I anticipated finding many more liberal family backgrounds among early bloomers in general and among those under thirty in particular than I found in the total survey group—but such large differences in background did not emerge.

Early bloomers of all ages more often learned about sex from peers or books than from parents. Over one-third of them came from what they described as "conservative" to "repressive" families. Only a small percentage, less than 15 percent of the under-thirty early bloomers and 11 percent of the total, got overwhelmingly positive sexual messages from Mom and Dad; though another approximately 25 percent of all early bloomers report the absence of negative messages.

"My parents never talked about sex," writes Janet, a twenty-four-year-old multiply orgasmic woman who has two regular sex partners. "Their attitude about my sex education was one of benign neglect. On balance, I think it was a positive thing. They let me come to my own conclusions rather than forcing theirs upon me."

Not all of the women who refused to link sex and love also reported such active sex lives, but, what they did have in common with each other, and with early bloomers of every age, was early experience—which, more often than not, led them to be, or feel they were, castigated by their peers.

The Peer Connection

Jennifer, a twenty-two-year-old Seattle college student, filled in the blank following "Number of sexual partners" with: "Fifteen, but I've only been 'in love' with five of these. Call me 'easy.' My friends do."

When I interviewed Jennifer, she said, "I'm not typical of my generation. I like sex. It embarrasses me that I do, but I do."

She had her first orgasm via masturbation, in the shower with a hand-held shower nozzle at age twelve and lost her virginity —a planned event—on her fifteenth birthday. Her memories of it are positive, except for "the bad part, involving what happened when the other girls found out." Let Jennifer explain.

"We had a lot of oral sex before he penetrated me," she says. "He was three years older, not a virgin, and knew how to prepare me for the first time. I was very lucky. I had an orgasm with cunnilingus. That orgasm made me feel opened up, so penetration wasn't difficult really. I loved it. I really loved sex, right from the first time. When I was having sex with him, I thought I loved him too.

"But my vaginal lips were red and sore and swollen the next day. He hadn't shaved. Remember the Don Johnson look from 'Miami Vice'? He had a tough beard; and his two-day or however many days stubble had irritated me, but I didn't know that at the time. I thought he'd given me a sexually transmitted disease. So, I told my best friend, Kara, about it. I was panic-stricken. She went into the john at school with me to look at it and pronounced it herpes. Don't ask me why I believed her. Had she ever seen herpes? No! But, I was fifteen.

"So, I had to tell my mother, who took me to the doctor, who said I had whisker burn. What a relief! Mom was cool about it. She told me she wasn't happy about me being sexually active yet, but if I was going to be, she wanted me to use protection. She had the doctor put me on the pill *and* bought me condoms. Now, that's cool.

"My friends were another story. Kara had told everyone I had herpes while I was absent for my doctor's appointment. When I got back, everyone acted like I was contagious. They wouldn't get near me. I went off on Kara and told everyone the truth, but I don't think they ever believed me. It was almost the end of the school year, and we moved over the summer, thank God, because I was never part of the group again. Before I left, Kara told me it didn't matter that I didn't have herpes because I could have had it—I was so stupid."

Jennifer says the experience taught her: "You can't trust women." At her new school, she kept quiet about her sexual activity, made easier because her partners were again older boys, not students at her school. Now, in her senior year of college, she's more open with women friends about her sex life.

"They 'dis' me in a gentle way," she says. "I've been monogamous the last year, so it's okay. All is forgiven. Jennifer, you can come home to the bosom of sisterhood! The year before, I had five partners in one year and was always getting lectured about my 'values.' The big question was: 'Don't you want a relationship with a nice guy?'—meaning I wouldn't get one if I was too easy.

"Definitely, women believe sex and love should go together. I think that's the ideal, but it isn't realistic to expect it will always be that way. It's hard to make the distinction while you're having sex anyway. When I'm making love, I can believe I'm in love. Afterward, when my body cools down, so do my emotions. To make other women feel better, however, I have said I didn't like the 'empty' feeling after loveless sex.

"Well, you have to say something!"

The Early Bloomer's Attitude Adjustment

Repeatedly women tell each other: You *shouldn't* have sex without love. A plethora of women's magazine articles in the Eighties came down hard on "casual sex," which was typically defined as any sexual activity outside a relationship. If you read *Glamour* and *Mademoiselle* faithfully in the late Eighties, you might have reached the conclusion "loveless sex" was both responsible for, and in itself almost as bad as, the AIDS epidemic. Unfortunately, such logic leads women to put even more faith in its corollary belief than they already do: Sex with love is "safe." But not every woman internalizes the message. Some, like Jennifer, pay lip service to the concept, while going their own way.

Again, remember, women who respond to sexual surveys are thought to be more sexually liberal than the general population. With this in mind, I was still surprised when a whopping 90 percent of the women I surveyed said that sex was *not* wrong without love (26.6 percent of the respondents were women in their twenties). Nearly 60 percent of the total group had had sex on the first date at least once in their lives, though most said they no longer would. They most often cited "fear of disease" as a reason for changing this behavior, with almost 80 percent of the women under thirty-five adding: "If you have sex too soon, a man won't commit."

New research indicates that women over thirty-five are more likely to have sex for physical than emotional reasons—unlike women under thirty-five, whom we've repeatedly been told are more likely to have sex for emotional rather than physical reasons. No sex researcher working with the typical undergraduate student population has yet to make the case that women *under* thirty are capable of enjoying sex without love. Repeatedly, the younger respondents report substantially the same sexual attitudes as were purportedly held by their mothers at their age.

Early bloomers, however, are more apt to go their own way. As a group, they certainly did not accept delivery of many negative sex messages, including the ubiquitous "Don't touch yourself down there." Whether alone or with a partner, they *do* touch.

Women Who Touch Themselves

Here is what some women said about manual clitoral stimulation:

"My mother told me not to touch myself in the bathtub when I was eight years old. So, the next time I touched myself without the water and learned how to masturbate."

"The big secret about sex is playing with your clitoris. You never read in sexy novels 'and then she rubbed herself like crazy while he was fucking her and she came.' Oh, no! They want you to think the penis stands alone. I learned the secret early. I was a curious child."

"I tell guys this little finger won't keep us apart. It will pull us together. Unless I don't get to use it. And then this little finger will keep us apart for good!"

These women believe an involvement of the hand, not the heart, is *necessary* to sex.

Anne, a twenty-six-year-old public-relations junior account executive from California, expressed strong opinions about the importance of manual stimulation during sex. A victim of date rape, she was also the product of a family in which "Mom was extremely liberal to the point of being 'loose,' while Dad was extremely uptight.

"I've never actually seen him kiss anyone," she continues. "Now they are divorced. Big surprise! Maybe I developed a good attitude about sex by adding their extremes together, dividing by two, and finding the middle. Really, I'm not even sure where I learned about sex. I don't remember either of them talking about it."

Anne masturbated to orgasm at age thirteen—after "accidentally discovering my clitoris in the shower"—and lost her virginity when she was fifteen. She's had fourteen partners, one abortion, and for the past three years has been living with a man in a monogamous relationship. They have sex five to seven times a week, and it is, she says, "extremely satisfying." She is nearly always orgasmic.

"I've been orgasmic with all my partners but two," she says. "They were very young and so was I. In each case, he wouldn't touch me; and he didn't want me to touch myself. And he came too fast. I slept with them a few times and moved on. If a man doesn't want me to play with myself in bed with him, I don't need him. I know how to get my pleasure. Sometimes I have to get it that way, and when I do, I don't want some guy's ego standing in the way.

"The man I live with is great about that. He loves to see me come, and he doesn't care how I come as long as I do."

Interestingly, Anne believes this relationship has made her "respectable."

She says: "I always had more partners than my girlfriends did; and I got away with it by concealing some of them and also by being a 'stat.' [Slang for "status," meaning one of the chosen with good clothes, good looks, good grades.] With this guy, I'm legit. We live together. We're in love. We're monogamous. My friends approve of it. They have been worrying about me for years.

"I remember when I was sixteen someone telling me if I didn't stop fooling around with so many guys I wouldn't get a good date to the prom. It's funny now, but it made me uncomfortable then. I was always different from my girlfriends. They always had to be 'in love' with somebody. I pretended to be most of the time."

What Early Bloomers Can Teach You About Sex

Being an early bloomer definitely looks like a more enviable condition years later than it does when the bloom is passionately bursting. If you weren't an early bloomer, don't waste any time envying us now. We wanted to be more like you then. Women in every category have something to share with their sisters. The positive early bloomer behavior traits can be translated into the following good advice for all women:

- *Masturbate*. Sex therapists say masturbation is the surest learning path to orgasm for women. Even if you have little or no difficulty reaching orgasm in most of your encounters, masturbation is a valid sexual expression for both the single and the coupled woman.

- *Insist on manual stimulation during sex, if you need it*. Most women do. If a man tells you, "No other woman has touched herself while I am making love to her," reply, "I'm no other woman. I'm me." There's no point in telling him the other women were probably faking orgasm. He won't believe it anyway.

- *Don't let any discomfort you may feel about the disapproval of other women squelch your libido*. If you're involved with a man not deemed suitable partner material by your friends, or you're having an extramarital affair or having sex with more partners than they are, keep your own counsel. If you feel troubled about your behavior, talk to a therapist. Don't let friends run your sex life.

- *Learn to use love fantasies, rather than be used by them as many women are*. Some of us need the pretense of "love" to let go sexually. So, pretend. But, don't pursue relationships based on nothing more than sexual attraction and strong love fantasies.

The Love-Fantasy Connection

Love fantasies are the romantic scenarios women weave around the objects of their sexual desires. Many women are prisoners of those fantasies, held captive inside the shiny webs they've woven. They need to justify their lusts with love fantasies, and then they feel compelled to make the fantasies real. Victims of convoluted thinking, they are ready to commit to a man as soon as their libido rises around him. Some men think with their groins, and some women commit by theirs.

One woman, a self-described "woman who loves too much," and a late bloomer who wasn't orgasmic until age thirty-four, labeled her behavior "sexual idealizing."

"I was always more focused on how good it could be, rather than on how mundane it really was in a relationship," she wrote. "I idealized men, sex, and relationships. I was fooled by my idealizations. When you live like that, you're half-blind. Groping, you're always looking for 'signs' of his love and magnifying every good thing. You con yourself into believing so-so sex is so spectacular sex! Otherwise, you have to admit the whole thing was just a fantasy and it's just sex."

Other women, including the early bloomers I interviewed, use their love fantasies during arousal and masturbation or lovemaking, but relinquish them when the sex is over. The fantasies give them permission to surrender to their erotic feelings ("It's okay . . . if I'm in love. Let's pretend I'm really in love"). Often they don't understand what they're doing, even as they're doing it. These are some of the comments women made in explaining how or why they used love fantasies:

"Fantasies have always been an important part of sex for me. When I am masturbating, I imagine the whole relationship from meeting the man to The Consummation as I'm diddling myself.

Even in a masturbatory fantasy, I look at him a little askance after it's done."

_____

"It's hard for me to let go with a man unless I can see him in my mind as my true lover. With some men I've known, that's been quite a mental leap, one I can only make at the height of lust. Afterward, I think, 'Who, him?' "

_____

"Now that I am older [thirty-three], I can masturbate to real down-and-dirty scenes in my head. Men fucking me in every opening, that kind of thing. When I was younger, I had to have the hearts and flowers in there somewhere."

_____

"They say sex takes place mostly in the head, and I can buy into that. In my head, I always love them. I couldn't do the things I want to do with them if I didn't love them in my head at the time."

Knowing What You Need

Cheryl, a thirty-eight-year-old Georgia teacher, describes her early sexual experience as "an orgy of emotion and a modicum of physical stuff." She had her first orgasm early, at fourteen, via masturbation. And she wasn't shy about showing her boyfriends how to touch her so they could bring her to orgasm too. She also pretended every boy who touched her was her "soul mate," who had "survived tortures, including whippings," for the pleasure of pleasuring her.

"I was a cheerleader in high school," she says. "Southern girls can get away with murder if they're cheerleaders. Well, maybe not murder. Certainly not pregnancy. Getting pregnant was the end of life as we knew it. So, the point was: You didn't go all the way. You did everything but. We had the boys totally fooled. They thought we were swooning over them; and we thought we were too. But, it was the sex, not them. All that gushing over how 'cute' they were when what we really meant was how hot!

You know, I didn't have it figured out until just this past few years.

"And, they thought we were too good to go all the way, but the truth was we didn't want to risk it. Why should we risk it when we could have delicious orgasms without intercourse? My steady boyfriend senior year was an absolute expert at cunnilingus. He loved to 'eat me out.' It was years before I got it that good again. Him, I was crazy about. To this day, I couldn't tell you if I was blinded by the sex or if I loved him.

"That kind of sex was actually better, because you always got an orgasm. When I started having sex in college, I was a little disappointed at first. As soon as I had intercourse with a guy, he stopped spending so much time arousing me. I learned to speak up and ask for what I wanted, or to take care of it myself. In other words, sexual satisfaction is often in a woman's own hands. I really believe it is.

"I don't know why some women are shy about it. When I need to come, the need is so overpowering, I don't have to think about it. I just do what it takes to get the release."

By "need" she means an intense desire for touch centered in her clitoris, a need many early bloomers described in equally strong terms. Perhaps their need is greater than other women's, or perhaps they are just more aware, for whatever reason, of that need.

The Hormonal Factor

We don't know exactly how great a role individual hormonal development plays in differentiating the early bloomers from their less-sexually-active contemporaries. But, experts say the level of sexual desire—or the sex drive, which is determined by the androgen testosterone, present in both sexes, to a lesser degree in women—varies widely from one individual to another. Dr. Ruth Westheimer says more than half her mail from spouses is about "the basic problem, one partner wanting more sex than the other does."

Early bloomers want more sex, and they may want it because

their bodies are different than other women's, in that they produce more testosterone. Women become more easily aroused in their mid- to late-thirties due in part to the increased ratio of this androgen to female hormones in their bodies caused by the decrease in the natural production of estrogen while the androgen level remains constant. Many women, however, have naturally higher androgen to estrogen ratios throughout their lives. Perhaps this is true of early bloomers. And perhaps being orgasmic at an early age or easily orgasmic at any age is more dependent on body chemicals than we recognize.

I was easily orgasmic at thirteen. Other women who report precocious sexual development also had early orgasms via masturbation—years before many young women thought about masturbation. Almost 6 percent of the women I surveyed were masturbating before they were *ten* years old, three women as early as age *five*. Are early bloomers less mindful of prohibitions against touching themselves? Were they driven by stronger sexual feelings than other girls experienced?

For whatever reasons, early bloomers were not perfect buds waiting for love. Nor did they wait for the passage of a "suitable" amount of years to open.

CHAPTER 3

Wildflowers

"Looking back, I can see that I had no boundaries. I just didn't know how to say no. I did anything any guy wanted me to do because I had no clear sense of myself and what my sexual needs were and how to get them met."

—Renee, thirty-nine, a former wildflower

SHE MAY BEHAVE more outrageously than any early bloomer you've ever known, yet not be one at all. While early bloomers want to get their needs met without getting pregnant or losing status within the peer group by being labeled "sluts," wildflowers flaunt their behavior. Responding to something other than their own sexual needs, they seem to desire the the labeling, negative attention, and judgments their behavior invariably elicits.

Some wildflowers are, or later become, sexual explorers, a category we'll examine more closely in Chapter 22. Like all wildflowers, sexual explorers have more partners and/or report greater participation in sexual variations, but they differ from other wildflowers in that they are motivated primarily by their own pleasure drives, *and* they protect themselves from the negative consequences of sexual exploration, disease, and unwanted pregnancy. Rarely, however, is a woman a true sexual explorer in her youth.

"I was a bad girl for four years," says Jessica, age twenty-nine. "The last year of high school, I was totally wild, out of control. In one week, I had five partners. Don't ask me why.

None of them were any good. I don't know how I kept from flunking out of school.

"I just had to touch somebody, have somebody hold me. It sounds sick, but my drive wasn't sex, it was a touch-me drive, hold-me drive. I had to have the physical connection the way guys had to get their rocks off.

"In college, it was a little different, the sexually frenetic periods corresponded to school breaks and summer vacations. I was either very controlled and serious about my studies—or totally out of control. My roommate at college didn't know I had this other life until our second year rooming together when she went home with me on break. My parents were in Europe. The first night I had a party. I can still see the look on her face when she walked into my bedroom and saw me naked, tied to the bed with pantyhose. The guy who'd tied me up had gone to the bathroom.

"During those wild years, I didn't have many orgasms. I didn't masturbate until I was twenty. Orgasms didn't matter that much. It's funny but, at the time, I thought I was doing it for pleasure. It was crazy. Even after I started having orgasms, I wasn't having good sex. I would be attracted to a guy and go to bed with him, but it was just me getting off on using him for a change.

"I don't know why I needed to feel that. I don't know why."

Who Is She?

Wildflowers are 19.1 percent of the total survey group. They are women who:

- *Reported five or more partners during any given year.*

- *Had more than the average number of lifetime partners, men with whom they've had sex at least once, for their age groups.* The average figures are: for the twenties, eight partners; the thirties, twenty-nine partners; the forties, forty-seven partners; and the fifties-plus, nineteen partners.

- *Reported greater than "occasional" or "once only" participation in anal sex, bondage, and S&M activities.*

Almost half are sexual explorers, women who are in charge of their sex lives, who choose to participate in sexual variations, and who have multiple partners—or have made such choices in the past. The explorers are more often easily or multiply orgasmic than are other wildflowers. Their behavior is motivated by the quest for more exciting experiences, more or better orgasms, and the need for more variety and stimulation than the average woman has. Generally regular users of birth control and condoms, they protect themselves against the negative consequences of sexual experimentation.

But the other half of the wildflower group, the subject of this chapter, was rarely or never orgasmic during lovemaking. And, 34 percent of this group had never had an orgasm with a partner. Unlike explorers and early bloomers, these wildflowers are not strongly focused on orgasm. And they are appallingly casual in their approach to birth control and disease prevention.

How People Respond to Them

Wildflowers, though a minority, get a lot of attention. Writers of magazine articles huffily cite them as examples of negative behaviors in articles about sex and relationships. Other girls' mothers point warning fingers at them and admonish their daughters, "Men don't marry girls like that!" And they are the personification of modern moral laxity held up for scorn by everyone interested in controlling female sexuality, from the pulpit to the press. Feminists and conservatives alike often attack them.

Wild boys, of course, are another story. They are accepted or tolerated and even forgiven for their errant ways—by women, the very group most hurt by their behavior. Several recent studies on the double standard—conducted again on the ubiquitous eighteen- to twenty-two-year-old collegiate population—indicate how little attitudes have changed. A study published in *The Journal of Sex Research* found women students more condemning of their sisters for playing around, or in therapeutic jargon, "participating in extrapremarital intercourse," than they were of male students behaving the same way. The women were also harsher in their judgments of each other than the male students were in their judgments of women. A different study in another issue of the same journal found women participants rating women with multiple partners as "less responsible" than men with multiple partners. And the authors of a third study concluded, not surprisingly, that the double standard "is declining, but still persists—especially in the hearts and minds of women."

Yet, nearly everyone forgives wildflowers if they renounce their wild ways by "settling down" in a monogamous relationship, entering a period of voluntary celibacy, or coming out as a sex addict and seeking help within the sex addiction treatment industry or through Love and Sex Addicts Anonymous, the newest offshoot of the twelve-step programs.

What are they getting out of sex if they're not getting regular orgasms? A lot of attention.

The Negative Attention Needs

Karen, who is twenty-one, has already had "more than fifty" sexual partners though she is rarely orgasmic with a lover. The youngest of four children, she comes from a "straitlaced" working-class family, who were not overly religious. "It started when I was sixteen; and I decided I wanted to have seventeen partners before I was seventeen. Things got out of hand. I'd say yes without thinking about it. Sometimes I think I get more out of talking about it and watching my friends react than I get from doing it."

A self-described loner, Karen doesn't belong to a group of peers. She has two close female friends, and though neither of them lives nearby, she does give them "fairly regular bulletins" about her sexual escapades. They aren't censorious. In fact, she sometimes thinks they live vicariously through her.

"They've both been involved in monogamous relationships for at least the past two years," she says. "Kerry is living with her boyfriend, who she's been dating since they were both sixteen. She's twenty-one, been having sex for five years, and only had one partner. That blows me away! We're totally opposite.

"She rags on me for not using condoms all the time. I know she's right, but I just don't do it. I've been lucky, no diseases, only one abortion. If they use condoms, I'm glad, but I don't ask. I look at the penis to make sure there's no obvious signs of disease; and I milk it, looking for froth.

"I don't think she's got any concept how it can be with guys who aren't really involved with you. They aren't that worried. But she's fascinated by what I do. When I had sex with three different guys in the same day, I called to tell her about it. She pretended to freak out, but she was loving it. She asked me all the details, like which one had the biggest whang and what did I do about the semen leaking out and did one of them sniff the other one on me."

Karen can talk easily about sex. She says she likes large penises, "doing it hard," and having sex in semipublic places. What she doesn't articulate well is what she gets out of sex.

"I don't know why I've had so many partners. Even I think I'm crazy for doing it. I did have one brief monogamous period. I was ready to marry this guy when I found out he was with someone else. Then I went wild with other guys. I had to get my confidence back. He'd really hurt me. I'd been caught up in this fantasy of love, marriage, and children, and he rejected me.

"I can live without sex. I quit once for four months, cold turkey. Sometimes I don't think it's just sex. I feel like I have a loose end without a steady boyfriend, but I've rarely had a steady boyfriend. Mostly, I am alone and having sex with a lot of people to take care of that loose end. It's just how I am. I don't think about orgasms when I'm being wild. I just want to do something, to get somebody close to me. Orgasms don't matter as much as having somebody with me.

"Only a few of those guys were good sex partners, but it's still sex. You know. Just doing it is fun. I can get off when I masturbate, but I don't like that as well. I have to have sex. I don't know why I feel this way, but I do."

I asked several psychologists, psychiatrists, and sex therapists the question Karen has asked herself: Why?

The Psychoanalytic Opinion

The experts I spoke with who weren't involved in the sex addiction treatment industry either downplayed or flat out debunked the theory of sex addiction. What may be going on inside women like Karen, they say, is a struggle against a repressive childhood background, or she may be responding to real or emotional abandonment, especially by a father. Her quest for sex may really be a search for the love and attention she doesn't get, or perceives she isn't getting, at home. Here I should caution against applying pat answers to difficult questions. It is interesting to note, however, that Karen never knew her father, who left when she was a toddler. Her mother's succession of boyfriends have ignored her. Some wildflowers may be victims of childhood sexual abuse. Of the 15 percent of the women in my study who reported such abuse, nearly three-fourths were wildflowers.

While there may be a diversity of opinion on why she behaves the way she does, there is no dissent on one aspect of the wildflower's life: Her behavior puts her at serious risk.

The Risks

"I've had to talk myself out of some scary situations," says Linda, age twenty-five, who has sex with strangers on an average of twice a month. "I was handcuffed to a bed in a hotel room by a security guard who threatened to open the door, walk out of the room, and leave me there. He made me beg him. Another time, a man did it to me so hard, I bled. He was a little bigger than average, but it was his roughness, not his size, that hurt me. I've never been fucked that hard before or since.

"Once, a guy had trouble performing. I blew him until my jaws ached, but he couldn't get hard enough. He was so angry about it, I thought he was going to hit me. So, I told him it was my fault, that I was really dumb about sex. He was okay then. But he scared me. I think that man was capable of hurting a woman."

Women like Linda put themselves in positions of incredible vulnerability when they have sex with a stranger. Maybe he'll become violent. Maybe he'll infect them with an STD. If they aren't using a reliable form of birth control, maybe he'll leave them pregnant before vanishing from their lives.

Rarely does the one-night stand result in the kind of steamy sex depicted in such encounters on movie screens and in glitzy novels. In a study of 805 nurses published by *The Journal of Sex and Marital Therapy*, about two-thirds had faked an orgasm, with most saying they did so in casual, often one-night stand, encounters. Other studies, particularly of younger women, report similar, and even more dramatic, findings.

Why then would the wildflower put herself at such risk for so little pleasure? The experts tell us some of these women are looking for punishment, not pleasure, but others undoubtedly are looking for adventure. Danger excites them.

"It's probably sick," Linda says, "but the element of danger excites me. Whenever I go into a room with a man I don't know, I'm so scared in the pit of my stomach, I'm excited. It's a kind of erotic dread. Though I'm not orgasmic then, for days afterward I'll masturbate to orgasm to the fantasy of whatever we did."

For many women, the wild phase is a short period of time in their lives that will at some later point be clearly identified as a response to sexual rejection. A woman in her fifties describes it as the "I Want to Fuck the World to Get Even" response. Other women call it "revenge sex." They do it to show the man who left that they're still attractive to other men, if not to him. Or they do it to jolt themselves back to life sexually.

"I married at nineteen, divorced at twenty, and was the wildest gal in town at twenty-one," writes a twenty-four-year-old Texan, who is one year into her second marriage and pregnant with her first child. "In that year I slept with forty men, but they weren't exactly strangers. I knew them from work or school. I was working as a legal secretary, and a lot of them were clients. You know I almost never planned to have sex with anyone. It just happened. I only saw three of them more than once. And I don't know how many of them gave me orgasms. I wasn't thinking about orgasms that much at the time.

"Really, I was lucky. No violence, except for spanking. But, I did get some strange requests, guys wanting me to crawl naked around the room on all fours, things like that. Mostly, they wanted to hear my fantasies. Two older men wanted me to talk dirty while they masturbated. We didn't even have sex.

"I didn't see an ob-gyn the whole year. Often I asked the guys to use withdrawal as a form of contraception, because I wouldn't take the pill. It's a wonder I didn't get pregnant sooner. It took almost a year. Then I had an abortion, and I sobered up. I said to myself, 'This is never going to happen to me again.' I was tested for every disease imaginable and didn't have any. Can you believe the luck in that?"

Of the wildflowers in my study, 74.1 percent reported multiple abortions as compared to 14 percent of the group as a whole, and 51 percent have contracted multiple STDs as compared to 27.7 percent of the total.

Their stories have common elements, including:

- *They are aware of the risks their behavior entails.* Unlike women who make bad partner choices because they are mired in fantasy, wildflowers know what they're doing.

- *But they don't know why they take these risks.* If they were still practicing risky sex, they were not sure why they did. They are orgasmic and do masturbate, so they know exactly what they're missing in their partner encounters. "What exactly am I getting out of this?" is a question they ask themselves.

- *They do, however, report being driven by the need to be touched and held at any cost.* Over half come from sexually repressive family backgrounds and/or have been given intensive religious training. Almost 60 percent lost their fathers at an early age through death or divorce.

- *They are keenly aware of how others regard their behavior, which they don't keep secret.* Many, in fact, describe their adventures in detail to their friends, unlike sexual explorers who tend to keep their own counsel.

The Long View

Women who had put their wild phase behind them seemed to have answered more of their own questions about motives and rewards.

Meagan, who calls herself a "bad girl," is analytical about her sexual behavior. At thirty-eight, she is a successful executive in a conservative corporation. She is the last person you would expect to pick up strangers in bars when she's out of town on business trips, but that is what she did at one point in her not that far distant past.

"In my early and mid-twenties, I was really a wild child," she says. "I had one-night stands, wild weekends with strangers. You name it, I did it. Bondage, S&M, anal sex, anything. I've had hundreds of partners. As my career progressed, I became more careful because I had a higher level of visibility in my job, an image to protect.

"I was good at home and only bad on the road. For example, I spent a week in the Bahamas where I met a French painter who'd just been dumped by a rich older woman—literally dumped. She'd thrown him off her yacht and sailed away. He was the most decadent person I've ever known. I'm sure he'd slept with men as well as women and done drugs. He represented a serious risk and without thinking, I took it, but he was the last of my bad partners. When I got back home, I began to worry about AIDS. I was tested, and when I found out I was okay, I decided to change my behavior.

"When I was younger, I didn't have orgasms with most of my partners. I was acting out sexually. I know that sounds like therapy jargon, but I've been in therapy. I was angry. A lot of things had happened to me in my childhood, sexual things, with my older brothers, even my father, though it stopped short of actual penetration. I didn't remember those things until I was in therapy in my early thirties. I had blocked them out.

"One day in therapy I realized there was something inside me, like a big black cocoon. Eventually the cocoon broke open, and I could see my father and my brother and they were naked and their penises were huge. Then everything came back to me.

"Until that memory returned, I was mindless about sex. Sometimes it didn't matter who I did it with, as long as I did it. Now, I am wild when I choose to be wild because it's fun. I like it. I'm always the one in control of it. In the past, I wasn't. A few times I got myself into pretty scary situations. Once, I had to talk a man down from some weird psychotic high. He was hurting me. He was going to hurt me worse, but I talked him down. Another time, a man threw me out of his apartment. I was naked. I stood whimpering at his door until he threw my clothes out too. But he kept my shoes and my handbag. I had to walk home, more than thirty blocks, barefoot, in the middle of the night.

"But, the good news is that I don't do that stuff anymore. I have great sex, and I am by no means ready to settle into monogamy with anyone. I use condoms. And I take care of myself in other ways too, by not having sex unless I want to have sex for me, not just because the man has asked—and by making sure I get the kind of sex I want."

What You Can Do to Change Your Own Behavior

If you are a wildflower perhaps you are having a lot of sex and not enough pleasure. But, you can change the status quo, as Meagan, and many other women, have done.

- *Take a sexual time-out.* Give yourself a break from sex partners—even if it's only a week or ten days!—and spend that time examining your sexual behavior in a nonjudgmental way. Look at what you've done and what it's done for you—not what you think it says *about* you. What do you want from sex? Are you getting it? If not, why not? If you can afford to do so, talk to a therapist about these issues.

- *Give yourself permission to say "no."* Therapists say you can't really say "yes" until you've learned how to say "no." You don't have to go along with the sexual demands or requests of the men in your life. If you're always responding in the affirmative to any sexual request, you aren't saying "yes," you're just not saying "no."

- *Find positive ways of getting your needs for attention and nonsexual physical contact met.* Some women get pets and/or become more physically affectionate with family friends. They take lessons in sports, sign up for classes in creative activities, join drama clubs—anything to get positive attention for their activities.

- *Masturbate.* Consider masturbation an act of self-love as well as a means of releasing sexual tension. Fantasize about loving encounters with men who please you sexually.

- *Make better partner choices.* Draw up a list of the qualities you want in a man, focusing on how these qualities are reflected in his treatment of you. And, don't go to bed with a new man until you are confident he meets the requirements.

- *Most important, don't judge your sexual behavior or let others judge you.* Stop telling your friends the details of your sex life. Many people live vicariously through the exploits of others and even unconsciously encourage the continued wild behavior.

CHAPTER 4

Perfect Buds

"I envied the girls who didn't get hot and bothered. I think they were the same ones who never got pimples. There has to be a connection."
—Margot, a thirty-nine-year-old early bloomer on perfect buds

P ERFECT BUDS SEEM to do everything "right."

They fit the tight bud theory of slowing developing female sexuality. Often not orgasmic until her early twenties, the perfect bud is sexy without being threatening because a man typically sees her as a blank and beckoning canvas on which he can imprint his own fantasy. She is the sexual ingenue, a role many women continue to play even after they have adult children.

I envied them in my youth; and, perhaps, so did you. Even now, at midlife, when the differences rippling between most of us have smoothed out just as the wrinkles we share have suddenly appeared, I think of the buds as those women who got it all right. Many of them, however, tell me they consider themselves ordinary, dull, or boring. Truly, no one is ever completely satisfied with what they have, whether the subject of comparison is accomplishment, beauty, or sex drive.

More often than the other women in my survey, perfect buds reported that linking sex and love exclusively to each other has worked for them.

"I didn't think about sex in my teens," says Madeleine, a forty-three-year-old perfect bud from southern Illinois. "I thought about love. Sex was what boys tried to get you to do to them in cars. Sex was what you didn't do if you were smart. Love was what you got from boys when you were good.

"My mother told me two things: Don't make more than Bs in your classes, because boys don't like girls who make As. And, don't let them touch you below the waist until you're engaged.

"It was the early Sixties and some girls weren't listening to their mothers, but it never occurred to me not to listen to mine. I thought she knew what she was talking about. She had my dad and a beautiful split level house and my brother and me, everything she wanted. I wanted the same things.

"Still, I liked kissing and petting above the waist. So, I did those things with boys I dated steadily. When I was nineteen, I got engaged to Michael. We were engaged for six months before we got married. While we did a lot of things, including pet to orgasm, we didn't go all the way. My first orgasm came as a tremendous surprise. He brought me with his hand inside my pants. I knew I'd be a goner whenever he finally removed those pants if his hand could feel so good.

"I honestly don't know why being a virgin bride was so important to me then, but it was. By the time we got married, I was exhausted from holding him off. My nerves were shot. I cried at the drop of a hat. Between him pushing for sex and my mother asking if I was still a virgin—it was horrible the last two months before the wedding! When I went to my doctor for the premarital check-up, he put me on Librium."

Madeleine and Michael will celebrate their twenty-fifth wedding anniversary in a little over a year. She hasn't ever had an affair, and she's confident he hasn't either. Their sex life has been—and still is—"*highly* satisfactory."

"Being a virgin bride doesn't mean you're going to be uptight for life," she says. "We've done everything, oral, anal, bondage. He is a tender and passionate and very imaginative lover. When I was writing that on your questionnaire, he was looking over my shoulder, and he said he would say the same of me.

"What makes our sex life work is the level of intimacy we have achieved with each other. I could never make love with such abandon if I didn't absolutely trust him and know he knows me as well as one person can know another."

Perfect buds often seem to end up married and are likely, though not necessarily, monogamous women who place a high value on intimacy and also enjoy sex—the target audience for *Redbook* magazine. They do conform fairly closely to the tight bud theory of female sexuality: When, in the fullness of time, they flower, they delight in their newly discovered sensual nature.

Who Is She?

Perfect buds are 23.3 percent of the total survey group. They are women who:

- *Began to masturbate after age sixteen, but no later than twenty-one.*
- *Had their first sexual experience with a partner between the ages of seventeen and twenty-one.*
- *Had their first orgasm during masturbation before twenty-one and first orgasm with a partner before twenty-five.*

Nothing in their collective family backgrounds struck me as being different than the norm for their ages, socioeconomic brackets, religious affiliations, and other factors—but, they did seem to be more closely influenced by their mothers during adolescence than other women. Perhaps, like Madeleine, they paid closer attention to their mother's admonishments against touching themselves than early bloomers or wildflowers did. They do report less frequent, as well as later, masturbation than early bloomers.

Delayed Masturbation

"I didn't masturbate until I was twenty-one," says Jane, a twenty-seven-year-old law student, wife, and mother of an infant son.

"I wasn't taught not to touch myself. I just didn't do it. It never occurred to me to do it.

"My boyfriend taught me how. He was my first lover, and we had been together for nearly two years when he brought me a copy of *Penthouse Forum*. We read the stories and letters together, and that got me hot. He told me he would leave them with me so I could use them to masturbate with, and I told him I'd never masturbated. He didn't believe me.

"But, the next time we were together I was able to convince him I wasn't kidding. He said it was time I learned to masturbate, so he took my hand and showed me how to touch myself in the same way he touched me when he made love to me. I was embarrassed, and it took a long time for me to get hot. But I did. Then he took his hand away and told me to keep masturbating myself. I didn't want to, so he masturbated, too. It was an incredibly arousing experience. When I had an orgasm, he did too."

Other perfect buds report similar experiences. About delaying masturbation until their late teens or older, these women said:

"I lost my virginity at eighteen, had my first orgasm at twenty and two years after that, masturbated for the first time. As I look at these numbers, I wonder if I did things out of order? But, I wasn't interested in masturbating any sooner."

"I masturbated for the first time at nineteen or twenty (fuzzy on the years), because it took me that long to work up an interest in touching myself. In a Corvair of all places! My girlfriend and I had gone out driving and she had stopped at her boyfriend's place. I was sitting alone in the car in the driveway wondering what they were doing inside. She was always telling erotic stories about being with him. I got in the mood, and I did it, just like that. I didn't have an orgasm, but I got close. I was afraid I would lose control and she would come out, so I stopped. When I got home, I finished the job."

"I masturbated for the first time at age twenty-two—because I thought it was time I finally did."

"I was twenty-two and pregnant before I masturbated. My hormones were acting up at the time."

Repeatedly, perfect buds said they didn't masturbate early, because they simply weren't that interested in doing it. While many said they'd been warned against touching themselves, they received no more, or seemingly no more frightening, negative messages from Mother than early bloomers did. As one woman said: "Of course my mother said don't do it! My mother said don't do anything that could potentially be fun."

What also sets them apart from others in addition to their later masturbation is their early recognition of themselves as people of value. The phrase, "I didn't want to give myself away too easily," was repeated in one form or another by many perfect buds in explaining why they delayed having sexual intercourse longer than many of their peers. They were less likely to use the phrase "hold out" than other women in describing the struggle with men over sexual surrender. Early on, they seemed to grasp a distinction between giving freely of your sexuality and having it taken from you, and they decided when to give.

They not only get chosen, but they choose. Unlike many other young women, perfect buds choose their partners carefully. Not surprisingly, the men they describe as ideal mates sound like they possess the fairly traditional requirements: older, taller, stronger, richer or able and willing to make a good living.

But no matter how they describe their men, perfect buds talk about the need for "intimacy" first, sex second.

Early bloomers describe their sex drives; wildflowers talk about the terrible need to not be alone that drives them to precocious behavior; but perfect buds talk about their "intimacy needs."

The Intimacy Factor

They aren't the only women who want sex within an intimate relationship, but they are the most vocal about that desire—and the most insistent about not having sex any other way.

"I need intimacy" is the modern woman's way of saying she won't have sex without "love." Love, we have long been told, is necessary to the flowering of female sexuality. Perfect buds, more than any other women, believe this to be true.

"I can't have sex without true intimacy," says Shyla, a twenty-six-year-old from the South. "Too many people have sex too soon because they are using sex to avoid intimacy with each other."

And a thirty-eight-year-old New Yorker says, "Good sex can only happen in an intimate relationship. It takes more than two naked people to make an intimate bond. It takes time and trust and caring."

Melanie, a thirty-five-year-old teacher, says, "I've had sex a few times when I didn't feel intimately connected to the man, and I cried, once during and once afterward. It was so empty. For me, sex is a deeper experience than a physical one. I need to feel unified in all my being with my partner, not merely connected at the genitals."

Interestingly, 74 percent of the perfect buds said adultery is acceptable, whereas 81 percent of the total survey group found it acceptable. In most cases, perfect buds qualified that acceptance by adding "under certain circumstances," which nearly always meant, as one woman put it, "when the intimacy has died."

A thirty-four-year-old Boston mother of three, an ultimate perfect bud, said: "Adultery can only be acceptable when the intimacy of the marriage is irretrievably broken, while other factors make it necessary to continue the legal institution."

Typical perfect bud responses to "Is adultery wrong?" included:

"It's acceptable when you must stay in the marriage for financial reasons, but can't get your needs met there."

"If he's impotent and you're still functioning."

"It's certainly understandable when one person needs a lot more sex than the other does and is able to have an affair without destroying the marriage. No matter which is the one who needs more!"

What Perfect Buds Can Teach You About Sex

Whatever their opinions on sex and morality, perfect buds frequently express those opinions with more assurance than other women do. That self-confidence in the rightness of their own sexual choices is one of their strongest traits. I often found myself wishing all women could share it.

While they made up less than a quarter of my survey, the perfect buds represent the stereotypical female sexual ideal, and their evolution is the one by which most women are measured. Their strong positive behaviors include:

- *Acceptance of their own sexuality.* True, they have the weight of social approbation on their side. But we can all develop that same level of confidence simply by giving ourselves permission to accept our sexual desires and needs.

- *A strong focus on intimacy.* For them, the intimacy drive is greater than, or equal to, the sex drive, at least until they are well into their thirties. Because they save sex for relationships that hold the promise of intimacy, they provide themselves with better conditions for expressing and enjoying their sexuality than many women do. They find the emotional security they need to become sexual.

- *A strong sense of their own worth, sexually and otherwise.* Perhaps that attitude comes in part from living inside a body that is hormonally in tune with society's concept of how, and when, the sexual woman should respond—this seems to give them the confidence to make good partner choices. On matters of sex and love, they have the kind of inborn confidence rich women have in their ability to purchase cashmere and pearls, no matter where they actually fit on the socioeconomic scale. This is a good feeling to have—and one we can all have if we think of ourselves as valuable women.

The Sense of Rightness

"When I was in school, I had the feeling girls like me set the standards for the others," writes a forty-five-year-old Wisconsin

wife and mother. "Therefore it was incumbent upon me to behave well. I did not find that difficult. Nor have I found it difficult
to remain a faithful and virtuous wife for more than twenty-five
years.

"If you recognize that sex, though pleasurable, is only a small
part of your life, you will not let your passions get out of hand."

It is easier to recognize that about sex if indeed it is true. For
some women, "passions" are a bigger part of life than they are
for others. And, for many perfect buds sexual passion looms
larger when they reach their thirties and early forties, traditionally the peak years for women. Not all perfect buds would agree
with the Wisconsin writer. And some really do seem to have
worked very hard to keep their sexual development moving at
the appropriate stately pace.

"When I married at twenty-two, I was a virgin bride," writes
a forty-four-year-old Seattle executive. "I'd been engaged to another man before becoming engaged to my current husband. I
would have slept with the first one, because I was so sure we
would marry. But he insisted I keep my virginity in case things
didn't work. He knew me well enough to know I wouldn't want
to enter a marriage as 'damaged goods.' He was right. That's
how I felt then.

"In order to keep myself intact, I let my husband-to-be have
anal intercourse with me once a week. It hurt like hell. It left
me constipated. I cried every week. But, on my wedding day I
walked down the aisle in white with every feeling I deserved to
be wearing it. I was exultant. I felt like a real woman, totally,
for the first time in my life.

"The sex in my marriage was good after a difficult start. I got
honeymoon cystitis; and then I got pregnant the first year. But,
after I recovered from the baby, we got into sex with each other
in a very good way. We were close, as close as two people could
be, until three years ago when he suddenly began pulling away
from me.

"I won't bore you with the details of my marriage, but I am
having an affair now. While I am not free to divorce, I am totally
intimately involved in this relationship.

"The sex is better than any sex I've ever had. I am orgasmic with him in more ways than I was ever orgasmic with my husband. He is a good sexual athlete, with endurance, quick recovery, and great tongue muscles. He orgasms and so do I, with lots of fondling and positions, experimentation. It is a total experience, with closeness, talking, hugging, and holding. With him, I've had a deeper experience than any I've ever thought possible.

"It is right, and I have no regrets, no shame."

CHAPTER 5

Late Bloomers

"My husband performed oral sex on me once. He said he didn't like the taste. I felt awful, humiliated. Since my divorce two years ago, another man has tried to perform oral sex on me, but I wouldn't let him. I'm afraid to try that again."

—Leslie, thirty-nine, divorced, and rarely orgasmic

*I*MAGINE CINDERELLA AFTER the ball. Years have passed, and still the Prince has not come with the tiny glass slipper to fit her little foot. It is so many years after the ball, her foot has swollen to a bigger size from standing on it while sweeping the floor. It seems, in fact, like decades after the ball. That's how many late bloomers feel.

Or, to return to the book's metaphor: They fear their buds have frozen before they could bloom.

"I had my first orgasm at thirty-five," says Candice, a Midwestern public relations specialist. "It drove me crazy, wondering what I was missing. I was sure you could see it in my face, my body language, that I'd never had an orgasm.

"I'd been divorced twice. I'd been in a living-together relationship that had fallen apart. I'd spent more than twelve years of my life sleeping in bed every night next to a man. And I never had an orgasm in all that time.

"I didn't know how you got an orgasm, because I'd never masturbated. The idea of it was unappealing to me. Maybe I can blame that on my mother. She made it sound like an awful thing to do. Funny, she warned me against touching myself,

47

especially, she said, in the bathtub, but she never said anything about menstruation or pregnancy or any of the other woman things. When I got my first period, I thought I was bleeding to death. I hid six pairs of blood-soaked panties in the laundry basket and stayed in my room all day. She saw me putting the last pair in and told me what was happening.

"But, I guess it's not fair to say she had me so spooked I couldn't touch myself until I was thirty-five. I just didn't. I didn't make the connection between that and orgasms.

"I believed in love, in the power of love to move you like it says in the novels. I was very much into fantasies. I got myself terribly aroused fantasizing about the man I loved. Then, when I got into bed with him, he couldn't ever bring me quite there. None of the three really touched me down there, not in the way you need to be touched to have an orgasm.

"I would fantasize the love, feel the love, but the feeling never translated sexually. Eventually, I would begin fantasizing about another man. I used to keep journals, and they were full of my frigid angst and sex dreaming about other men. As soon as I married one man and it just didn't happen, I began thinking about another. It was sexual disappointment, but I didn't know it then. Both my marriages were sexless for years before we finally divorced. My first husband was seeing men on the side, but I didn't know it. The second one was seeing other women."

Somehow Candice didn't grasp the connection between orgasms and clitoral stimulation until she was thirty-five when she acquired a copy of Marc and Judith Meshorer's book, *Ultimate Pleasure: Secrets of Easily Orgasmic Women* from the Literary Guild. She would, she says, have been too embarrassed to buy it in a bookstore.

"I was astonished," she says. "I tried it, touching myself. Masturbating. What an ugly word! But it worked. Then I met a man who wasn't bothered if I touched myself while we made love. All those years I had been faking orgasms—and suddenly I was having them! It was wonderful. The first time it happened with him I let out a series of yelps that he said sounded like a cat with her tail caught in the door.

"All those years," she repeated. "What a waste!"

Who Is She?

Late bloomers are 23.2 percent of the survey group and are women who:

* *Began to masturbate after twenty-one, if at all.* Ten percent of this group have never masturbated and another 20 percent do so "rarely."

* *Did not become orgasmic until their late twenties or beyond—with over half not having an orgasm until past age thirty.*

* *Reported frequent difficulty in achieving orgasm during lovemaking and/or masturbation even after becoming orgasmic.*

One striking difference between late bloomers and the other women is their overwhelmingly negative responses to initial sexual experiences. Their comments ranged from "not memorable, at best," to "awful!" Another difference was the high number—over 60 percent—reporting dissatisfaction with their sex lives. They are also far more caught up in love fantasies than any other group of women, which may partially explain their perpetual disappointment with real sex.

Late bloomers were somewhat more likely to label their families as "highly religious" or "very conservative," and they did seem more judgmental or punitive about other women's sexual behavior than the survey respondents in general. However, they did not report significantly fewer sex partners than other women in their age groups. Many had multiple partners, even two and more marriages, without being orgasmic. And many reported extended periods of "sexlessness," in their marriages and in other relationships.

"In both my marriages, the sex died early," wrote a forty-year-old woman who had her first orgasm at thirty-nine. "The first time we stopped making love after two years, but we stayed married five more years. We slept, like nested spoons, in the same bed. It was affectionate.

"The second one was a little different. He was careful not to touch me in bed. He hardly ever even rolled into me. I don't know what went wrong. I never told either of them I didn't have orgasms. I thought I was a great fake."

The Late-Bloomer Mindset

No matter how sophisticated they might otherwise be, many of the late bloomers I interviewed struck me as women stuck in the sexual ingenue phase. They talked about love, not sex. Their fantasy lives were more active than their sexual realities, and the fantasies were of love more often than sex. Even after they became orgasmic, many, including Candice, expressed concern about whether touching themselves during lovemaking would frighten a man away.

Having a man, being in a relationship, even a bad one, is more important than sexual pleasure. Yet, the man was rarely described in real terms. He was idealized, as sex was idealized. Not surprisingly, these late bloomers seemed to make poorer partner choices than any group in my study except wildflowers.

One woman described as "the best relationship of [her] life" a few brief encounters with a man who was most likely married. She couldn't call him at home; he didn't call her from anywhere but the office. They put a weekend trip on her credit cards because he had canceled his cards, and he never reimbursed her for his share of the expenses. Rationalizing these and many other give-away details, she refused to see the obvious.

Maybe some late bloomers, like this woman, choose badly because they don't look closely at the man they're choosing. They are looking instead for men who will fit easily into a fantasy script. When a real man fails to hit his marks and speak his lines, the fantasy stops working for them.

What Does She See in Him?

This question can be applied more often to these late bloomers than to the other women I interviewed. They had more gay or alcoholic husbands; reported more physical, psychological, and sexual abuse in their relationships; were more likely to be left holding the bills or standing at the altar. Even when they professed to be happily involved in wonderful relationships, they, like the woman above, described situations with men which were clearly anything but "wonderful." One woman, for example, said her wonderful man "had to slap [her] sometimes, though he didn't like to do it." Often the sexual encounters they reported were exploitive or humiliating ones.

"My second marriage is good, except for the sex," says Claudia, a forty-one-year-old Seattle entrepreneur. "My husband doesn't have sex. He gets blow jobs. I think his need for blow jobs is a power trip. The first time we tried to have sex, on our third date, he couldn't. I'm sure it was because the sex was my idea. I'd been nervous about when to do it, so I met him at the door on our third date in a negligee. I said, 'This is making me nervous; let's get it over with.' He tried, but he couldn't keep it up long enough to do the job.

"The next time, he couldn't again, so I blew him. After that, he was okay in bed. He'd reasserted control in the relationship by having me blow him. When he's having problems, he wants me on my knees, mouth open.

"He blames me. According to him, I'm not sexy. Maybe he's right. I didn't masturbate until I was thirtysomething, and it took me a lot of tries before I had an orgasm. I still don't have orgasms very often, either by masturbating or with him. I dream about being with a man who would really move me sexually, and I would have an affair, but I don't want to take off my clothes in front of another man.

"My friends say, 'Why don't you leave him now?' because he's such an arrogant bastard."

Other late bloomers tell similar stories of being stuck, for one reason or another, in a relationship which they find far from sexually satisfying. Either they are not orgasmic or they are rarely so. Yet a small percentage of the late bloomers in my study have moved beyond becoming orgasmic to fully enjoying their own sexuality. This small percentage puzzles me: Why hasn't orgasm, when it finally happens after an anxious and long wait for it, produced a dramatic release from past repressions?

The Sexy Factor

Many of these women added disparaging comments to the questions, "How often do you have sex?" and "Is that satisfactory?"

Often, they seemed to feel the need to explain their lack of activity by asserting their own lack of appeal. "Who would want me more often?" one wrote. Others aggressively defended their low numbers.

"I'm not that sexual," wrote a thirty-one-year-old Florida secretary. "It's not that high a priority with me. I like my husband and my marriage. I like being married! But sex once a week is fine. I may or may not have an orgasm. For me to come is such a production, I would just as soon fake and get it over with. I don't like putting out that much energy."

And, "I'm not that interested in sex, so once or twice a month is enough," from a twenty-nine-year-old.

"I don't know how often we have sex," wrote a forty-two-year-old from Philadelphia who has never masturbated and had her first orgasm at age thirty-seven. "The last time was . . . let me think. . . ." She added, "It's quite satisfactory, however often it is."

Are their sex drives lower than other women's? There's certainly nothing wrong with wanting or needing less sex than other women do. Having sex less often doesn't necessarily make a woman less skilled as a lover. These women may, however, believe there's something wrong with them because they aren't as easily or as often aroused as they believe other women are. Late bloomers seem to have less confidence in themselves as lovers—and as "sexy" women—than any other category of respondents.

"I know I'm pretty," a twenty-six-year-old wrote, "but I'm not sexy. I don't feel sexy. If it's sex a man primarily wants, he doesn't want me."

Other women made similar comments, indicating their low sense of sexual self-esteem didn't extend to other areas of their lives. Some women, including most of the late bloomers who genuinely bloomed, say they either did, or had, consciously chosen to put other things before sex. Most often those "other things" were work or family obligations. Women between thirty and forty often had chosen demanding careers. A few women over fifty-five wrote about putting their sexuality on hold while they cared for aged parents, handicapped children, disabled husbands.

"You can decide not to let yourself be sexy," wrote a thirty-nine-year-old New Yorker. "That's what I did for years. I was a career woman. I was very busy. Where did sex fit into that equation? That I was also frigid didn't occur to me until I had a fling with a much younger man while I was on vacation last year. He taught me things about my body I never knew. No man had ever performed cunnilingus on me before. Once I discovered that, I was a changed woman.

"I'm sexy now!"

The Oral Factor

No other category of women in my study had such negative opinions of cunnilingus. Many seemed to have more opinions than their limited experience with the practice would reasonably warrant. Less than 20 percent reported being orgasmic via cunnilingus, compared to 90 percent of all respondents. Most were far more willing to perform fellatio on their partners than have cunnilingus performed on them.

"I've never liked it," wrote a thirty-eight-year-old divorced mother of two. "I've certainly never known a man who's done it right. The man I'm seeing now was very offended because I didn't want him to do it. I made up a story to placate him. I told him I'd had a terrible experience with it once. A man had bit me until I bled. Now, I explained, I can't let myself go and enjoy it. He was sympathetic. Well, why wouldn't he be? It's a good story.

"I was going to tell him my first husband had traumatized me by saying I smelled fishy down there, but by now, I reasoned, he would expect me to get over that."

Another thirty-eight-year-old woman wrote: "I don't mind doing it, but I hate having it done to me. Men are cleaner. We can't help it, but we're not."

And a twenty-nine-year-old wrote: "I think cunnilingus is overrated. It was only done to me twice. Both times I was self-conscious and uncomfortable physically. Maybe I'm not made right to have it done to me, but each time it felt like the man was gouging me with his chin while his tongue was not driving me wild. No more!"

A Maryland woman insisted she would enjoy having cunnilingus done more often, but that pantyhose get in the way. "My husband wants to do it," she wrote. "And, really I would let him. I like it. But, I wear pantyhose to work everyday. They leave me feeling sweaty and smelly at the end of the day."

The common elements in late bloomers' stories include:

- *Their inability to use love fantasies as arousal aides and to then let them go.* More than other women, they try to make their fantasies real and fail to take the mechanical steps necessary to make real sex better.
- *Their consistent poor partner choices, which they often rationalize and justify.*
- *Lack of sexual confidence in themselves.*
- *The tendency to become involved in sexless marriages and other long-term relationships.*
- *Their dislike of cunnilingus, which other respondents enthusiastically enjoy.*
- *Their greater dissatisfaction with their sex lives.*

If you are a late bloomer, don't be discouraged. The fact that you are reading this is proof you want more from sex, and you can get it.

How Some Late Bloomers Changed Their Lives

Late bloomers who now enjoy rich and satisfying sex lives have several things in common:

THEY GAVE THEMSELVES PERMISSION TO ENJOY SEX FOR ITS OWN SAKE. THEY REDUCED THEIR DEPENDENCE ON LOVE FANTASIES FOR AROUSAL

Learning how to recognize love fantasies for what they are isn't easy for many women. Some late bloomers have learned to become more orgasmic by replacing love fantasies with more graphic sex fantasies during masturbation—and discovered to their surprise that their changed fantasy life is reflected in changed attitudes toward men, love, and sex. Many sex therapists, in fact, use "guided fantasies" to help women become orgasmic, either for the first time or on a more regular basis.

"I don't let myself dwell on those love thoughts," writes a thirty-seven-year-old late bloomer, who in spite of being inorgasmic until two years ago, has a satisfying sex life now. "In the past, I masturbated to romantic scenes, and I was always trying to make my daydreams real with men. A year ago I bought a book of erotic stories and began masturbating to them. Now, I invent wild sex scenes with strangers. Screw the love stories!"

THEY GAVE ORAL SEX ANOTHER CHANCE

For those late bloomers who have moved beyond merely becoming orgasmic, cunnilingus often played a vital role in the sexual discovery process. More often by oral than manual stimulation, many finally became orgasmic after years of being sexually active.

"Becoming orgasmic changed everything for me," wrote a thirty-eight year old from Cleveland. "I was naive about emotions and sex and relationships before I had an orgasm. I invested sex with a mystery that doesn't have to be there. I learned how simple it was a few days after my thirtieth birthday. A man went down on me and gave me an orgasm. He wasn't the love of my life, but he moved me physically like no one else had ever done. I realized it wasn't dependent on a man, or rather, Mr. Right. I decided I would have orgasms on a regular basis."

THEY MASTURBATE REGULARLY

Being orgasmic via masturbation takes the pressure off a woman to have an orgasm during sex. She feels less desperate if she knows she *can* have an orgasm. When she knows she can have them regularly, she begins to feel more confident about herself, *sexier*. Some late bloomers say they began scheduling a time set aside for masturbation and did it, even when they didn't feel particularly aroused.

One woman wrote: "I made love dates with myself three times

a week. I lit candles, put on a silk robe, rubbed myself with oil or cream, played soft music. Then I read hot novels or watched a video until I was aroused enough to masturbate. After six months of this, I was confident in my ability to have orgasms, confident in my sexuality for the first time in my life."

THEY MADE GOOD PARTNER CHOICES

A few women do credit a man with changing their sex lives, and a good man can certainly make a difference in any woman's life. Many men, of all ages, find the relatively inexperienced woman, no matter her age, appealing, because they want to play erotic guide. But you don't even need one who's willing to be a teacher; any man who understands the basics of female sexuality will do.

"I had two children and three divorces before I had an orgasm two years ago," writes a thirty-six-year-old Chicagoan. "He was a married man. And for months I tortured myself thinking I loved him and wanted him to leave his wife. I begged him to leave his wife and marry me! I thought no one else could ever give me an orgasm since no one had before him.

"He explained it to me. When he said he wouldn't leave his wife, I threatened to kill myself. I told him I had to have him because only he made me orgasmic. Wasn't that true love?

"He said, 'Look, all I do is rub your clit while I fuck you. Any man can do that. *You* can do that, for God's sake!'

"I masturbated after he left. He was right. I could do it. Did I feel like a fool!"

PART 2

Pleasures
Denied

CHAPTER 6

The Woman Who Doesn't "Need" an Orgasm

"I know how to have an orgasm, but orgasms aren't that important to me. Sex isn't as important in a relationship as a lot of other things. I want more than sex."

—a thirty-one-year-old New Yorker

W̲HEN I INTERVIEWED men for my previous book, *What Men Really Want*, they repeatedly told me that one aspect of female sexual behavior bothered them more than any other. Women, they said, want more from sex than sex. Women, they said, use sex to get what they want from men.

One man said: "Sex isn't an item on her personal agenda. It's the credit card she uses to get a guy to turn her agenda into his shopping list."

Harsh words, but they were echoed by many men who spoke them as much from hurt as anger. The sexual revolution and the feminist movement might as well never have happened because, according to them, women still want to get most of their emotional and financial security needs met through sex. What they said is often true: Some women do use sex to get what they want from men. Their attitude—that men are responsible for women—reflects a lack of faith in their own ability to take care of themselves. Many women, particularly the daughters of middle and upper-middle class mothers who don't work outside the home, have never seen any other kind of relationship between men and women.

That the traditional sexual bargain seldom works today doesn't stop them from believing it should and blaming themselves, and men, when it doesn't.

"If she says she really wants you, she doesn't necessarily mean she can't wait to get in your pants, which is what you mean about her," another man wrote. "What she probably means is she wants your income added to hers or your sperm donated to her egg."

That's certainly not true of *all* women. Though cruelly stated, however, it could be applied to *some* members of this group of women, the pleasure deniers.

What Is a Pleasure Denier?

- *They are probably orgasmic*, at least some, and perhaps most, of the time, but orgasm is not their main sexual goal.
- *Nor do they crave sexual variety*, either in numbers of partners or types of experiences with the same partner. Often when they experiment with sexual variations, they do so to please their partner.
- *They are not free to pursue sexual pleasure for its sake alone*, because they have too much "invested" in sex.

Not that they don't enjoy sex, they are quick to say, *but* . . .

What Makes Them Deny Their Own Pleasure?

NEGATIVE SEX ATTITUDES

Some of them become pleasure deniers partly out of guilt. Maybe they don't believe women should enjoy sex. Maybe they were promiscuous in the past and believe salvation, of the social as well as religious kind, is dependent upon a period of denial. The impact of religion on sexuality in our culture, even for the relatively nonreligious, is tremendous. Our negative sex attitudes have their roots in Puritanism, even if they are expressed in other terms.

INVOLVEMENT IN RELATIONSHIPS BASED ON FINANCIAL AND/OR EMOTIONAL DEPENDENCE

Maybe they are inhibited within a living-together relationship much as their mothers and grandmothers were in marriages. For the sake of the relationship, they put his needs first and deny themselves little pleasures, behaving like "good wives" forgoing the last slice of chocolate cake, the best cut of meat, and the joy of regular orgasms.

"I enjoy sex," they say, "*but . . .* "

THE BELIEF THAT SEXUAL PLEASURE IS NOT AS IMPORTANT AS OTHER GOALS

The "but" precedes a denial clause explaining why other goals are more important to them than sexual pleasure. Both the wording of their denials and the social climate in which they are spoken give these dependent clauses the weight of the unassailable. Women who would never admit to having repressive sexual attitudes based in religious guilt have a new language in which to express their negativity, the language of intimacy, which has become almost as overworked and insipid as the word "relationship."

Intimacy is chic. Intimacy is warm, proper, and correct, like Hope Steadman, the good wife and mother on "Thirtysomething." Not to have intimacy is to flounder emotionally in a neurotic stew of our own making, as Ellyn, Hope's best friend, did before she met and married Billy, ending her neurotic singlehood, and as Melissa, Michael's single cousin, did. Yes, all three women might have had good sex on any given Tuesday night, but what Hope has—a marriage, home, and children—is much more important.

And, who can refute the argument that some things are more important than sex—especially now when STDs flourish and biological clocks tick wickedly away?

Because no one *can* argue against that premise without sounding like a holdout from the do-it-if-it-feels-good generation, women, especially the new conservative twentysomethings and the baby boom women in their thirties anxious to become mothers, are able to justify an old-fashioned idea, getting their needs met through sexual relationships, in a thoroughly modern way.

They lecture about the dangers of casual sex. They bemoan the emptiness of loveless sex. Getting into a relationship, finding a husband, starting a family—all sound in the newspeak like the laudable steps one must take in the quest for the Holy Grail, rather than what they really are: the same life moves every generation has made.

In many ways, the pleasure denier is an old-fashioned girl in Nineties' clothing, motivated by the same forces that pulled her mother's strings. That the pursuit of pleasure and the search for a relationship could be separate goals doesn't occur to her. And why should it when all the sexual messages handed down to her over the years have relentlessly linked the two? She wants to please her man, and she is motivated to do so in part because she wants, and feels she needs, a commitment to more than good sex. No wonder she insists on forging her own links, as if by denying one—pursuit of pleasure—she'll improve her odds of achieving the other—a relationship. In fact, sex has become the chief weapon in her arsenal of feminine wiles, though she probably doesn't realize it.

"If you have sex too soon, a man won't commit," she says, and she swears by the (no sex before the) "third-date rule."

Though considerable evidence to the contrary exists, she believes she can manipulate a relationship through the timely dispensing of sex, one sex act a time. Women's magazines advise: Don't have oral sex before the third encounter, or don't be the first to initiate oral sex. In an article asking, "Can You Be Too Good in Bed?" *Glamour* warned the reader that to display all her erotic skills before a relationship is well established would be to risk scaring the man away.

When you look at sex that way, it ceases to be an activity undertaken mainly for the pleasures it provides or even as the pathway to intimacy. (Can intimacy, after all, the closing of the emotional distance between two people, be achieved by such calculating means?)

The pleasure-denying woman in search of commitment is the target market for the marriage guides and the man-bashing books. While some of the sharp edges of difference between the sexes have blurred, women still seek identities primarily through intimacy and men seek theirs primarily through achievement. Intimacy is the womanly goal, the word around which those books turn. When a method of ensnaring him fails to work, she blames herself and him, not the method, not the mindset that creates and accepts the method. Bolstered by a media climate in which relationships are as sanctified as Mom, flag, and apple pie, she can be, and often is, sanctimonious about her position.

"I do look down on women who are having sex for the sake of having sex," admits a thirty-two-year-old Philadelphian. "Their values are all wrong. That kind of behavior doesn't work today."

She automatically assumes women who are "having sex for the sake of sex" are having it with many partners, indiscriminately. Many women do equate pleasure with promiscuity—especially if the pleasure is being enjoyed by another woman. And, some are almost palpably angry at women who openly acknowledge their ability to enjoy sex outside committed relationships. Pleasure deniers see sexually independent women as a threat—which, if we're being honest, they can be—and an insult to the established social order, an order which the pleasure denier hopes will reward her for her own good behavior.

Many have *deliberately* put pleasure on hold, temporarily or longer, while they are focused outward on finding the one, the man who can give it all to them. Another woman who is not obsessed with getting a relationship or keeping one going or moving the one she has into marriage seems as threatening as a sexy divorcee in a roomful of tired wives. She can only be forgiven if she changes her behavior by punishing herself through a period of public celibacy meant as much to purify her in preparation for a relationship as to atone for her "sins."

The pleasure denier wants other women to validate her position.

More important, she often wants a relationship so badly, she conjures them from the limited material men give her. Examining and analyzing, she finally rationalizes every word he speaks until she concludes he's said exactly what she wants to hear. Then she misinterprets his actions until they underscore the words she's hearing in her head. Making much of little, she pursues love fantasies as if they were realities.

It's easy to look from the outside in and see how she short-changes herself. It's easier to be critical of her, even smugly so, unless you are where she is. Many of these women are experiencing a pain their mothers and older sisters never knew. Maybe they waited too long to marry and mother. Maybe they chose men who've been there and don't want to go back—or simply aren't in any hurry to get there. And maybe they have to settle for living with a man who, a generation ago, would have been happy to marry them. For whatever reason, they haven't been able to get husbands and babies as easily as other women have.

"I want a baby so bad, I can smell it," writes a thirty-eight-year-old executive editor. "When I hold someone's baby, the sweet smell of its little head makes me want to cry. I never knew I'd feel this way. I have this terrible longing for my own child. The man I love could give me that child, could give me all of it, the city apartment, home in the country, everything.

"He has it, and he won't share it. He says he's been married before and had his child and he doesn't want to do any of it again. I can't tell you how hurt and angry that makes me feel."

She says the sex with him is "good," but "not the best I've ever had."

How could it be?

The following chapters focus on three distinct types of pleasure deniers. You may be one of them, or you may be denying yourself sexual pleasure without fitting neatly into any of these categories. You can still find help and solace in the stories of women who have moved out of the pleasure-denying phase.

CHAPTER 7

Revirginized Women

"I dated Bob for seven years—and he didn't get any for a long time, six or seven months. He stayed with me. I was the one who pulled away from him. If you want a man to stay, you have to make him wait for sex."

      —a twenty-eight-year-old retail manager, who was a
               wildflower in high school

T HEY TAKE THE Madonna song "Like a Virgin" to heart. Sex with each new man is supposed to be "like the very first time." At least, *he* should believe it feels that way to her. No matter her age and sexual history, she wants him to assume the role of more experienced partner, and she believes he wants it to be this way too.

Some women have revirginized a dozen times or more in the course of a dating lifetime. They don't really expect a man to believe they're virgins—only less experienced, especially of late, than he is. While some lie about their histories, most simply don't offer any, or many, details from their pasts, letting their actions, or lack of them, lead the man to his own conclusions. Their motives for revirginizing behavior vary. Some women become celibate for a period of time to atone for periods of promiscuity. Others deliberately withhold sex as a technique for forcing a man to commit to a relationship in some way.

Maggie, a thirty-five-year-old New York publishing executive who's revirginized several times, has a lot of dates, but would like to marry before her "biological time runs out." Like many New York women, Maggie has a roommate to share the cost of a one-bedroom apartment in a good neighborhood. This year, she has the bedroom, and her roommate, Cheryl, a graphic artist, is sleeping on the futon. They've been sharing the same apartment for five years, and each New Year's Eve, they trade places, alternating bedroom with futon.

"Each year one of us is promising herself she'll get married before she has to spend another year on the futon," Maggie says. "And then it's New Year's Eve again and we're toasting each other and rearranging the closets and drawers together. I love Cheryl, but it gets a bit depressing.

"Two years ago she bought this book everyone was reading at the time, *How to Marry the Man of Your Choice*, by Margaret Kent. It's the one with the money-back guarantee if you followed her advice and didn't get married within two years. Anyway, Kent said don't have sex with him for a lot of dates. I think it was twelve. A great number, anyway. I'd check the book, but we threw it down the incinerator chute this past New Year's Eve.

"I won't say the book alone made me reexamine my approach to men, but it was a contributing factor. Cheryl was really into these books, really heavy into the theories. For a while, it looked like the concept was working for her. She almost got married. So, I decided to give it a try. When I met Matt, I knew instantly he was someone I wanted to marry. I didn't have sex with him until the fifth date. I'm not kidding you . . . the *fifth* date. In my twenties, I went to bed with men I'd met at *parties*, sometimes hours after meeting them.

"So, okay, I gave the system a shot. I held him at bay. I'll admit he was intrigued. He goes, 'Why won't you have sex with me?' And I go, 'Well, I just can't do that with a man I don't know very well. It's how I'm made.'

"Can you believe it?"

The important question is: Did Matt believe it?

"Yeah, I guess he did. Whether he believed it or not doesn't matter. We were together about six months. Then I caught him in bed, actually *in bed*, with another woman. It was one of those awful scenes you read about in books. I thought he was cheating on me. He kept going alone to his place in the Hamptons in the middle of the week. He said he needed to get away from the distractions of the city and work. I rented a car and went out there to spy on him one night. I saw them go in together—and, just like a character in a movie, burst into the room when they were in the act of doing it.

"That was the end. He said he was sorry, she didn't mean anything to him, he really loved me and didn't want to lose me, all the usual garbage. On the other hand, he didn't exactly behave as if I meant so much to him either."

But, she reflected, "I think I know where I made the first mistake with him. I made him wait for sex. I got that right. But, I let him do it anally the very first time. Big mistake. Men don't respect you if you let that happen too easily. Anal sex should be a very big deal with the woman. She should say, 'Oooh, I don't know . . . only because I love you so much!' Ridiculous sounding, but true.

"I happen to like anal sex, which must put me in the minority of women. Men are always telling me their former partners wouldn't let them do it. Who are these women?"

She's seeing another man now and "not exactly, but sort of, following the [how-to-catch-a-man] system." The revirginizing part—making him feel like the seasoned lover to her less experienced woman. She made him wait, but not so long. They had sex on the third date, but she plans to "postpone anal sex indefinitely this time." She'd already decided she wanted to marry him on the first date, two weeks before their first sexual encounter.

"Oh, I always know that on the first date. I can always tell if I'll want to marry the guy or not."

Maggie has a lot in common with other revirginizers, not the least of which is the tendency to think in terms of bridal white almost from the first hello.

Who Is She?

Nearly 20 percent of the women I surveyed wrote about their revirginizing behavior—and half of them were repentant wild-flowers. Over half were in their twenties, with most of the remainder between the ages of thirty and thirty-five. Only two women over forty reported revirginizing behavior.

Revirginizers are women who:

- *Were currently single, either unmarried or divorced, and reported periods of voluntary celibacy lasting six months or longer.* These are not women who wrote complaining of their inability to attract sex partners for extended periods of time. They had the opportunities, but chose to say no.

- *Expressed a strong belief in their need to atone for past promiscuous behavior by abstaining from sex.* Almost half were motivated to change their sexual behavior dramatically in the aftermath of an abortion. Rather than determining they wouldn't be careless about contraception again, they decided they wouldn't be "casual" about sex.

- *Held a strong belief in their ability to force a commitment by withholding sex for a certain length of time or controlling the sexual relationship in some way.*

They almost unanimously—98 percent—answered yes to the question, "Do you risk losing a man by having sex too soon?" Alas, so did the group as a whole, with an astonishing 91 percent answering yes. Although 74 percent of revirginizers (and 67 percent of the total group) have had sex on a first date, at least once in their lives, they said such behavior was "wrong," "stupid," "proof of your unmarriageability," and "a bad tactical error."

Or, like this twenty-eight-year-old woman, they couched their negative sex judgments in intimacy terms. She writes:

"Sex too soon destroys the fragile bond between two people and makes it impossible to have true intimacy. Sex is too often used in place of intimacy by women as well as men, though men do it more often. If you want to be sure you'll never see this man for a second date, have sex with him."

The Instant Choice

Revirginizers decide early, often on the first date, this man is the one. An overwhelming majority of them can list the reasons why they instantly knew he was right; and their lists read like a catalog entry for "Husband, Upper Middle Class." They probably more often than not force the man beside them to fit the list just as they force the fit between love and sex.

"I didn't have sex with the man I'm seeing now until the fourth date," writes a twenty-six-year-old revirginizer, "because I want to marry him. He is everything I want in a husband: good job, tall and good looking, sense of humor. I'm not going to make the same mistake women in my office have made, waiting too long to settle down. There's nobody left for them. It's sad."

Other women claim their targeted mates are sensitive or kind, intelligent and understanding. How do they determine these qualities exist in a man, and in abundance, early in the first date, in time to realize they must delay sexual activity to manipulate him into a relationship with marital potential? How can they possibly decide this is the man they want to marry before they've had sex with him?

"You just know these things," insists Maggie. "And, once you know you want him you aren't going to get him if he thinks you're too sexually experienced or too easy."

No one is more goal-oriented than the revirginizer. No matter how many times she's tried the system and failed to marry, she believes in it. And the key to the system is immediate implication. You can't revirginize with a man after you've gone to bed with him on the first date. Therefore, if you follow the logic, you have to decide quickly.

"I made the mistake of having sex on the first date with a great guy," writes a twenty-seven-year-old. "And I never regained the lost ground with him. I won't do that again! I met a terrific man the next weekend; and I'm sure he's the one for me. This time, no sex for several weeks. I've mapped out my strategy already."

Maybe they can't point to success stories, but revirginizers believe in the strategy and may not stop believing until after it's failed to work for them.

"I sublimated my sex drive during the courtship," writes a newly divorced twenty-eight-year-old from Florida. "I got into that whole traditional wedding thing, picking china patterns. After we were married, reality reared its ugly head.

"Before I married him, I'd had some hot affairs. As soon as I met him, I became this vestal virgin. I'm taking a psychology course now, and I think I was acting out the Madonna-whore complex. I'd been a whore, so I became a Madonna to get married.

"Do you know how I got him to marry me? I begged him, literally begged him to marry me after we'd made love one day. He agreed. Why did I want to marry a man it turns out I can't stand? I don't know. I thought he would be a good husband. I didn't think he'd hit me.

"I should have seen it coming on our third date when he got so mad at me because some guy flirted with me that he slammed me against the car door. But by then I'd already made up mind to marry him. He's a lawyer."

Many revirginizers told stories similar to this one, though often the reported abuse—physical, psychological, and financial—occurred in relationships, not marriages. And so strong is the revirginizer's determination to make the man fit the myth that the reality doesn't deter her from wanting to marry him. Sadly, this behavior is not limited to revirginizers.

The February/March 1991 issue of *Modern Bride* published a survey of 500 readers, 61.6 percent of whom were college graduates working in professional or managerial jobs, in which 29 percent reported major personality flaws in their intended husbands, including jealousy, anger, and an unwillingness to talk things out. These are indeed *major* flaws, the kind that lead to battery in some cases and divorce in others. Yet the brides-to-be march eagerly toward their altars with blinders on beneath their veils.

Maybe they really think marriage will change their men for the better. Or, more likely, they don't think, have stopped themselves from analyzing data about the man the minute they made the decision to marry him, way back there on date one or date two. Having made the early choice, the instant commitment almost upon meeting the man to marry him, they didn't give themselves permission to reconsider.

Nor do many revirginizers permit themselves true lust. Over half of this survey group reported sexual dissatisfaction with their partners—the very same partners they still hoped to marry. Why don't they hear the warning bells signaling later marital and sexual problems?

"So many things are more important than sex," writes a thirty-three-year-old from Alabama. "I want a life I can't get on my own."

The sex with her boyfriend, the man she wants to marry, is, she admits, "not very good." She describes a sexual relationship in which his needs are met, while hers are not.

"He doesn't like to go down on me, and he hates it if I touch myself during sex. He says, 'Why do you do that? No other women I've been with have done that.' So, I am pretty much doing it his way now.

"I give the best blow jobs he's ever had, or at least he tells me I do. Someday those b.j.s will pay off for me bigtime."

The Desire to Control Relationships Through Sex

The revirginizer believes she can control a relationship by behaving in the "right" way. She may believe she won't get what she wants unless she is an effective manipulator of her man, his emotions, and particularly his penis. And she *can't* control the man if she can't control her own sexual desires, which she does by deliberately putting them on hold.

The control extends beyond *when* they will have sex to *how* they will have it. Each step of the sexual relationship has been carefully orchestrated in advance.

"First time, it's missionary position," writes a thirty-six-year-old revirginizer, "or they think you're too comfortable with having sex with a new guy. No oral stuff until the third time. And, anal and bondage and all that—much later on, much later. You have to make him believe you've never done this stuff with anyone before he came along."

Seventy-seven percent of these women insist missionary is the only acceptable first-time position! But, even more interesting than their allegiance to the concept of the man on top, dominating, is their attitude toward birth control. Revirginizers don't use anything in more than half their sexual encounters, and withdrawal is the favored method for over 30 percent of them —"until a relationship is established."

In other words, they fail to protect themselves from pregnancy and disease in the early encounters with a man, when they have no assurance from him that he isn't having sexual relations with other women. Without a monogamous commitment or even a hint or promise of one from him, they risk their health. Why? They don't want to appear "ready" for sex, because they want the man to think they were swept away.

"The whole issue of birth control and disease prevention is so tricky," writes a thirty-four-year-old management consultant. "You look like a whore if you have a basket of condoms in your nightstand. You can't be on the pill if you haven't been dating and ditto for the diaphragm. What are you doing with the protective gear if you aren't playing the sport?

"Here's how it has to be. Hold a man off until you decide to have sex, then insist he provide protection. If he has nothing with him, make him pull out before he comes. I confess, I haven't always been successful at speaking up or, when I do speak up, getting the man to go along. But I've been lucky."

The fear of appearing "ready" or "easy" even affects women who are discreetly on the pill. Many of them won't carry condoms for protection against STDs. The reality of protection clashes with the romantic sexual message they're trying to send: "I'm vulnerable, not sexually sophisticated or experienced. Take care of me."

Sometimes, however, everybody's lust gets out of control. She isn't taking care of herself, and he isn't taking care of her either. The resulting pregnancy or STD deals a blow to her commitment campaign as well as her body.

"I was afraid I'd gotten pregnant during the first month we had sex," writes a twenty-seven-year-old law student who is dating another law student, two years younger than she. "That would have been awful! A baby now is out of the question, but an abortion would have killed this relationship.

"I've had my wild days. This is different. This man could be my husband and true life partner. I imagine us setting up a practice together, raising our children, and bringing them into the office when they are babies so I can nurse."

Another twenty-seven-year-old writes: "I've been seeing him for two months, but I'm not going to have sex with him until I have a sense of commitment from him. Sex isn't the most important thing. However, I'm on the pill though he is not aware of this. I've had two abortions, and I don't want to go through another one. In each case, it left me feeling awful and also ended the relationship.

"With so much bad stuff behind me, I want this one to be perfect. When we finally do have sex, it will be like starting over."

Another woman in her late twenties writes: "I know what I want and am willing to defer my own sexual pleasure to get it. You can't get a man if you let him have everything too soon, and you can't get him if he thinks you're too experienced. I know I'm taking a real risk, but I won't ask him to use condoms. A woman can't bring up this issue without appearing to be experienced.

"I know this sounds like something my mother would say, but it's true. Men still marry less experienced women or women they believe to be less experienced."

I don't know what her mother would say, but to me it sounds like a Nineties update on the old Fifties philosophy that put women in a double bind by telling them they could, and should, control their sexual desires but allowing them no back-up protection when they couldn't and didn't.

The revirginizers' stories have common elements—all familiar to women who came of age in the Fifties—including:

• *Their acceptance of popular dictums determining when sex is permissible—and how it should be performed.*

- *The "instant choice" syndrome, in which they decide very early that a man is the one.*
- *The failure to protect themselves from unwanted pregnancy and disease because they don't want to appear experienced or ready for sex.*

Residual Sex Guilt

Is it all manipulative logic or do many of these women revirginize in part as a way of purging themselves of past sexual "sins"? Nearly 80 percent of them describe earlier promiscuous periods in punitive terms, castigating themselves for their behavior.

"I was wild, out of control," a thirty-year-old woman wrote. "I'm lucky terrible things didn't happen to me, because I was asking for them. I was pushing the edges of the envelope.

"During my wild days, I picked up strangers in clubs. I let them tie me up with silk scarves. I had sex in bathrooms at parties held in houses and apartments of people I barely knew. I was depraved. Last week I took an AIDS test and found out I'm okay. It's a new lease on life, and I'm not going to have indiscriminate sex anymore."

Some women even blamed themselves for becoming victims of date rape.

"I was drinking," a twenty-four-year-old wrote. "Men have no respect for women who drink. He took advantage of me. It was awful, but maybe it wouldn't have happened if I hadn't had too much wine, if I hadn't given the appearance of being sexually easy."

Surely unacknowledged sex guilt plays a role in the decision to revirginize for some women, especially those who describe their pasts in such negative and self-blaming terms.

"I slept with fourteen guys in my senior year of college," writes a twenty-five-year-old. "It started with me rebelling against the guy I was seeing. I just said, 'Fuck it, I'll sleep with someone else. I'll show him.'

"When I got pregnant, I didn't have a clue as to who was the father. I didn't tell any of them, not that they would have wanted to know. I didn't tell anyone. I went by myself to have the abortion. It was weird, not exactly painful. They were nice to me at the clinic. But they kept asking me if I wanted to cry, and I didn't.

"After the abortion, I cleaned up my act. I didn't have sex for almost two years. Now, sex is not enough for me. I could do it all the time, but I'm not going to. I could have sex on the table, the floor, the backyard with this guy I'm seeing, but I'm not going to.

"He's going to marry me, and I'm going to do everything right. Someday I'll have a baby. Maybe after that, I'll tell him about the abortion, but maybe I won't. It's my private business to carry around, not his."

Many revirginizers do carry around "private business" of this sort. The heavy weight represses them sexually and makes them highly critical of themselves and other women.

How You Can Move Beyond Revirginizing Behavior

If you have chosen to remain celibate for a period of time because you need the emotional space for positive reasons—good for you. But, if your behavior is motivated by the desire to atone or to control a relationship, you're cheating yourself of sexual pleasure. The best advice for moving on comes from women who've done that, the former revirginizers.

STOP READING MAGAZINE ARTICLES AND BOOKS THAT GIVE ADVICE ON THE RIGHT TIME TO HAVE SEX

"I stopped reading all those articles on the New Celibacy," writes a twenty-nine-year-old Atlanta woman. "If you read this stuff, you get convinced that nobody is having sex or should have sex because sex is too risky. The authors make you believe that everything will turn out perfect in your relationships if you have sex at the right time. When you're searching for a relationship or coming out of yet another failed one, as I was, you're desperate to believe anything. I tried withholding, and it didn't lead to great relationships. I'm in a great relationship now. We had sex on the first date, and he's been nuts about me ever since. So, go figure."

DON'T COMMIT TOO SOON

"I used to believe you have sex on the third date and then don't have sex with anyone else but him and all will be well," writes a thirty-year-old Northeastern retail executive. "So, for most of my twenties I had two kinds of relationships: With men who cheated on me and with men who had sex the same way I did, so that we both committed too soon. The last time around I said, 'I am not promising I won't be with anyone else,' and I held to that for six months. We're getting married next week, and he's wonderful."

BE RESPONSIBLE ABOUT BIRTH CONTROL AND DISEASE PREVENTION—BECAUSE FAILURE TO PROTECT YOURSELF OFTEN STEMS FROM UNACKNOWLEDGED SEX GUILT

"I learned in therapy that I was punishing myself for being sexual by taking chances with my body," writes a twenty-six-year-old New Yorker. "I am on the pill now, and I use condoms. I feel so much more in control and freer. My sex life is better, and I don't feel as desperate to commit."

On reading their letters, I often wished I could say to revirginizers, "Lighten up!" This happily married broadcast executive in her thirties does say it: "My husband and I had sex on the first date. Six months later he was the one who wanted to get married, and I was the one on the fence. I'm glad I let him talk me into it. He's often said, and I believe it's true, that men don't decide whether or not they want to marry a woman based on when she has sex with them. For men, wanting sex and wanting to marry are separate issues.

"You ask, 'Does a woman risk losing a man by having sex too soon?' I say no, because the kind of man who will dump her as soon as he's had her will do it whether she has sex on the first date or the sixth—as soon as his goal is achieved.

"On the other hand, why not ask if a man risks losing a woman by having sex too soon? Conceivably he could. What if he prematurely ejaculates the first time? She might decide he isn't worth the trouble and not give *him* another chance."

CHAPTER 8

Living-Togethers

"When we first moved in together, we had sex all the time. Now, it's not such a big deal anymore."

—a twenty-six-year-old cohabitant

TWENTY YEARS AGO, living together was daring, but it isn't anymore. Living with a man to whom you are not married isn't likely to get you banned from the family reunion, though it may put you just outside the comfortable fellowship of married couples and church, and may not please your mother. Surprisingly, the arrangement also may not guarantee that your sexual needs will be met.

According to several studies conducted in the late Eighties, women in living-together arrangements were more likely both to be the victims of domestic violence and to have the kinds of sex they didn't want than were either single or married women. Some experts blame the violence on isolation, explaining that these couples are to some degree distanced from social controls of family and church because their relationships aren't sanctioned by either church or state. Other experts cite the woman's precarious standing, both economic and otherwise, within the relationship as the source of the power disparity at the heart of such behavior. Women often live with men who earn more money and want marriage less than they do. Some women aggravate this power imbalance by holding on to the belief that a relationship can be "controlled" through sex, rather than being equalized through financial parity. If she gives him what he wants sexually, she reasons, he'll give her what she needs outside the bedroom.

Many women do live with men in joyously egalitarian arrangements. They choose to live together for reasons mainly of pleasure. Obviously they aren't pleasure deniers, the subject of this section of the book. Therefore, the women discussed here, who are pleasure deniers, shouldn't be considered representative of *all* the survey respondents who live with men.

"I've been living with Kevin for two years now," writes a twenty-eight-year-old Chicago professional. The themes of exploitation and abuse in her shocking story were echoed in several other women's stories. "From the start, I've guessed he cheated on me, but have no proof. He doesn't try as hard at sex as he did when we were dating. The sex isn't less frequent, but it feels less valuable. He doesn't have to phone or make plans. I'm just there.

"Sometimes things get really bad between us. A few weeks ago we went to a party where he had too much to drink. They were showing porno movies in this one room. He insisted on having sex there where other people could see what we were doing. I didn't want to do it. He didn't seem to care about my feelings. I didn't say no, but I was hoping he'd get the hint when I wasn't enthusiastic. I cried all the way through it.

"He didn't get the hint."

But, why didn't she just say no? She wanted him to do it for her. Though he obviously wasn't respectful of her feelings at all, she kept silently hoping he would suddenly recognize and respect her needs—and take care of her, not himself.

According to several women in similar situations, the option to say no either doesn't exist or has to be used with discretion. It's useless to argue about whether or not that's true. Many of you reading this would take issue with that statement, but if the women in the relationships believe this to be true, then it becomes true as they hand over their power to their men. They fear that if they exercise their option to say no they might have to make new living arrangements, and many of them are both financially and emotionally trapped.

Who Is She?

Living-togethers represent 14.4 percent of the total survey group. Women in their twenties make up 67.2 percent and women in their thirties 30 percent. The remaining less than 3 percent are women in their forties. The criteria for defining them is obvious and simple:

• *They are living with men to whom they are not married and with whom they are sexually involved.*

Slightly more than half do want to marry their lovers. Another 20 percent are ambivalent. The remainder, mostly women older than thirty, do not want to marry the men with whom they live. That the living-together women I surveyed may be somewhat less inclined to marry than other cohabiting women interviewed in other studies—where as many as three-fourths typically want marriage—might be explained by two factors: A disproportionate number of my group live in big cities where the pressure to marry may be less intense while the need to find a roommate to share expenses is greater than in other parts of the country. Furthermore, more than 30 percent of my group are over thirty, older than the typical collegiate study participants, and are often divorced. Perhaps the older, divorced woman is less inclined toward marriage than her younger never-wed sister.

Why Women Live with Men

According to several studies conducted on couples in their twenties, men live together for sex, while women live together for commitment, hoping the arrangement will lead to marriage though the odds are against it. A 1985 Columbia University study found that only 19 percent of cohabiting men marry their partners. And a 1988 study commissioned by The National Bureau of Economic Research in Cambridge, Massachusetts, concluded that cohabiting couples who do marry have an 80 percent higher chance of divorcing than couples who haven't lived together before marriage. (Perhaps, the authors of the study suggested, they are less committed to the concept of marriage.)

But, the living-together women in my study cited "financial necessity" and "logistic convenience" as often as love or the hope for marriage as motives for their living arrangements. Women over thirty-five particularly say they simply got tired of carrying changes of underwear and make-up bags in their briefcases. They moved in with him because it was easier than dividing their time between his place and theirs.

"I got tired of schlepping my stuff across town every night and morning," writes a thirty-seven-year-old mortgage banker. "It was exhausting, and I was almost always the one who schlepped. He had a zillion excuses. But, the bottom line was: His apartment was better than mine."

A twenty-three-year-old writes: "I can't afford to live alone, not even in a closet. I was sharing an apartment with two women and one man, who was a boyfriend to one of the women. It was too much. No privacy. I wanted to read paperback mysteries in a bubble bath with no one banging on the door—or not to have to listen to hot sex in the next room."

Most of these women make less money than their men— which, many are savvy enough to realize, is the underlying basis for the inequality in their relationships, an inequality that extends to sex.

Sexual Frequency and Security

A study conducted by the National Center for Health Statistics says that unmarried cohabitants have more sex than either married couples or singles. Other research supports that claim. A major study on premarital cohabitation among never-married women in the United States reported in the August 1987 issue of *Journal of Marriage and the Family* found these women have more sexual intercourse than other women. For the women in my study this is also true. Living-togethers reported having intercourse or other sexual activity an average of four to six times a week as compared to two to three times a week for marrieds and once or twice a week for singles living alone.

Live-ins seem to expect their relationships to be even more sexually oriented than they are because the phrase "living together" smacks of lust not socially sanctioned, always the hottest kind. Or they may feel pressured to meet a frequency average they believe to be higher than it is because they fear losing their partner's interest if they don't. For whatever reasons, this group of women worried more about whether or not they were having enough sex than any other group, except wives who knew their husbands were having, or had had, affairs. Even when they say the sex is good, they don't sound secure in the knowledge.

"We have great sex," a thirty-six-year-old cohabitant writes. "But I'm afraid to be complacent about it. Living with someone is like always being on trial. I was married for ten years, and I felt more comfortable about the sex. I didn't feel like he'd leave me if we had a temporary lull in the bedroom. However, it was a false security. He did leave me—for an affair with another woman. Then he came back, but I left him. So, it's hard to tell if I worry now because I'm not married or because it's happened to me before."

A 1986 survey by *New Woman* magazine found cohabiting women felt more insecure about their love relationships than did other women. Perhaps like the woman above they feel "on trial" or easily disposable because they aren't married. They may have good reason not to be complacent. Studies, again largely conducted on college-age people, show live-in males sleep around more than married men do. The men are also more likely to suggest a break-up than the women, while in marriages the reverse is true, with women instigating more of the divorces.

All the evidence seems to point to a situation in which the man more often than not has the upper hand, which forces the woman to put her faith in the one power card she thinks she holds: sex.

"I've been living with my boyfriend five and one half years," writes a twenty-seven-year-old Seattle woman. "And I know why he stays with me. I perform fellatio almost every time we have sex. If I didn't, he would be out the door. Believe it!"

Sexual Coercion

The truly shocking statistics on cohabiting couples concern incidences of violence against the women.

"Swinging—and Ducking—Singles," an article in the September 5, 1988, issue of *Time* labeled couples who live together before marriage "the most violent of all." Among other sources, the article cited a University of New Hampshire study that found the levels of aggression among cohabitants higher than among daters or married people. Violence against live-in women ranged from slapping to rape. *Time* concluded that "live-in arrangements, which are not the norm, put added pressures on the couple."

Even more pervasive among cohabitants than "swinging and ducking" is sexual coercion. Forty percent of the cohabiting women in the 1986 *New Woman* survey reported they had endured a kind of sex they didn't want or didn't enjoy. Other surveys and research studies had similar findings. Sometimes, that "endured" sex was painful. And again it often included rape.

The cohabiting women in my survey did report frequent incidences of coerced sex in their relationships. Their most common complaints were either being forced, or feeling compelled, to perform fellatio more frequently than they would like, or to swallow semen, which they found objectionable, or to submit to anal sex, which they found either distasteful or painful. Ten percent have been raped or assaulted by their live-in partners. A few said they had unwillingly played the submissive role in spanking and S&M games. Overall, in fact, a higher percentage of this group than any other did participate in S&M activities, though many said they willingly did so.

The repeated theme running through many of their stories was one of sexual powerlessness.

A forty-eight-year-old Baltimore writer remembers her living-together phase, when she was forty, this way: "I look back on it and get the same feeling I had as a young woman when a man

I was seeing literally forced my head down so I could fellate him. The first time it happened, we were sitting in my parent's driveway in his car. I was nineteen and home from college for the summer. Now, I don't know why I continued to see him, but I did, for two more years.

"If I didn't get the message right away when he wanted me to fellate him, he forced my head down. Once I had bruises from his fingers on my neck. Twenty years later I lived with a man who had the same impact on me, but psychologically, not physically. He never actually pushed my head down with his hands. But his control over me, over the sex in our relationship, was so complete, I felt as if he did.

"I only lived with him a year. It was a difficult year in my life. I'd lost both my parents, my job, my condo, and my cat. When I got my self-esteem back, I left him."

Many cohabiting women project a low sense of self-esteem. Either they don't think they can make it on their own financially or emotionally, or they fear they won't be able to attract another man with the qualities they want. They seem to think the men have more value than they do. Some are hoping for marriage, and perhaps because the man doesn't offer it, they feel devalued.

"I know a modern woman shouldn't think this way," a twenty-five-year-old cohabitant writes, "but I would feel better about myself if he wanted marriage. I wonder if something is wrong with me that he doesn't [want marriage]. Maybe a little of that Catholic school education did take after all."

Others are struggling to survive a period in their lives that the living arrangement was supposed to be making easier. A few cite fear of disease as a reason for staying where they are. Among the women over thirty-five, the primary reason for staying was: "Where would I go if I left? All the men are gay, married, or rejects." Their attitude is: "This is as good as I can expect it to get."

And most continue to believe sex is their currency of exchange in their relationships even after the man has clearly wrested sexual control, devaluing the currency in the process.

"I lived with Mark for two years," writes a twenty-four-year-old. "It seemed like a great idea at first, because it was the only way I could afford to live off campus. I hated the dorms. My roommate was a raving beauty from South America . . . rich, rich, rich. Her parents insisted she stay in a dorm because they thought it was safer. I was truly miserable sharing space with her. Then came Mark.

"I really knocked myself out to please him in bed, but he got more and more demanding, especially about anal sex. Why do I meet the men who want that? After we'd been together a year and a half, he raped me. He was drunk, but that doesn't excuse what he did. He really hurt me. I wanted to leave him, but I couldn't. I was in my senior year of college, no money, no place else to go. I stayed with him six months after that incident. It was hell. Luckily, I met another man during that time and spent most of my nights at his apartment."

She is, she reports, living with the second man now. While he isn't abusive, he doesn't satisfy her sexual needs either. He has a problem with premature ejaculation, which she's never discussed with him for fear of "hurting his feelings."

"I want to be with him," she says. "I want a real commitment from him, but this is the best he's going to give me for now. I want to get married, but he doesn't. Given those circumstances, I'm not going to give him any trouble about sex.

"I don't always have orgasms, but he doesn't know it. I fake. He thinks he's a great lover, and I'm great at letting him think it. To me, he does have a problem with sex, though probably not to him. I think he ejaculates prematurely. I like intercourse to last.

"But I've said or done nothing. I don't want to hurt his feelings, mess with his ego. I want him to marry me."

Even women who don't want marriage often feel unable to stand up for themselves sexually in a cohabiting relationship. Some perhaps are drawn into these relationships because their submissiveness makes them appealing to dominant men. But, if it's truly satisfying for these women, who are we to judge?

The stories of living-together women have common elements, including:

- *Their secondary financial position within the relationship*. The younger women especially nearly always earn less than their lovers.
- *Their belief in the power of sex to hold him*. Perhaps they are less inclined to speak up for themselves sexually than other women because they fear losing him if they do so.
- *A greater level of sexual activity than other women experience.*
- *Their insecurity about the relationship.*
- *The likelihood of sexual coercion on some level.*

The Bottom Line

Surely many cohabiting women do allow the sexual coercion to take place because they are not financially equal to their partners.

"You make compromises in life," explains a thirty-five-year-old journalist living with a forty-three-year-old corporate executive whom she does not want to marry. "I can't have this lifestyle on my own. I do love him, in addition to appreciating the advantages his income gives me. He is not the best lover I've ever had. But, you can't have everything all at once.

"I met him six months after his divorce. He'd been married twenty years. She let him get sloppy. He doesn't try as hard in bed as other men I've known. So, I try for both of us.

"He'd always wanted anal sex from her, and she wouldn't do it. I told him I would—though, if you can believe this, I'd only done it once, in my extreme youth. You know the old joke about anal sex. Every woman does it twice, once to see what it's like, the second time to see if it's really as bad as she thought it was. You can imagine how bad my first time was if it took me over fifteen years to try again!

"He's not huge, but a little bigger than average. We use plenty of lubricant, but the first time was still a scorcher. He just slams right into me, sometimes I think harder this way than he does when we're having regular intercourse. Maybe it just feels harder. But, I've gotten used to it, and I would never tell him he's hurt me sometimes. Why spoil it for him? We do it this way once a week. I drink a glass of wine and make sure I'm really hot before we get to that part. I can even have orgasms during anal sex if I start out hot and rub my clitoris while he does me.

"Look, it goes with the territory."

As long as women continue to believe the answer to lower incomes lies in living with men, it probably does.

How You Can Get More Sexual Satisfaction

You're a cohabiting woman denying her own pleasure for the sake of holding a man, forcing a commitment, or from a sense of inequality based on financial disparity. Are you stuck in a sexual rut? No, other women have improved their sex lives and you can as well by:

- *Asserting your own right to sexual pleasure.* Communicate your sexual needs and desires to him. You may be pleasantly surprised to discover that your pleasure improves the quality of the sex for him too.

- *Refusing to be intimidated into performing sexual practices you don't find arousing or satisfying.* You don't have to swallow semen, have anal sex, participate in bondage, or allow him to spank you. Some women enjoy these activities. If you don't, say so.

- *Put a time limit on the relationship if marriage is important to you —and not to him.* Be careful about issuing ultimatums. They only work if you carry through. But, in your own mind, set a deadline by which you will look for other living arrangements if he hasn't set a wedding date.

- *If money is an issue between you, work toward financial parity.* Some women report their relationships improved when they found higher-paying jobs or assumed a more equitable share of the living expenses. If he's paying more than half, he may feel subconsciously resentful.

CHAPTER 9

The Clock Women

"I broke up with a wonderful man. The sex was good, but he didn't want to get married. He's been married, had a child. I can't afford to waste my time with him,"
　　—a thirty-eight-year-old victim of the ticking biological clock

WHETHER MARRIED OR single, she wants to get pregnant before her biological time runs out. Now her sex life is run by her biology. If single, she puts tremendous pressure on herself and the men she dates to make a commitment early. If married, she has sex by the calendar. Desire is a casualty in the military campaign launched to fill her womb.

Because I became a mother at twenty-one, I've never known what it is to yearn for a child. He was there, before I scarcely had time to think about what it would be like to be a mother or how not being a mother could feel. The clock woman, on the other hand, may have postponed thinking about motherhood, then suddenly discovered one day she had trouble thinking about anything else.

"I never wanted a child before, and I'm astonished at how much I want one now," explains a thirty-seven-year-old professional, who has had five abortions, the most recent one four years ago. "I wish I'd known then what I know now. I wouldn't have had the last abortion. I've kept looking for the right man so I could have it all, the perfect little family. I was so picky. Everything had to be perfect, maybe to make up for the hell that was my own childhood. My father abused my mother. He didn't actually beat us kids, but most of the time we were scared to death.

"So, I kept looking for the Hallmark card relationship, or as, one of my friends puts it, the International Coffee commercial marriage. There always seemed to be time to start over again with someone else, to get it right. But I'm ready to think about being a single mother. If something doesn't work out within the next year or so, I'm going to get pregnant by any reasonable gene pool. I know I'm fertile.

"I recently broke up with a man I love, and he loves me. But, he doesn't want to marry and have another child. He has two by a previous marriage, and he says he's not prepared to take on the responsibility again. I don't blame him, really. He has two kids to put through college now.

"The sex was good in this relationship, some of the best sex I'd ever had. We had fun with sex. He's playful, and so am I. One of the best things about him was the way he didn't come unglued when I did whatever I need to do to come, whether it's use my hand or lock around his leg and rub after he's come. He was great. But, it got to the point where I was crying after sex. I was so sad that he didn't want to marry me and give me a child.

"We had all these horrible long talks. And I cried and cried. I had to stop seeing him. I couldn't do it his way.

"Ironically, this is the sexual relationship I longed to have in my twenties when I didn't know how to get what I needed in bed. I went into therapy. I learned how to get my needs met. And in my thirties I'm walking away from that to try to get my womb filled."

Who Is She?

I defined the clock woman as:

- *A childless single or married women over thirty, who anxiously wants to get pregnant as soon as possible.*

Almost 40 percent of the survey respondents are in their thirties, and slightly over half that group are childless. But married
or single, fewer of them are anxious to have a child than I
anticipated—with, ironically, the single women being more anxious than their married sisters. A mere one-fourth of the married
and childless women say they are "desperate" to conceive.
Though media coverage of infertile couples would lead one to
believe the bedrooms of thirtysomething America are little more
than would-be breeding grounds, only a handful of married
women wrote about their long and futile efforts to become pregnant. Perhaps a woman who is fixated on her biological clock
isn't as likely to respond to a sex survey as other women are.
After all, sex isn't uppermost in her mind.

Because she has been the subject of numerous newspaper and
magazines pieces in the past several years, the woman whose
clock is ticking has come to epitomize the career woman in her
mid- to late-thirties. According to the stereotype, she's a hard-
driving executive who didn't think about having children until
she'd accomplished everything else, and then suddenly realized
she was nearly out of biological time. Coffee mugs, greeting
cards, and T-shirts bear a version of her epigram: "Oh, no! I
forgot to have kids!"

Why Did She Wait So Long?

Many women, who did have children earlier whether they could
afford them or not, regard her as a self-centered conspicuous
consumer of lifestyles who wants a baby now because motherhood is the only lifestyle badge she hasn't sewn on her scarf filled
with merit badges. Other women consider her naive for believing
that Mr. Perfect Father would show up at the right moment and
then her womb would just as magically be filled with his perfect
seed. "Nobody really gets to have it all," they delight in telling
her.

But in reality many clock women haven't achieved enormous
success. Some of them would like to become single mothers, but
can barely afford to be single women on their salaries. Some
delayed marriage and pregnancy because they were on arduous

personal journeys, working through the psychological problems caused by childhood abuse. Others may have been married—to alcoholics, abusive men, or simply men with whom they weren't compatible. For whatever reason, they decided that having a child in that marriage wasn't a good idea. Still others didn't find the man they wanted to marry until they were over thirty.

However she got to post-thirty-five and childless, she likely didn't reach this destination by planning to wait until the last possible moment to conceive.

"I thought I had time," explains a thirty-eight-year-old office manager, who is childless after two divorces, both from alcoholic men who physically abused her. "I wanted a child, but I wanted to do it right. Both my marriages were disasters, the kind you don't bring a child into. And, I wasn't capable of mothering until only recently. Now I know I would make a good mother. It's taken me this long to get my life together."

Biological Dating

"My best friend calls it 'sexual entrapment,' but I am trying to get pregnant by a man without his knowledge," writes a thirty-nine-year-old college professor. "He is married. I've been seeing him for two years, and I know he's never going to leave his wife, as promised. I've given up on that. I just want his child. I don't want him to do anything to help.

"For the past six months, I've arranged to have him here during my fertile period. The sex is wonderful. I've never had unprotected sex in my life, and I love it. I feel so vulnerable, so womanly. I'll do anything for him, including oral sex. The only problem is making sure he doesn't come in my mouth and waste his sperm.

"He loves the way I make love now. I'm doing things he's wanted me to do. Yesterday we made love in a chair on my apartment balcony. I just sat down on him. It was the strangest feeling, sitting straight down on his penis. I felt him penetrate me so deeply, and I thought, 'Maybe this will help me get pregnant.'"

Several women have told me they know of women who are

trying to get pregnant without their partners' knowledge or consent. Many of these partners are married men. The whispered stories of deception would be funny if they were written into a movie script, but are far less amusing in real life. One woman continues to fill her prescription for birth control pills and keeps them in the medicine cabinet, carefully flushing one down the toilet each day, so her lover won't suspect. Another, a district sales manager, schedules her travel to precede her fertile period, so her lover will be as interested in having sex as she is on the right days.

Not all of them find the experience of trying to get pregnant behind his back a liberating one that enables them to make love with abandon.

"Spontaneity is a thing of my past," writes a thirty-seven-year-old who "would rather be pregnant than orgasmic." She is seeing two different men, neither on a "very regular" basis, adding to the difficulty. "My whole life revolves around my fertile cycle. When my temperature is right, I'll cancel social engagements with friends or even business associates and try to get one of these guys into my bed.

"I've become very inventive about getting them over here. But, that's not the same as spontaneous, not by a long shot. I've never faked so much in my life."

Like other women in her position, she only confides in a few close women friends who, more often than not, don't endorse her methods.

"I'll bet half the thirtysomething women in Victoria's Secret shopping on their lunch hour are driven by baby lust, not sex lust," speculates a "happily married mother," whose two closest friends are both trying to get pregnant without the knowledge or consent of the would-be fathers. "They used to talk about their multiple orgasms. Now they talk about their fertile days. The funks they go into when their periods start are as bad as the agonies they suffered when a man didn't call back.

"Personally, I think it's wrong to do what they're doing behind the man's back. It's not fair to a child to be conceived this way. But, I'm keeping my mouth shut. The odds are they won't get pregnant this late in life anyway."

The odds are she's right. A woman's chances of conceiving drop by 75 percent from age twenty-one to age thirty-nine according to various medical sources, including infertility specialists. Those numbers take the fun out of sex for a woman desperate to conceive, even if she's married—and even if her husband shares her passion.

Reproductive Sex

"We've been through some of the most dehumanizing experiences known to couples," writes a forty-year-old Midwestern wife. "My husband has been sent into restrooms to ejaculate into test tubes. I've been poked, prodded, examined—have spent so much time in the splayed position I feel more like a trussed chicken than a woman. Trying to get pregnant has ruined our sex life, and I'm NOT pregnant!

"I know I need to let it go. We're going to lose each other if I can't, but I haven't been able to do it yet."

Like other women in her position, she didn't try to conceive a child until she was past thirty-five. As she describes her life, she sounds more like the quintessential clock woman than most I interviewed. Yet, it's easy to understand why she waited. A late bloomer in every sense of the word, she didn't marry until she was thirty. She and her husband were both working and going to college. When they had each earned post-graduate degrees and saved the money for a down payment on a house, she was thirty-six.

"I expected it to happen," she writes. "Just like that. I don't know why I was so naive. We should have thrown caution to the winds and tried to have a baby years ago, before we could afford it. Now I think we were anal retentive to say the least."

Lulled by the baby boomer's belief in eternal youth—*our* eternal youth, anyway—and encouraged by news accounts of late motherhood, many women delayed starting families until everything else was "right." Ironically, the biological urge has put their sex drives in the backseat at exactly the point when they should be enjoying their sexual peak years.

"I read about women who have multiple orgasms and peak

experiences," writes a thirty-nine-year-old from Michigan. "I'm missing that whole scene. All I have are peak temperature readings—followed by peak depressions when my period starts. I hate menstrual blood!"

Another woman responded to the question, "Do you have sex during your period?" by printing in huge block letters: "NO! I CRY DURING MY PERIOD. SEX DURING PERIODS IS FOR PEOPLE WHO STILL KNOW HOW TO HAVE FUN IN BED."

Yet success, in the form of late pregnancy, can also deaden desire.

"I'm pregnant at thirty-eight," writes a New Yorker. "All I can think about is my own body and what's going on inside it. I am filled with awe and wonder and a sense of triumph and a little fear. What if something goes wrong?

"What I am not filled with is lust. My husband hates this. He already has a child; and he agreed to this one to please me. I don't think about sex anymore. I stopped thinking about it as soon as I knew I was pregnant. The most time I've spent thinking about sex in four months was this evening in filling out your questionnaire.

"No wonder men have traditionally strayed sexually during their wives' pregnancies. I understand it now. But if he does, I'll kill him."

Separating sex from procreation may be the most difficult pleasure hurdle a woman has to leap. But she can do it. In the next chapter, other women will talk about how they have.

CHAPTER 10

Why Sacrifice
Pleasure?

"My husband and I weren't getting along. We'd been trying so hard to conceive a child, and there was tension between us so thick it was like fog. That month, he was out of town on business during my fertile days. I was frustrated, angry he hadn't postponed the trip, and then he called from across the country. First, he sounded tired, then sexy. He asked me if I'd masturbated today, and I realized he was masturbating as we talked. So, I started touching myself. We talked each other to orgasm, and all the tension was gone between us. After that day, we made love like lovers, not reproductive machines. I'd still like to get pregnant, and I haven't, but we've stopped putting that goal ahead of giving each other love and pleasure."

—a thirty-seven-year-old professional woman

Women in the pleasure denial phase insist, *"Other things are more important than sex."*

Those smug, self-righteous words mask the erotic bargain they're making with God or fate or whatever. What they mean is: *"I am denying myself sexual pleasure until I get whatever else I want."*

A fifteen-year study of dating college couples in the Boston area about why couples do or do not marry highlighted one of the differences between the sexes. Men, while they wouldn't marry for good sex alone, were not likely to marry if they didn't find high sexual satisfaction with the relationship. Women, on the other hand, reported no such correlation between high sexual satisfaction and the decision to marry.

Women, the study concluded, are willing "to trade sexual satisfaction for commitment."

Unfortunately, too many women are willing to make the trade even though it can't be made. Sexual pleasure for commitment is an oranges-for-apples trade. It can't be done. Women have been encouraged to believe that limiting the role of sexual pleasure in their lives will enable them to achieve relationship, marriage, and mothering goals—as if enjoying sex and getting other needs met were an either-or proposition. Consciously or not, women are influenced by our culture's two-hundred-year history of promoting sexual denial—especially by *women*—as a means of obtaining salvation. Our bedrock American beliefs hold that sex is only good under certain limited circumstances and that denial of our sexual desires is almost always the best way to handle them.

Women who deny pleasure limit the amount of physical pleasure they will allow themselves, as if this wearing of the erotic hair shirt will in some mystical, religious way grant them their other wishes. But, the penance isn't necessary. Enjoying sex and getting pregnant or establishing a relationship (or finding one, for that matter) aren't incompatible goals.

Unlike the woman (discussed in later chapters) who has lost the capacity for pleasure through some traumatic event such as rape or contracting herpes or being sexually rejected by a spouse or lover, the woman who denies pleasure is still orgasmic in some, if not most, of her encounters. Certainly, she hasn't cut herself off from sexual relationships as the traumatized women have. She isn't foregoing sex, but, she's quick to explain, having an orgasm during sex isn't really the point. Rather, she's *using* sex as a means to an end, because she wants so much more from her sexual relationships than erotic pleasure. The nonsexual needs weigh heavily on her, suppressing her ability to respond.

Many women, especially women in their forties and fifties, told me they regretted not allowing themselves to be more sexual at an earlier age. They described having lived their lives as "good girls," putting their own sexual satisfaction at the bottom of their needs list, or focusing on getting a man, getting married, getting pregnant to the exclusion of pleasure—until something happened to make them realize they were missing an important part of life for no good reason. It made some of them angry at themselves or at the men in their lives. The majority, however, wanted to send a message to younger women: Enjoy yourself now.

"I spent the second half of my thirties trying to get married and or pregnant by two different men," writes a forty-one-year-old television industry executive. "I was obsessively goal-oriented. Can you believe I actually begged both of these men to marry me, and if they wouldn't marry me to let me move in with them where I planned to trick them into fatherhood by getting pregnant 'accidentally'? I thought they would make 'good' husbands and fathers. Where was my head? How can a man you have to drag kicking and screaming to the altar and trick into fatherhood be a 'good' husband and father?

"The sex was only so-so with both of them. Looking back, I blame myself for that. I didn't tell them what I needed sexually, because I was too afraid of scaring them away if I did. I thought I had to please them to get them to marry me, and I thought pleasing them meant keeping quiet about my own needs. As time went on, I became less responsive sexually. When I got to the point in each relationship where I was begging the man to marry me, I was no longer having orgasms with him. Now I think I was nuts. Then I thought getting pregnant was more important than having an orgasm.

"But something happened to connect me with my sensual side again. I had a once-in-a-lifetime, never-to-be-forgotten sexual experience with an old lover who was in town on business. Maybe the chemistry between us was responsible for part of the fireworks, but I'm sure the sex was so good, at least in part, because I wasn't trying to get any commitment from him. I was in bed with him because I wanted to be there for the moment, for nothing else beyond the moment. That night opened my eyes. I'm not getting sexually involved with a man again unless I want to have sex with him. I don't care anymore about what kind of kid they might produce. I'm tired of looking at men, at my sex life, as the vehicle for reproduction.

"I'm not denying my sexual needs anymore."

No, she isn't married or pregnant yet. Perhaps she never will be. She didn't get married or pregnant during those five years of "obsessive goal-oriented" behavior with men either. But, she is enjoying her sexuality now, and she didn't enjoy her sexuality then. By sacrificing pleasure, she gained nothing.

Why Sex Is Good for You

The following letter illustrates how joyful sex can be between a man and a woman.

"I recently ended a six-year relationship because he doesn't want marriage and I do," writes a forty-three-year-old Californian. "While we didn't want the same things, the sex was very good. For whatever reasons he won't marry me, he loves me. We were sexually free with each other. We had many beautiful experiences together, including the last time we made love. The most stunning flood of warm and sweet feelings washed over both of us when it was over. That afterglow lasts and lasts and will always be with me.

"What I want from sex, I had with him. Orgasms, yes. The freedom to be adventurous and do different things. Really, in sex I believe both men and women are seeking a deep affirmation of themselves, a validation of life. We found that with each other."

I was struck by the beauty of her words, so different from the sentiments expressed by a woman who wrote about her "wasted" years with a man who would not marry her.

"It didn't go anywhere," one woman writes, dismissing a love affair as if it had been a bad investment on the stock market. "I can't believe I wasted all those years with him and got nothing out of it. He didn't even buy me any jewelry."

I hope the California writer finds the husband she seeks. Whether she does or not, she'll undoubtedly have another fulfilling sexual relationship, because she finds pleasure in sex. She doesn't link her sexuality to her desire to marry as goal-oriented women do. I'm sure nobody needs to tell her that sex is good for us, physically and psychologically. Some women do need to get the message that we are entitled to sexual fulfillment just as we are entitled to fulfillment of all our other needs.

Recent research on hormones has credited regular sexual activity, especially if it culminates in orgasm, with everything from regulating menstrual cycles and alleviating premenstrual and menopausal symptoms to improving skin tone and promoting the health of bones and the cardiovascular system. Many of these benefits occur due to the increased production of estrogen encouraged by sexual activity. In addition, the release of endorphins in the brain, triggered by orgasm, alleviates minor aches and pains and elevates mood. Endorphins play a significant role in helping maintain emotional stability by making us less irritable, more relaxed, and better able to sleep.

Sex *is* good for you.

How to Stop Limiting Yourself

The best advice on how to pull yourself out of the denial phase comes from the many women I surveyed who've done just that. Some, who were in cohabiting arrangements that stifled them sexually, either learned how to ask for what they needed from their men or, in some cases, left them. Others, who had been so determined to find "relationships" or husbands that they used sex as an entrapment method, finally conceded that this deception ultimately didn't work. And some, who'd sacrificed desire to the demands of a rigorous program for conception, rediscovered the erotic passion they'd felt for their lovers.

Whether or not they reached their goals isn't the point. Some did find the man, conceive the baby. Others didn't. But they all came to realize that sexual pleasure was an entirely separate pursuit of happiness.

Their stories had these elements in common:

THE EPIPHANY

Nearly every woman described a sexual experience that seemed as powerful to her as her first orgasm. One woman called it, "a deepening of my orgasmic response," and insisted that once she'd experienced this, she could never say sex wasn't important again. For these women, the epiphany was an intense experience all the more noticeable for its occurrence in the midst of a sexually unremarkable period.

"I'd just broken up with a man I'd been seeing for three years," writes a Connecticut professional, age thirty-four. "I had done everything 'by the book' with this man and still no marriage proposal. I also hadn't had a good fuck in three years. I wanted to take a month off, but I could only afford five days in the Caribbean, where I met this Brazilian banker who spoke Portuguese to me while he was making love. I couldn't understand a word he was saying. It was the best sex of my life, wild, and completely free.

"When I went back home again, I promised myself I'd never spend another three years of my life doing everything by the book and faking more orgasms than I was having."

A Cleveland wife had a more prosaic, but no less personally astonishing, experience.

"My husband and I had been trying to make a baby for a year," she writes. "Our sex life was in the toilet. We were snapping at each other all the time. This particular night we were going to a dinner party at a friend's. I was running late. From downstairs, he kept yelling out the time to me. I was almost ready when he came upstairs. 'Oh, great,' I thought, 'A lecture on my tardiness.'

"Instead, he looked at me with this curious expression on his face and asked if I had a new dress. I did. He said he liked it. The next thing I knew he was kneeling in front of me performing cunnilingus until I was weak in the knees. I will never forget how that felt, standing there in my high heels, my dress pushed up around my waist, my pantyhose pulled down past my knees, while he licked and sucked me to orgasm.

"That night we put our sex life back on track."

Other epiphanies manifested themselves at a turning point in some women's sexual lives.

"I had been living with my boyfriend for two years when I discovered masturbation," writes a twenty-six-year-old. "Sex had been okay for me, I had orgasms most of the time we did it. But sex was mostly for him, because I lived in fear of sexually disappointing him. I was afraid I would lose him if I didn't please him sexually, and I couldn't bear the thought.

"The orgasms I had when I was masturbating were awesome. They inspired me. I told him I wanted to masturbate for him, and he was put off. I don't think he wanted me to have that much control over the sex. But I was really bold that night, though I never had been before. Instead of saying, 'Okay, honey,' in my Valley Girl voice, I did it anyway. He was knocked out totally. We had incredible sex.

"I promised myself that I was going to stop playing little Miss Good Girl, and I have. I ask for what I want now instead of worrying about whether or not the kind of woman he would marry would want this thing. If it scares him away, too bad for him. But the truth is, he loves it."

And this one:

"I am freer now," a thirty-eight-year-old graphics designer writes. "Six months before my thirty-fifth birthday, I went into a panic about being single. For two years I obsessed on getting married before it was too late to get pregnant. I had three disastrous relationships with men who didn't want to get married or have any more kids. One of those relationships cost me thousands of dollars, because I used my savings to bail out his business, which failed anyway. I'll never see that money again. I wouldn't have invested it if I hadn't convinced myself the guy would be my Mr. Right as soon as his financial troubles were over.

"And the terrible thing is that I didn't even let myself go sexually with him the way I am capable of letting go. I tried so hard to please him. I gave him my money and daily blow jobs. Finally he dumped me, and when he did, he said I was 'rigid' in bed.

"A little after my thirty-seventh birthday, I said to myself, 'Enough of this!' I had a wonderful sexual fling with an unsuitable man. He was twenty-three, definitely not marriage material. I didn't care. I just wanted the sex. One weekend, he had eight orgasms. I can't imagine how many I must have had. He was expert at cunnilingus. He could even make me come by nudging my clitoris with the end of his nose.

"I like sex. I've always liked sex, except for those two years out of my life when I was trying to get married. I don't know how I felt about sex then, but I wasn't doing it for the fun of it."

THE DECISION TO MAKE PLEASURE A PRIVATE GOAL

Interestingly, most women said that they had never shared these experiences, neither the details nor the attitude changes inspired by them, with their friends. Considering how much intimate information women do exchange with each other, that's surprising. Why have they kept quiet? They say female friends "won't understand," "will think [they] are sex-obsessed," or "criticize" them.

A single woman in her thirties writes: "If you tell your friends you are really into sex, they will tell you that you're a sex addict. Nobody drinks more than one, maybe two glasses of white wine anymore for fear of being thought an alcoholic. And nobody has sex for fun."

Other women, both single and married, make similar assessments of the moral climate surrounding them.

"If you believe what they say, nobody is having sex anymore, unless it's for a good reason," writes a thirty-four-year-old Midwesterner. "This is not the time to talk about your hottest-ever experience in bed. Last year I had one of those experiences, with a stranger. It propelled me out of my dull relationship with the kind of man I'm supposed to marry.

"But, I never told my friends, not even my closest friend. I said I left him because I had commitment phobia, which is understandable. If they knew about the sex part, they'd think I was nuts. I would never admit I left him because I promised myself I wouldn't endure that kind of sex anymore.

"These days, you don't leave for sex, or, for that matter, stay for sex. It's a secondary consideration."

Today, women talk to each other about their "relationships" in the language of "intimacy," which conveys socially acceptable attitudes about sex.

"If you have another opinion about sex, you feel a little funny," writes a twenty-three-year-old who had sex with her current boyfriend on the first date. "I didn't tell anyone how soon I slept with him. I'll bet I'm not the only one, but nobody else is talking either."

Even married women say the expected things. Several of the wives who wrote about how striving to conceive had hurt their sex lives hastened to assure me it was the same for other women in their position. The phrase, "getting pregnant is more important than sex," was repeated again and again, with none of this generally well-educated group of women recognizing how counterproductive this attitude can be.

"It's okay to say you don't enjoy sex anymore because you're trying so hard to conceive," explained one. "It's not okay to go to your support group for women who are having trouble getting pregnant and tell them you had a great sexual experience with your husband. Definitely, *not* okay.

"Women who've given birth have their labor horror stories. We tell each other how we're too tense to enjoy sex anymore."

The female solidarity behind negative sex attitudes, which was exemplified in many early bloomer's stories, inhibits many women from speaking honestly about their sexual experiences and attitudes, which is ironic, considering how often we berate men for their inability to communicate "openly." But, I would certainly advise women to keep their own counsel. Why invite someone to castigate you?

THE MENTAL "LETTING GO"

Following their sexual epiphanies and the often concurrent decision to keep their sexual attitudes private, women reported a mental "letting go," a shedding of restrictive inhibitions and sex guilt that freed them.

"I've turned a corner with men," writes a thirty-seven-year-old Philadelphia banking executive who has recently "stopped focusing" on finding a husband. After her own epiphany, she recognized, "Sex has to be an 'I' decision. I can't do it for any reason or not do it for any reason other than I don't want to do it. Now that I have separated my sexuality from all the other issues, I can let go in a way I never could before.

"Recently I was making out on the sofa with a man. It was our second date. I didn't want to have sex with him, but that had nothing to do with the timing. I just didn't want to have intercourse. But I wanted to make out. It got me very aroused. We had our shirts off and we were kissing, touching, and rubbing against each other. I made sure I had an orgasm, because I wanted to have one. I didn't feel obligated to make sure he had one. In my promiscuous past, I would have felt obligated to give him an orgasm too, either by intercourse or blowing him.

"In my more recent past, when I was trying to find a husband, I would have monitored my sexual responses very carefully and stopped the action before I got near orgasm. I would have been telling myself the second date is too soon for sex.

"Now I let myself go. I carry condoms in my purse, so I am prepared if I want intercourse. If I don't, I'll ride with it only exactly as far as I want it to go."

Some women say this mental letting go has allowed them to reach a level of sexual satisfaction they never before experienced. They have stronger orgasms or more orgasms or multiple orgasms. Suddenly they find themselves asking their partners for more stroking, fondling, kissing, caressing, or more oral sex—without blushing. A woman who has always wanted to experiment with bondage but was too embarrassed to ask handed her boyfriend silk scarves and told him what she wanted.

"My sex life has never been so good," a twenty-nine-year-old writes, "as it has since I gave up on trying to get my boyfriend to marry me. I feel sexually liberated! Nothing is on my mind when we have sex now except the sex.

"I finally told him I want more cunnilingus. He said he was glad to know that, because he enjoyed doing it but never was sure if I liked it that much or if he was doing it right. Last night when we made love, I held his face while he ate me out and I moved him where I wanted him to be, even regulated the speed until I was so blown away I couldn't do anything but orgasm. He was blown away too!"

When I saw the Steve Martin movie *L.A. Story*, I thought of these women's stories as the sign on the screen flashed, "Let your mind go . . . And your body will follow." It will.

PART 3

Orgasms

CHAPTER 11

Some Observations
from the Survey

"There have been a few times when the earth rocked, everything was perfect for us . . . but, I don't think I've ever had a 'best ever' sex experience. It would be a vaginal orgasm. Once I really came close to it. I'd like to have one at least once in my life."

—a thirty-eight-year-old television producer

MY SECRET WISH is that, if the proponents of reincarnation are right, Sigmund Freud is doomed for eternity to keep returning to earth as a woman agonizing over her inability to have the "right" kind of orgasm, which is a "vaginal" one, of course.

If I were in charge of new life assignments, he would never be one of the minority of women who do reach orgasm via intercourse alone. He would require direct clitoral stimulation —a lot of it!—but he would be too ashamed to use his hands during intercourse. And, he would keep marrying men who are as ignorant about female sexuality as he was during his reign as the great psychiatrist.

His contributions to the world as founding father of the psychoanalytic process notwithstanding, Freud's legacy to women is a form of sexual hell. In his book *Three Essays on the Theory of Sexuality*, written in 1905, he said that the mature woman "transfers" from the clitoral orgasm she experienced via masturbation in puberty to the vaginal orgasm in intercourse. He wrote:

When at last the sexual act is permitted and the clitoris itself becomes excited, it still retains a function: the task, namely, of transmitting the excitation to the adjacent female sexual parts, just as—to use a simile—pine shavings can be kindled in order to set a log of harder wood on fire. . . .

When eratogenic susceptibility to stimulation has been successfully transferred by a woman from the clitoris to the vaginal orifice, it implies that she has adopted a new leading zone for the purposes of her later sexual activity.

He labeled the woman who never achieved orgasm without direct clitoral stimulation immature and/or frigid. Those damning appellations persist in doing harm today even though Alfred Kinsey, Masters and Johnson, Shere Hite, Helen Singer Kaplan, and others have documented that the majority of women, at least 66 percent, require direct clitoral stimulation to reach orgasm. In fact, Kaplan puts the number at closer to 80 percent.

Yet, educated and intelligent women berate themselves for not being able to reach orgasm without manual or oral stimulation to the clitoris. In a study recently published in *The Archives of Sexual Behavior*, more than one-half of the thirty women, aged eighteen to fifty-nine, who participated were dissatisfied with their orgasms because they were not achieved during intercourse alone. In another study published by *The Journal of Sex and Marital Therapy*, both men and women saw women who required manual stimulation to reach orgasm as "less functional" and "less mature" than women who didn't. The study's authors, however, were heartened to note the women requiring additional stimulation were only rated "somewhat dysfunctional" by most participants.

The Most Surprising Survey Result

The women in this book have generally satisfying sex lives, but they still idealize the "vaginal" orgasm.

- *Over 70 percent of my respondents are not orgasmic during intercourse alone.*

- *Over half of them described an ideal sexual experience as one in which they would be "vaginally" orgasmic.*

- *And, while masturbation is considered by sex therapists to be the surest learning path to orgasm for women, 10 percent of the late bloomers, the women who have the most difficulty achieving orgasm, have never masturbated at all and 20 percent do so "rarely."*

Sadly, women seem to set themselves up for sexual disappointment by expecting their bodies to respond in ways they simply don't.

The Truth About Orgasms

An orgasm is an orgasm, no matter where it seems to have originated. Most sexologists, including Masters and Johnson, believe all female orgasms are triggered by the clitoris, though some women have orgasms they term "vaginal," because these orgasms occur during intercourse without manual stimulation. The clitoris may be larger in those women or located in such a slightly different position that it is stimulated more effectively during intercourse than the average woman's clitoris. Or, she may have learned to move in a certain way in a certain position so the clitoris receives sufficient indirect stimulation for orgasm. Or, she may have learned to delay intercourse until she is on the brink of orgasm. (Or, she may be easily orgasmic from many different forms of stimulation, which stimulate nerve endings in the clitoris even when the stimulus is as far away as the breasts, neck, or earlobes. A small percentage of women are orgasmic via these routes.)

She isn't sexier, more mature, or more in love than the woman who can't have an orgasm without direct clitoral stimulation. To become orgasmic, or more fully satisfied with her orgasmic capabilities, a woman must accept the reality of female biology. Striving for the perfect vaginal orgasm will only keep her frustrated.

"Women need to cut themselves a break," a twenty-three-year-old New York University graduate student wrote. "Can you imagine a man agonizing over whether or not his orgasm came from the right place? We do such a number on ourselves, don't we?"

We do, but we can stop doing it. Being orgasmic, according to the women in this book, really is as simple as one, two, three.

Step One: Eliminate Guilt

Sex guilt permeates much of women's thinking about female sexuality, including orgasms and specifically, where they do, or "should," originate.

"I never heard about Freud and the vaginal orgasm thing until I went back to college ten years ago," writes a forty-five-year-old nursing administrator from the Midwest. "When I read about him and his crackpot theory in a psych class, I thought, 'That man was a nut! Why didn't anybody figure it out?' Since then, people have. Now it turns out he was probably dismissing the real stories of sexual abuse little girls told him as childhood erotic fantasies. Freud didn't get women.

"Anyway, I hadn't heard about Freud when I started masturbating at thirteen. I naturally assumed I was doing the right thing for myself sexually, because it worked, and I taught my partners how to do it too."

On the other hand, a lot of women who hadn't specifically heard of Freud's theory were influenced by it. Without knowing why, many women, and men, believe there's something wrong with a woman who doesn't have an orgasm during intercourse, or they think something is wrong with her partner. The penis, they reason, should be enough to produce ecstasy in both of them. When it isn't, they blame each other or themselves or the penis. That thinking instills a kind of sexual guilt in women and sometimes men: The guilt of not being, or loving, enough.

"I thought there was something wrong with me if I couldn't have an orgasm during intercourse," writes a twenty-nine-year-old divorced woman from Florida. "My husband thought so, too. I faked a lot of orgasms during sex and then had them secretly when I masturbated. This made me feel guilty.

"It also made me think there was something wrong with my marriage. I remember lying on my bed and crying after I had masturbated and telling myself, 'I have to find a man who can do this for me!'

"Maybe the marriage would have worked out if we'd been smarter about sex. I didn't understand that I was normal—that this is how women are sexually—until just last year."

Several women wrote about their moments of realization when they finally understood that their need for direct clitoral stimulation was a fact of sexual biology, not an indictment of them and their relationships, or an indication of their inability to love enough or in the right way.

"It was like a sexual epiphany," a forty-two-year-old writes. "I'd borne two children before I was orgasmic during lovemaking, because I never figured out that what I did when I masturbated was also what had to be done during intercourse. That opened a new world for us. We began to experiment orally, manually, every which way."

Another woman said simply: "It freed me."

She, like many other women, was "freed" by reading *For Yourself*, by Lonnie Barbach, a sex therapist and author who puts to rest Freud's theory about orgasm in clear, concise, and reassuring fashion. Available in paper, it's one of the two books on sex every woman should read.

Step Two: Use Your Hands

Barbach's book also encourages the use of masturbation as a learning path to orgasm. The majority of women in my survey, 69 percent, were first orgasmic via masturbation and learned to be orgasmic during lovemaking by teaching their partners how to touch them during intercourse or by touching themselves. In most cases, masturbation proceeded the first sexual experience, but that was not always the case.

"I was sexually active for several years before I masturbated," wrote a Virginia accountant. "But, I did not have an orgasm until I masturbated. After that I found it easy to have orgasms during lovemaking. I was relaxed about my ability to have them. I didn't get nervous anymore when men stimulated me orally or manually, so I could be orgasmic.

"Before I masturbated to orgasm, I stopped whatever they were doing when I got too excited. I was afraid of losing control. I didn't know what would happen. I thought I might pee all over them or something. That sounds silly now, but it isn't when you're there."

Another woman wrote: "I couldn't bring myself to masturbate for fun, but I finally did it in order to learn how to have an orgasm. It was my husband's idea. He bought me a book and a vibrator and then went bowling so I could figure it out. I did."

Many women wrote about their vibrator experiences. Some claim they never would have become orgasmic without the more intense vibrations the little machines provide. Others said they had trouble weaning themselves from that intensity and transferring to manual or oral stimulation.

"I couldn't have an orgasm no matter what we did," wrote a sixty-two-year-old wife and mother. "We were in sex therapy when it was a new concept. Our therapist, who'd been trained at Masters and Johnson Institute, suggested a vibrator. That worked, but I had a hard time getting off it. Eventually I was able to have orgasms most of the time during sex with additional manual stimulation. Whew!

"I've often wondered if it's this hard for the younger generation. I hope not. It shouldn't be so hard for anyone."

Unfortunately, it is. Many women under thirty experience difficulty in reaching orgasm, particularly during lovemaking, even after they have learned to give themselves orgasms via masturbation. They want intercourse to be a no-hands experience.

"I didn't have an orgasm during sex for the first three years of our marriage," writes a twenty-seven-year-old St. Louisan. "It takes me a long time to have an orgasm even during masturbation. I didn't feel right asking my husband to masturbate me, and sex didn't work until recently when I figured out a way to do it.

"Before we have sex, I go into the bedroom alone and masturbate myself almost to orgasm. Then, I call him, and we make love. I usually come this way. Maybe it sounds crazy, but it's the only way I can make sex work for us."

Step Three: Use Your Sex Fantasies

While sex therapists say that nearly everyone fantasizes, and Masters and Johnson maintain the average person has eight sexual fantasies per hour—ranging from the fleeting thought to the full encounter—a surprising 30 percent of my respondents claimed they did not have fantasies. The majority who did not fantasize were late bloomers, women whose love fantasies rule their lives.

Others described such tame favorite fantasies as:

―――――――――

"I am making love to my boyfriend by the ocean, and it is perfect."

―――――――――

"I surprise my husband in the shower, and we make love standing up."

―――――――――

"My boyfriend is sleeping and I tiptoe into the bedroom, remove the covers from his naked body, mount him, and have my way with him."

―――――――――

The majority, however, described variations of the fantasies Masters and Johnson label the most common: idyllic sex with a stranger; group sex; homosexual encounter; bondage or forced sex. Perhaps many women deny their fantasies because they fear a fantasy is a secret wish. It isn't.

A rape fantasy, for example, doesn't indicate that a woman wants to be raped. It merely signifies her desire to have sex without feeling guilty or restricted by fears of how she might look, or sound, or smell during sex. In fantasy, she frees herself from all constraints by imagining she is forced to enjoy herself. She has no control—and no guilt. (Men also fantasize about being forced to have sex, for the same reasons.)

One creative woman wrote: "I have two favorite fantasies. In one, I am being ravished by a clan king in a cave while the entire clan watches. In another, I am having sex in the stands of a crowded football stadium. These are my standby favorites for masturbating, and sometimes I turn them on in my head when I'm not quite there during sex."

Most women do use fantasies for arousal during masturbation and sometimes intercourse. The use of fantasy, either blatantly sexual or the more romantic love fantasy, during lovemaking does not imply that there's something wrong with you or him or something lacking in your feelings for him. Some women also use fantasy as a means of arousing themselves before sex. Marc and Judith Meshorer, the authors of *Ultimate Pleasures*, the other sex book every woman should read, call this "starting on warm," and it's one of the secrets of easily orgasmic women.

"I lead an active fantasy life," wrote a Michigan woman. "I think about sex a lot before bedtime so I'll be hot when my husband touches me. Sometimes I'll read erotic books and magazines or watch an X-rated video at home alone. That really puts me in the mood. Fantasy is my way of preparing my body for the shift from everyday life to sex."

Women who can use fantasy as an arousal aide, accept their need for clitoral stimulation, and teach themselves to become orgasmic via masturbation—if they aren't already orgasmic with their partners—have reached the first stage of female sexual evolution: discovering pleasure. They know what sexual pleasure is and how to get it.

This is where it stops for some women, while for other women it never really gets started at all. But for you, it's only the beginning.

PART 4

The Pleasure
Claimers

CHAPTER *12*

How Pleasure Claimers Get Better Orgasms

"Should sex only be an expression of love? Nah! It can be both loving and animalistic—or only animalistic. I love my husband. Sometimes we make love like animals. I have never loved my lovers. The sex is good with all of them."

—a thirty-nine-year-old adulterous wife

*P*LEASURE CLAIMERS MAY be married or single, monogamous or not, but sex is *important* to them. Orgasms do matter. They don't say, "I don't care if I have an orgasm or not," very often.

For them, having *an* orgasm isn't always enough either. They want, and frequently have, multiple orgasms or enjoy extended lovemaking sessions leading to intense orgasms. Or, they are orgasmic in a variety of ways, including through oral genital stimulation, a favorite of pleasure claimers. They have freely explored their own, and their partners' bodies, and the knowledge they have gained has given them sexual power. Whether monogamous or promiscuous, they like to experiment sexually. When they are faithful to a man, they do so by active choice, not fear of the consequences should they cheat. They make active, not passive, choices.

For some women, sexuality really does bloom more fully

within the confines of an emotionally secure monogamous relationship, while for other women, that same description reads like the specs for an erotic straitjacket. Women who have claimed their sexual pleasure from within themselves know what they need, and they go after it. They are not easily influenced by the antisex messages they get mainly from other women, but they are seldom rebels either; they do not flaunt their behavior in society's face. There is often a considerable split between their private selves and public façades, especially if they live in small communities where sexual behavior is closely monitored by others or work in a conservative profession or firm.

Profile of a Pleasure Claimer

Over 70 percent of my survey respondents are pleasure claimers. Breaking pleasure claimers down into the four major categories, I found:

- *56.7 percent were early bloomers*
- *15.2 percent were wildflowers*
- *20.1 percent were perfect buds*
- *9 percent were late bloomers*

I defined them as women who:

- *Masturbate and are comfortable with asking for, or giving themselves, manual stimulation during intercourse.*
- *Report being orgasmic in nearly all their sexual encounters.*
- *Have a high degree of satisfaction with their sex lives.*
- *Answered the key attitude question, "Do you think sex should only be an expression of love?" with "No."*

Pleasure claimers often experience orgasms through more forms of stimuli than other women. Several are orgasmic during dreams or fantasies. A few reach orgasms merely from having their breasts stimulated. They also report more multiple orgasms (40 percent experience multiple orgasm anywhere from infrequently to often). In general, less than 12 percent of women are thought to experience multiple orgasms. Those pleasure claimers who do have them say they first had multiple orgasms during masturbation and then learned how to have them during sex by varying the kinds of stimulation they receive.

"If I want to have multiple orgasms, I can have them almost any time," writes a thirty-seven-year-old monogamous wife. "I have my first orgasm during cunnilingus. Then, we have intercourse, varying the positions and the intensity of thrusting. I can usually come once or twice again during intercourse, sometimes by adding manual stimulation. After my husband has ejaculated, I can have several more orgasms if he or I continue to stimulate me manually while he's kissing me deeply and holding me. At this point, they come one right after another because I am so high, there's very little needed to get me back to the peak.

"If he's tired after sex, I sometimes masturbate while he watches."

Many women describe the sessions in which they were multiply orgasmic in a similar way. Varying stimulation is a key element in their lovemaking styles. Some use the same technique to delay orgasm and prolong excitation by stopping one form of stimulation at the brink of orgasm, thus obtaining a stronger response when they do have an orgasm. Not all sexually confident and satisfied women have, or even care about having, multiples. The pleasure claimer, however, seeks a more intense experience than she did during her sexual discovery phase.

Interestingly, few pleasure claimers were late bloomers, suggesting, for the participants in this survey at least, a connection between earlier masturbation and a satisfying sex life.

One notable exception, a thirty-three-year-old waitress from St. Louis writes: "Raised a devout Catholic, I didn't have sex before marriage and can't remember how old I was when I first masturbated. You see, I've blotted it out of my mind! I was lucky in my choice of husbands. He is sensitive and giving in sex. I also think I was fortunate in having sex for the first time at an older age, into my twenties, when I'd read and heard enough to know what to do and not be traumatized if it wasn't good the first time. I didn't have an orgasm for two years. But now I have multiple orgasms."

Whether married or single, the pleasure claimer has a rich fantasy life that doesn't threaten her real life, a healthy, positive attitude about sex, and these basic traits:

- *Sexual confidence, in her ability to attract and please a man—and in her ability to be orgasmic.*
- *Communication skills, which enable her to tell and show her partner what she needs in bed, without self-consciousness and without making him feel threatened or "lectured."*
- *The ability to separate sex from the rest of her emotional and financial security needs, even from love.*
- *Willingness to experiment sexually with her partner.*

How She Claimed Pleasure

1. SHE GAVE HERSELF PERMISSION

Sex, especially good sex, begins in the brain.

"You must have the right mindset to achieve fulfillment," writes a twenty-nine-year-old yoga instructor from the Northwest. "In an ideal world, young girls would be given a better sense of their sexual capacity—instead of a guilt trip. Sex would not be treated as something dirty. This is not an ideal world, is it?

"I can't even tell you when I learned the basics about sex. I feel like I always knew them. Even as a young girl, I had sophisticated fantasies. On the other hand, I am still learning about sex and always will be.

"This is the right mindset: Recognize and respect your body's tremendous capacity for sexual pleasure. Don't criticize your body for being made this way or your spirit for wanting to follow its lead. Be open to new ways of experiencing and giving pleasure."

It is a cliché, but one of the few worth repeating: *Sex takes place largely in the brain.* No woman will have a joyous sex life until she's given herself permission to enjoy sex. Many pleasure claimers, including the above yoga instructor, come from families they characterize as rigid, Puritanical, or strict, but they somehow developed their own attitudes, often helped by the silence their families kept about sex.

"What probably saved me from having my mother's bad attitude about sex," writes a thirty-six-year-old computer programmer, "is the fact she was too embarrassed to tell me much about sex. I sensed her negativity, but I didn't get it put into a lot of words."

And another woman writes: "At least I didn't have to overcome a lot of negative teaching about sex in my family. Not that they didn't have negative attitudes! They just never talked about sex. My mother always said you don't talk about religion, politics, or sex. I learned about sex from the kids in the neighborhood. When I was thirteen I believed sex happened when a man and a woman put their private parts together and peed into each other. I was already masturbating, but I didn't know what I was doing. I didn't get the connection between that and 'sex.' "

Few pleasure claimers grew up in families where sexual information was comfortably presented in a nonjudgmental, nonpunitive way, but they don't use their backgrounds as an excuse for remaining stuck in a negative sexual rut.

"You make your own life," writes a fifty-year-old Catholic mother whose parents wanted her to be a nun. "I was embarrassed to tell my mother I was pregnant after a year of marriage, because she would know I'd been having sex! We didn't ever use the word 'pregnant' between us. I told her I was 'expecting,' and she relayed the information to my father who was waiting in the next room. It was unthinkable for me to tell him such an intimate piece of news! To him she said, 'Our daughter is in the family way.'

"Somewhere along the line, after a baby or two, I thought, 'This really should be more fun. Making babies was wonderful, but I wanted to get something out of the times when we weren't making babies.' "

2. SHE IDENTIFIED HER OWN SEXUAL NEEDS

After she decided sexual pleasure was good and her right, the pleasure claimer, whether consciously or not, developed her own mental erotic needs checklist, beginning with regular orgasms. But, that was only the beginning.

"I know what I need sexually," writes a New York designer, age thirty-one. "A lot of oral and manual stimulation. My idea of 'foreplay' is an orgasm orally or manually before intercourse."

"I need a lot of variety in sexual activity," says a West Coast television executive. "And I'm not ashamed of this. I can be monogamous, but not with a man who isn't into experimenting. I'm very oral. Before my period I get into mild pain. I like to be spanked and fucked in the ass. I know what I like and when and how I like it, and I don't let anyone's idea of what's suitable influence me."

A happily married woman, on the other hand, writes: "I need emotional security to enjoy sex. I couldn't let myself go with a total stranger. Trust is important to me. I can do anything with my husband. But I could never do those things with someone who doesn't love and cherish me."

The pleasure claimer recognizes her needs, both the conditions under which she can "let go" and the ways in which she needs to be stimulated for arousal and orgasm. That may sound elementary, but many women don't know what they need sexually. Their fantasies are of love and romance, and they expect the men in their lives, like romantic heroes, to know exactly what to do for them. They think men can make *it* happen, though they aren't quite sure what "it" entails.

"When I got married at age nineteen I thought my husband would be able to make the earth move," writes a fifty-two-year-old stock analyst. "Or at least make the bed rock. When he couldn't, I was disappointed. I withdrew from him sexually for several months, only granting him an occasional quickie. Then I discovered masturbation, which taught me I could rock my own bed. I became a full sexual partner in the marriage at that point. My, was he relieved!"

3. SHE DIDN'T LET ANYTHING STOP HER FROM GETTING HER NEEDS MET

Many of these women initially intimidated their husbands or boyfriends when they spoke up for themselves sexually. Their new assertiveness represented change, which is often scary, even when it's recognized by both parties as a good change. Other women got heavily critical messages from friends when they became involved in "for-sex-only" relationships. Some were even shut down temporarily or longer by doctors, ministers, priests, and rabbis who either wouldn't answer their questions about sex or gave moralistic and preachy or outrageously chauvinistic sex advice encouraging them to deny their pursuit of sexual pleasure.

"When I was first married twenty-five years ago, I asked my gynecologist what was wrong with me that I couldn't have orgasms during sex with my husband," writes a forty-four-year-old Michigan public relations specialist. "I was too ashamed to admit I could have them during masturbation, and he didn't ask. He said I needed to relax and give myself fully to my husband! Ten years later I asked another gynecologist the same question. I did admit to masturbating, and he said, 'Why don't you just continue faking orgasms with your husband and masturbate for release after he's asleep? You'll probably save your marriage!'

"By this time Masters and Johnson were household names. He should have known better. Luckily for me, I was outraged. I bought some books, and I discovered things no doctor ever told me, mainly that it's okay to do the same things during sex you do during masturbation. Nobody had ever told me most women need direct clitoral stimulation to reach orgasm during intercourse. For ten years I thought I was a woman who didn't love enough."

And a fifty-one-year-old Midwestern primary school teacher writes: "My husband and I went through some real bedroom battles when I became assertive about sex. He was convinced I'd taken a lover for a while, because, he asked, how else would I know about that 'stuff'? And he balked at changing things. When I asked for oral sex—and remember this was thirty years ago when nobody we knew had ever heard the word 'cunnilingus'—he said, 'You want me to kiss your box? Only lessies and sissies do that!' You see what I was up against.

"I persevered, because I recognized how scared he was. He always knocks on 'queers' and 'sissies' when he's scared out of his pants. Also, I had begun our marriage by faking orgasms like mad. When I stopped faking and started asking for the real thing, he was thrown off-balance.

"But, he learned. Oh, did he learn! We've had, and still have, a wonderful sex life."

4. SHE HAS KEPT HER OWN COUNSEL

The censure of friends and family, and even the pervasive sexual negativity of the right-wing crusading ladies who seemed to dominate the talk shows in the late Eighties, keeps many women from more fully exploring their sexuality. Not pleasure claimers! They don't ask their friends for sexual advice.

"I made the mistake of telling my best friend about my first extramarital affair," writes a twenty-nine-year-old Philadelphia wife. "She really came down on me, in a loving way, of course, and 'for my own good.' The next day following my 'confession' to her over glasses of wine at happy hour, she called me at the office. She said she hadn't been able to sleep all night for worrying about me.

" 'You're going to wreck your marriage,' she said. 'I wouldn't be a friend if I didn't tell you how I feel and try to talk you out of this terrible thing.'

"She sort of hinted she might have to tell my husband if I didn't agree it was madness to see this man, and so I agreed. I was shell-shocked. I didn't see the man again, but a few months later another man came along. And I didn't share the details with my best friend. To this day, she thinks she saved my marriage. She would die if she knew I've been playing around ever since."

The pressure to conform sexually is also strong on single women who are inundated with advice from their friends, and their favorite magazines, on how *not* to behave if they want to get or keep a man.

"Everybody tells everybody else, 'You shouldn't have sex outside a relationship,' " writes a twenty-six-year-old New Yorker. "It's such a repressive mindset. Fear of disease is just the excuse for reverting back to our Puritanical roots. If everyone really thought in disease terms, they'd all use condoms, which they don't. Women just hate to think about other women having a good time in bed.

"I never admit to most other women the truth about my sex life. A few of my friends are open, but most aren't."

Pleasure claimers have confidence in their own sexual choices, and they don't subject themselves to critical scrutiny of their intimate lives. They don't need validation. Unfortunately, many women do, and they aren't likely to find it in today's social climate.

What She Does in Bed

Not surprisingly, she is more likely to experiment beyond the sexual basics than other women, and many are sexual explorers, those women who are willing and eager participants in sexual variations.

Pleasure claimers report that:

- *Over 90 percent regularly receive cunnilingus and are orgasmic this way.* The same percentage performs fellatio, with three-fourths enjoying it, though the majority say they receive more oral sex than they give in their relationships.

- *Most have tried anal sex at least once*, with almost 50 percent enjoying it on at least an occasional basis.

- *More than 60 percent have experienced bondage*—both as the one bound and the one doing the binding—and most enjoy it.

- *Nearly 40 percent have participated in spanking and other light S&M activity*, most often at their own initiation.

- *Over 80 percent have watched an X-rated video*, with three-fourths of the group being the partner most likely to rent them.

- *Over 80 percent have used a vibrator or other sex toy.*

- *Nearly 60 percent masturbate on an average of once a week.*

- *Most describe having more graphic and frequent sexual fantasies than other women.*

- *They make love in places other than the bedroom and positions other than missionary*—with nearly half having made love out of doors at least once.

- *Unlike the majority of women in magazine reader polls and other research, they don't let dissatisfaction with body size or tone prevent them from being assertively sexual.*

"I'm not as skinny as I used to be and sometimes I don't feel I'm quite as sexy looking, especially to a stranger on the street," writes a thirty-two-year-old California journalist. "But my husband is still avid for me. And in bed, I'm a far hotter number than I was ten years ago.

"I think I could seduce any man I really wanted, full hips and all. And once I got him in bed, I know he'd come back."

The pleasure claimer does attract men. They look into her eyes and know that if she should decide to take them into her bed, they will find pleasure there.

CHAPTER 13

What Does She Know About Sex That You Don't?

"The quality of the sex in our marriage had been disappointing me for a long time. I dressed up and took my husband out to dinner. In the restaurant I told him, 'Look, from now on sex is going to be for both of us, not just you.' I was braced for a negative reaction. He was delighted. 'I've always been disappointed that you weren't more interested in sex,' he said."

—a forty-year-old Canadian wife

*A*T SOME POINT after her sexual epiphany, the pleasure claimer begins to own her sexuality. Even if she has never gone through a denial phase, she still reaches a point where she wants more, sexually, than the knowledge she can and will be orgasmic in most of her encounters. As she moves to a higher level of sexual enjoyment, the claiming pleasure stage, she is no longer sexually tentative, insecure, or selectively naive, if she ever had been.

She wants to please her man, but not at the expense of her own pleasure. That he is most often happy with this changed attitude that leads her to take a more active role in sex often surprises her, though it shouldn't.

What She Knows About Male Sexuality

Numerous research studies show men are more highly aroused by their partner's excitement than her erotic skills. The older they get or the longer a relationship endures, the greater is their need for active female participation. Few things give a man of any age more pleasure than bringing a woman to orgasm, preferably more than once.

Pleasure claimers know the two most important things about men and sex:

- *The female orgasm is the new male performance indicator, the orgasm count replacing notches on the bedpost as proof of his virility.*
- *Men do not know as much about female sexuality as women think they do.* When women expect them to know automatically how to please them, they're expecting too much.

What She Knows About Sexual Assertiveness

According to men's magazine reader polls and other sources, a sexually assertive woman is most men's partner of choice. More responsive, more easily orgasmic than other women, an assertive woman is probably, but not necessarily, in her thirties, when her biology is responsible for an increase in sex drive. Whether she has multiple orgasms or not, she is orgasmic in most of her encounters. She is, of course, a pleasure claimer.

Often more educated about both male and female sexuality than he is, the pleasure claimer doesn't expect her partner to "give" her orgasms. Rather, she helps him bring her to orgasm by showing and telling him what she needs. She also freely uses her own hand to stimulate her clitoris during intercourse when she needs to do so. Some women, especially early bloomers, reach this stage in which they fully claim their sexual pleasure before age thirty. Unfortunately, some women never do.

A woman needs a certain level of confidence in her body's ability to become aroused and respond in orgasm before she can stand up for herself sexually. When she's worried about whether or not she'll be able to have an orgasm, she's not likely to get much more from sex than that orgasm. She isn't free enough to surrender to her own sexuality—to let her mind go so her body can follow.

What She Knows About Sexual Communication

With confidence comes a greater ease in sexual communication. Many of the women I surveyed remember the first time they voiced their sexual needs to their partners—when it wasn't so easy.

"I was thirty-two and divorced," one woman wrote, "and I felt I had nothing to lose with this particular man. I wasn't looking for another husband yet. So, I asked him to touch me where I wanted to be touched. The sex was the best I'd had up to then. That taught me an important lesson: Ask! Men love it! I love it! When I think of all those years I wasted sending my husband mental signals he didn't pick up. . . ."

Another said: "The first time I asked a man if he would perform cunnilingus on me, I almost died of embarrassment. But he quickly, and happily, revived me."

Only a few women reported negative reactions from their partners to their direct sexual requests. One woman followed the advice in a magazine article that said "Don't discuss sex in the bedroom." She told her husband over morning coffee that she wasn't getting the clitoral stimulation she needed during intercourse, and he accused her of "critiquing" his performance. I don't know why some experts advise talking about sex while fully clothed and in any other room of the house than the bedroom. The men I surveyed said they want a woman to tell them what she needs while they're in bed together making love, not while they are folding the laundry together or driving to his mother's house for dinner.

Pleasure claimers can ask for what they want without sounding like they're either demanding or criticizing. They can also separate sex from other aspects of a relationship, including love, which we've been told women just can't do. (How they do so is discussed in depth on pages 140–141.) Sex is a priority for them.

They don't stop wanting sex because the husband doesn't do his share of the chores or the boyfriend won't commit. The stories of pleasure claimers in the next three chapters will show you *how* they do it.

"My husband and I have drawn invisible lines around the bed," writes a monogamous wife of twenty years. "The rest of our life stays outside the lines."

A happily single woman writes: "It's just so much b.s. that women can't make love without being in love. I'm tired of the sentimentality and hypocrisy! Every act of sex, even between married people, is not a holy consecration of love."

You would expect the pleasure claimer to have a better sex life than other women. She may also have better relationships, because she doesn't expect to get all her needs met through sex. She doesn't use sex. Nor does she regard sexual pleasure as something that "happens" to her, that is, as something men make happen to her.

Without apology or waiting for consent, she claims her own pleasure. Married or single, so can you.

CHAPTER 14

Monogamous Women

"My husband and I take a weekend away from the kids four times a year, even if we can only afford to check into the local Days Inn. One of the most erotic hotel weekends we ever had took place when I was six weeks from delivering our last child and couldn't have sex anymore. We masturbated each other. He bathed me, rubbed lotion into every crevice of my skin. He even shampooed my hair and sucked my toes dry.

—a Maryland housewife, age thirty-six

DEPENDING ON THE survey cited, anywhere from 30 percent to over 50 percent of married women are having, or have had, extramarital affairs. While the infidelity statistics vary, experts generally agree that women's sexual behavior in general, and particularly in this area, has changed more than men's has since the early Fifties when Kinsey first surveyed sex in America. In recent years, we've been inundated with stories about wives who cheat and why they do it. Reading those numerous stories one occasionally gets the impression the faithful are an undersexed minority.

Some women do remain monogamous because of religious beliefs or family and social pressures, fear of the consequences if they're caught, or simply because they have little interest in sex. But other women stay in the marital bed because the sex is so good there.

"I am not morally opposed to adultery," says Nan, a forty-year-old computer programmer who has been married for nineteen years. "One of my friends is married to a man she won't leave for economic reasons, but they haven't had sex in two years. If there were no sex in my marriage, for whatever reason, I would find it elsewhere. I can't imagine living a life without sex!

"Fortunately, we have, and almost always have had, a good sexual relationship. Every long-term relationship will have its ebb and flow of desire, and we've had a few low points, like when I was pregnant both times and then after the babies were born, and when Jeff lost his job a few years ago. During those times, we were so consumed with other issues, we didn't think about sex as much. Or, at least, one of us didn't think about sex as much.

"But, we always get it back! Sex works well for us for two reasons. One, we have a strong physical attraction to each other, even after nineteen years. Two, we are both willing to experiment, even to do silly things. Years ago, when our firstborn was only nine months old, we made love in her wading pool. We'd both lived in the Midwest, away from major sources of water, all our lives, and making love underwater was a fantasy we'd shared. Late one night, we were sitting in the backyard sipping wine and talking about that fantasy, among others, and one of us, I don't remember which one, said, 'There's the water!' So, we did it.

"I think a lot of wives lose their husband's interest sexually because they get stuck in sexual ruts. They won't go much beyond the missionary position, and they think sex belongs in the bedroom, after the kids are asleep, with the lights out, when everything else is done and they're feeling happy with their husbands. What they don't get is how much you can improve your life by being open to the moment. Sometimes we've even had great sex when we weren't particularly happy with each other in other ways.

"Sex to me isn't connected to whether he remembered to stop at the market on the way home."

Who Is She?

Married women made up 34.2 percent of the total survey group. Nan, like 62 percent of these married respondents—or just under 20 percent of the total group—has been monogamous throughout her marriage and is satisfied with the relationship. I defined the happily monogamous wives by these obvious and simple criteria:

- *They are married.*
- *They are not having—nor have they had in the past—an extramarital affair.*
- *They report being satisfied with their sex lives.*

I expected to find several clear differences in the backgrounds of the monogamous wives and the ones who'd had, or were having, extramarital affairs, but I found only one area in which they significantly differed.

Not surprisingly, happily monogamous wives had fewer partners before marriage than most adulterous wives did. Nearly half the monogamous wives had never had another sex partner, though they had dated other men before marriage and, in all but a handful of cases, had had sex with their husbands before marriage. Yet, happily monogamous wives were also *less* likely to have been virgin brides. Six percent of the wives involved in affairs were virgins on their wedding day, compared to 4 percent of the happily monogamous group.

The real surprise, to me at least, was that happily monogamous wives are *far less career-oriented than the other wives—with less than 10 percent of them holding management or professional jobs.* While slightly more than two-thirds were working, or had worked at some point in their marriages, more often they have jobs rather than careers. Several wrote to say they credited their happiness in part to fitting their own schedules around their husbands' more demanding careers.

Their Shared Behavior Traits

Their secondary economic position does not, however, carry over into the bedroom. Like other pleasure claimers, they generally have healthy, positive attitudes about sex, sharing these common behavior traits:

- *The ability to separate sex from the rest of the marriage.*
- *Sexual confidence.*
- *The willingness to communicate their needs and desires to their partners.* If anything, they seem even more willing than other assertive women I've interviewed to take the responsibility for making sex good for both partners.

In addition, the monogamous women, who report they initiate sex about half the time, say:

- *They make sex a "priority" in their marriages.* From the beginning, they were determined that both the marriage and the sex would thrive.
- *They accept the natural cycles of desire without feeling threatened by temporary periods of waning.*
- *And, they put high value on being sexually free with their partners.* In other words, they are willing to experiment with different sex practices, positions, and settings. The monogamous wives recounted stories of sex in unusual places as often as single women did, and they were often the ones who suggested the variations.

The Role of Sexual Initiator

For many women the phrase "initiating sex" means starting the encounter. But many of the monogamous wives said they not only initiated half, if not more, of their sexual encounters, but had also introduced into their marriages the sexual variety the couple enjoyed. Many said they taught their husbands how to make love.

This group of women have one strong message for the rest of us: *Don't wait for him to make great sex "happen." Make it happen yourself.*

"When we'd been married almost two years, we hit a snag,"

says Alice, thirty-eight, mother of two teenage sons. "And I decided I was going to unsnag us, not wait for him to take care of things. We had fallen into the typical married habit of having sex once a week, predictably on Saturday night, missionary position, in record time—or, so it felt to me. He didn't last long enough, and I didn't have orgasms. But I was faking them. I just knew if I didn't change things then, we were going to be in trouble. The orgasm issue aside, it was boring.

"I bought some books on sex. There weren't as many then as there are now, and they were more devoted to basics than extras. But I got enough out of them to know what we were missing. A lot! I also discovered that sex had only worked for us by fluke. We were doing everything wrong.

"We had developed this pattern in courtship that lasted a few months into our marriage. We petted—mostly above the waist, because we were too shy to finger each other's genitals much— until I was fairly excited and then had intercourse. By the time he ejaculated, I was pretty hot from all the rubbing, but of course I wasn't having an orgasm because neither of us was touching me. But, because he was young and enthusiastic, we petted until he got another erection and had intercourse again. By this time, I could have an orgasm during intercourse most of the time because I was so aroused I didn't need much more stimulation. But, timing was critical. If he came the second time before I came at all, I faked. And we quit.

"Of course, after we'd been married a few months he stopped being able to have intercourse twice in a row. So, I stopped coming, but continued faking. This is where things stood when I took charge of our sex life.

"I knew he would be crushed if I told him I'd been faking, so I didn't. I did let him know I hadn't come the next time we made love. He was surprised, but he shrugged it off. Then the following time, I let him know I didn't come. After several times, he was worried. I had his attention. He kept asking me what was wrong.

"I pulled out the books and read the parts about clitoral stimulation. I told him I thought I needed more stimulation now than I had when we were courting, because my body was probably changing and just required more. He accepted that. He also took the books out of my hands and began reading.

"That changed our lives. It sounds like a simple thing, but neither of us knew that one of us needed to touch me in the vicinity of my clitoris. I had never even heard the word 'clitoris' until I got those books. I had to check the dictionary to see how to pronounce it. I introduced us both to my clitoris. And over the years, I have continued to be the one who introduces something new. I'm probably the only wife in suburbia who introduced her husband to X-rated videos!"

A few of the wives who related similar stories had more sexual experience than their husbands when they married, but most didn't. Like Nan, they got their information from books or the daytime talk shows. A number of women said they learned more about orgasms from watching Donahue or Sally Jesse Raphael or Oprah than they'd ever learned from their mothers, peers, or ob-gyns. Maybe these women became the sex instructors in their marriages because they were home during the day.

"He just didn't know how to touch," one woman wrote about her husband. "I expected him to know everything, and when he didn't, I was disappointed. Then I started watching daytime TV and learned he wasn't the only husband who didn't know how to touch. Obviously somebody has to learn and teach the other. I taught him. I'm a good teacher."

They also gleaned information from magazine articles, movies—X-rated and mainstream—and the confidences of friends. And they were careful of their husbands' feelings as they brought new ideas into the marital bed.

"At first my husband was suspicious," a Chicago wife wrote. "Then I started reading out loud to him from magazine articles so he'd know where I was getting my ideas. He loved it!"

Making Time for Sex

The typical complaint in two-career marriages is: no time for sex. Monogamous wives believe someone has to conform to the other's schedule to make time for sex, and they are comfortable being the partner who does.

"In any marriage at any given time, one partner wants more sex than the other does," says Rachel, a fifty-four-year-old mother of four. "It's been a long time since he's wanted more sex than I have! More often than not, I initiate, but I haven't had any complaints from him about it.

"When the kids were born, he didn't always like sharing me with them. The most difficult years of our lives were when they were small, and again when one of our sons had a problem with drugs. But I set aside time for my husband alone. Sometimes I was so tired I fell asleep before he did, but I told him to wake me for sex, and he often did. I always said I was never too tired for sex. Don't wake me for anything else but sex.

"We put a sign on our door that said, 'Do Not Disturb' on Saturday and Sunday mornings so we could make love while they watched cartoons. They understood they weren't supposed to bother us, and most of the time they didn't. If they called us to mediate their fights, we ignored them.

"We took weekends away together whenever we could. We were totally different with each other when we were away from the family. Now that the kids are grown, I travel with him on business. Other men's wives can't do that because they have careers of their own. Sometimes women ask me if I don't regret not having a career. I made a choice when I married him to put the relationship ahead of everything else.

"A few years ago I had a heart problem. After it was diagnosed, Sam said he worried about me having so many orgasms that I would give myself a heart attack. I told him, 'I can't think of a better way to go.' I'm not going to stop having sex, or multiple orgasms, to protect my heart!"

Like Rachel, the other happily monogamous wives in my survey said that making time for sex, and the romantic interludes often preceding sex, was a priority in their marriages. It could be argued that they have more of this time than career women, but many of the career women in my survey somehow found the time to have affairs even as they were complaining about time constraints affecting their marital sex lives. It could also be argued that monogamous wives devote more time and energy to sex as a means of keeping their mates, upon whom they are financially dependent, happy. However, in talking to them I didn't get the sense they felt their positions were precarious; they seemed confident in their husbands' love.

The Ability to Separate

Men will tell you—and have told me—that sex begins to go wrong in a marriage the first time she says, "Not tonight, dear," immediately following some obvious and nonsexual transgression on his part. (Understandably, a wife could react to news of his infidelity by pulling away sexually.) As far as he's concerned, sex shouldn't be withheld as a form of punishment when he doesn't set out the trash cans on pick-up days. But steeped as we are in the female tradition of viewing sex as a link in a chain of love and duty, women often do just that.

This group of women, however, doesn't.

"I don't take anything else into bed with us," says Beth, forty-three, mother of two, and married twenty-three years. "There have been times when Dan drove me crazy over things he would or wouldn't do, but I never let that come between us sexually.

"I'll give you an example. For three years we couldn't put a car in our two-car garage because he had it full of parts to a vintage car he was rebuilding. Those parts were spread all over the floor, and I wasn't supposed to disturb anything. For three winters, I scraped ice off the windshield at seven-thirty in the morning because I had to get my kids to school. My mother said, 'You should tell him he won't get sex until he cleans up that mess in the garage.'

"You know it never occurred to me to do something like that. 'Mother,' I told her. 'I love sex. It's the mess in the garage I hate.' Eventually someone wanted to buy the car, so he put it back together and sold it."

Like Rachel, Beth says the biggest challenge to marital sex is children. "It's not just their physical presence," she says. "But they come between you in other ways. No two parents ever agree completely on how to discipline kids. And often one parent has a personality clash with one child, while the other parent has no trouble with the child. This happened in our family. Our older son, Danny, has never given me real trouble, but he and Dan have rubbed each other the wrong way since Danny learned how to talk.

"I made a decision years ago. As much as I love that child, I won't let him come between me and my husband sexually. I don't mean that Dan was physically abusive, because he wouldn't be. I wouldn't tolerate it if he were so inclined. Often I wished he could just ease up on the kid, on what he expected of him in school and sports, and I said so. But I would never turn from him sexually because of what went on between him and Danny."

Happily monogamous wives made a decision early in their marriages to keep sex separate from the rest of the marriage. And they seem to be reaping the benefits.

"I don't care what anyone says," Beth says. "Sex makes everything better between two people. Okay, you haven't solved the other problems by locking the bedroom door and making love for an hour. But you feel good about each other. You are gentler and kinder with each other, more tolerant of the flaws and quirks. It takes the edge off. It bonds you closer together.

"Would the problems go away if you didn't have sex? No! But you and he would be crankier when you tried to deal with them later."

In addition to separating sex from the rest of marriage, these women know how to tell fact from fantasy. Many women allow love fantasies to consume a larger part of their lives than their real marriages do. Not this group! They use their fantasies and then let them go.

The Fantasy Connection

Again, the ability to use love fantasies as arousal aides sets the pleasure claimer apart from the pleasure denier. Rachel, for example, says she occasionally has fantasies of other men during lovemaking with her husband to heighten her arousal. Rachel suspects that her mother had similar fantasies but let them destroy the sexual side of her marriage.

"My mother told me once, with great pride, that she had fallen in love with someone else after her marriage, but never did anything about it," Rachel says. "He was a friend of friends, and she'd met him in someone's home. They'd had a few brief meetings, always within groups of mutual friends. That's all. He worked at the Post Office, and after she realized she loved him, she said she never used 'his' branch again. She told me this story in a way that made me feel she expected a badge of honor.

"I don't know the truth and never will, since she won't tell me, but I doubt my mother ever had an orgasm. She probably had a sexual fantasy about this man, and the fantasy scared her. It irks me that she let the postman come between her and my father."

Rachel is probably right. Sanitized, her mother's erotic yearnings were not only acceptable, but also noble since she was sacrificing their realization for the sake of her family. The love fantasy provided her with an excuse for withdrawing sexually from her husband.

A Canadian study on the relationship between sex guilt and female fantasies conducted on women ages eighteen to forty-seven and reported in a 1988 issue of *The Journal of Sex Research* found a high level of sex guilt the most powerful predictor that women would have less varied and far less explicit sexual fantasies. Women who suffer from sex guilt, often subconscious, are more likely to experience the love fantasy rather than the purely sexual one. How many of these women do lay beside their husbands each night feeling sexually unsatisfied and dreaming of another man?

The sex isn't good, so they decide they've married the wrong man. They blame lack of love rather than mutual ignorance and guilt for the chill between their sheets. They fake orgasms, because that's what wives are supposed to do. They don't touch themselves during intercourse, because love and the right penis should take them to the heights of ecstasy, and they're convinced this man, this penis, beside them was the wrong choice. But another man, Mr. Right, who lives in their heads, slightly beyond reach, could make it all happen if only they weren't trapped— or too good and noble to run to him.

Happily monogamous wives don't fall into the love fantasy trap. They use their fantasies, which are more graphic and varied in content, as arousal aides during masturbation or intercourse. And they don't assume the love fantasies are any more an expression of their true desires than is the rape fantasy. They see this sexual daydreaming for what it is: a pleasant diversion from reality, not reality itself.

"After my first child was born, I had firestorms of sexual fantasies," one woman wrote. "For the first two or three months, I didn't want my husband. I wanted Paul Newman. Or the UPS man. But I knew it would pass. As soon as I was able to have sex, I took the fantasies to bed. My husband and I had a great time. He didn't have to know Paul Newman and the UPS man were involved."

Another wife, a forty-five-year-old mother of three from Atlanta, writes: "In general I think men are more honest with themselves about their fantasies than women are. A man looks and thinks about what he might do if he had the chance, but he knows it doesn't mean anything. A woman looks and couches her fantasy in different terms. She has to believe she wouldn't do the things she's thinking unless she were in love with the man in her fantasy—or not in love with the husband in her bed.

"I've been married twenty years. I've had a lot of sexual thoughts about other men in those years, but I have never confused those images dancing around in my brain with truth. My girlfriends have. I've seen marriages end over what we called crushes in high school."

The happily monogamous wife doesn't chase her daydreams. She uses them to add richness to her life.

CHAPTER 15

Independent Women

> *"I love the life of a single woman! The dirty little secret about us is we have much better sex than married women. I was briefly married. What a mistake! Masturbation is preferable to married sex."*
>
> —a thirty-six-year-old secretary from Buffalo, New York

*T*O PARAPHRASE THE ubiquitous Virginia Slims ad, if you want to look at how far we have *not* come, Baby, you need look no further than our attitudes about single women. Unmarried men are still viewed as social assets, while unmarried women, especially those over age thirty-five, are not. The self-help and psychology section of bookstores is clogged with man-hunting guides. You won't find anything in those sections telling men how to catch a woman. The basic assumption is: Women want to get married more than men do, and, therefore, men have to be coaxed, coerced, manipulated, and trapped into marriage. A single man is a bachelor whose lifestyle is acceptable, understandable, even enviable. A single woman, particularly one with little or no interest in getting married, is, after all these years, an object of concern, pity, or bewilderment to both her married and single friends.

Society may not be as overtly sexist as it was twenty or thirty years ago, but it is covertly sexist, particularly in its attitudes toward single women. Yet, many studies show the majority of single women are happy with their lives. The prevailing media stereotype, the desperately single woman, is not the norm. "Desperate" may be a passing phase in a woman's life, one often coinciding with the sudden realization her time to conceive a child is limited, but it is not the lifetime mindset of the unwed female.

Many single women wish their friends accepted that.

"If you're beyond forty and never married, someone you know thinks you're a closet lesbian," says Janice, forty-three, an administrator in a government agency, who has neither married nor borne a child. "And, somebody else thinks you're frigid. The phrase, 'I'll bet she's never had a really good fuck,' has been whispered behind your back.

"Friends and strangers are always psychoanalyzing me. If I read an article in a women's magazine about how some women fear commitment because they were sexually abused as children, I know one of my friends will read the article and try to get me to 'open up' about the abuse they're sure I've been hiding in my past. An unmarried woman is open to interpretation by everyone. It's different for married women. They can be half of the most neurotic couple you've ever met, but it's okay. They're married.

"Most of my friends are single, five to ten years younger than I am, and some, not all, are obsessing on finding the right man. I'm past this phase. My ticking biological clock has quietly run down, and the silence is wonderful. For a few years in my late thirties, I panicked too. I answered personals ads, bought into the man-catching mentality as promoted in bookstores and on "Oprah." It didn't work. Part of me really didn't want it to work. I'm happy the way I am.

"I've probably had a hundred sex partners since I lost my virginity at age sixteen. I love sex and don't regret my promiscuous days one bit. Sure, I've slowed down a lot in the past ten years. Who hasn't? I'm more cautious now. I use condoms. I wouldn't have sex with a man I met at a party like I did when I was twenty-one. There aren't as many partners at forty as there are at twenty anyway. I've had my share of nights alone with

Mr. Vibrator. But there's always someone if you really want, or need, to have someone.

"Now I'm seeing a man who is fifteen years younger than I and of a different race. Just seeing him naked excites me. When we no longer please each other, we'll move on, with no regrets."

Contrary to what many believe to be true of women her age, Janice is happily single and sexually active. She considers her life well-rounded, full of friends and work satisfaction, with time alone for hobbies and passions. And men.

Who Is She?

Single (never married and not cohabiting) women are 18.9 percent of the total survey respondents, and divorced (not remarried and not cohabiting) women are another 32.5 percent—making a total of 51.4 percent unmarried women who live alone or with roommates. Almost 75 percent of them—or almost 39 percent of the total—qualify as Independent Women, women who:

- *Either never married or divorced and have not remarried.*
- *Are both sexually active and satisfied with their sex lives.*
- *Report satisfaction with their lives in general.*

I searched for the common threads in socioeconomic and religious backgrounds, and once again, I didn't find startling differences between the happy and not happy, but the independent women included a high number, almost half, of early bloomers. As a group, their religious training, regardless of denomination, was more often "nominal" than rigorous. Whether one is raised Catholic (22.5 percent of the total survey), Protestant (47 percent of total), or Jewish (25.6 percent of total) seems to be less important than how rigidly the tenents of faith are applied to sexual behavior and enforced within the family.

The independent women in this survey do report currently having more sexual activity, including masturbation, than single women in other studies generally do. In both the most recent *Cosmopolitan* and *New Woman* magazine surveys, for instance, single women were sexually active on an average of once a week.

The independent women in my study report an average of intercourse twice a week and masturbation three times a week. And when they have a complaint about their sex lives, it's that they would like more.

This is not the woman in the local supermarket known as a meeting place for singles, hovering over the salad bar until she meets the one, their hands grazing while passing over the bean sprouts. You will not hear her say "I'm so tired of lying my head down on the pillow alone at night" over cappuccino. Chroniclers of post-AIDS society most often fail to interview her when they're doing stories on "the new single woman," because she doesn't fit their theory that women want to be part of couples or, more specifically, of those couples called "parents."

Within the smaller group of unmarried women, the 25 percent who did report dissatisfaction with their sex lives in particular and their lives in general, some did write poignantly of the empty pillows beside their heads or the intoxicating smell of freshly powdered babies. Of the unhappy group, 70 percent were over thirty, only 20 percent had been married, and less than 8 percent were mothers.

But only a few of my unmarried respondents (curiously, nearly all of whom were born and raised in the South) seemed to fit the profile of the desperately single women. One Alabama woman, the survivor of two traumatic marriages ending in bitter divorces, insists she can "only be happy as a wife." Another twice-divorced woman from South Carolina claims it was not possible to be both happy and single. If only they'd made the "right" choices in men or manipulated the right men in the right way, they insist, their lives would be blissful.

To be happily single, a woman needs a high lifestyle satisfaction quotient, and these unhappy women don't have it, but the independent woman does.

What Is Her Secret?

It's a matter of attitude. Independent women share common attitudes, including:

- *Self-confidence*. She feels confident of her ability to take care of herself, not only financially and emotionally, but also sexually. (Perhaps Southern women, more than any other group, aren't raised to think of themselves as capable in these ways.)

- *Ambivalence toward marriage and motherhood*. She has, doesn't want, or has given up on having children and considers marriage a state to which she may or may not someday aspire. Repeatedly, independent women told me they "might" want to marry "someday" with no sense of urgency in their words.

- *Considers sex a priority in the selection of partners*. The suitability factors are far less important to her than sexual attraction.

- *Separates love and sex*. She is definitely not searching for "the one" though she may have been in the past.

"Age thirty-five is the danger point for single women," says a thirty-eight-year-old Philadelphia editor. "For a few years, I was obsessed with getting married. I thought, 'It has to happen now. It's gotta' happen before my time runs out.' Every man who was vaguely suitable was him.

"I'm over it now. Women in this stage will do anything to get the man, including sacrifice their true selves."

The Many, Not "The One"

"I've heard so many women say, 'I'll give it six months, and if he isn't willing to commit, I'll move on,' " says Monica, a thirty-two-year-old magazine journalist. "Every time I hear that, I think the guy who commits to her is in for a life of starch in his jockey shorts. It drives me nuts! Like human relationships can be run this way! All these women who mark their calendars for the six month talk on "where this relationship is going" keep saying they have to do this because they're running out of time. But, the years keep going by, and they're still alone. You'd think they'd notice the system doesn't work, wouldn't you?

"I don't think this way. Marriage is not a goal for me, which is not to say I've ruled out the possibility of wanting to marry in the future. Maybe someday I'll be with someone I want to marry, and that's fine. Maybe I never will be, and that's fine, too.

"I love men, and I love sex. I've had great relationships. When they end for one reason or another, I look back fondly. My only goal in relationships is to be able at the end to look back without anger or regret.

"Sex plays a large role in my choice of a partner. For marriage-minded women, sex is secondary. A relationship would never work for me if the sex isn't good—and plentiful. When I am attracted to a man, my body sings. My heart palpitates. My stomach jumps. My body temperature goes up. I know after a few times in bed with him if it's going to be a relationship or not.

"Oral genital stimulation is key. I want oral sex at least half the time. My first orgasm with a man was via cunnilingus. He was so good at it, I felt like butterflies were kissing me. We lived together for two years. Then he was transferred to California, and my work was here. It was a hard choice, but one I'm not sorry I made. My mother devoted her life to my father. When he died suddenly in his early fifties, she was bereft. She had nothing of her own, no inner resources to fall back on. My brother and I feel so responsible for her. If she isn't happy, which she never is, we feel responsible.

"My sexual history is mostly one of serial monogamy. I don't consider myself promiscuous, and I probably haven't had any more sex partners than the women who are out for commitment. But I'll bet I've enjoyed them more!"

Like Monica, many of the independent women in my survey said sexual attraction played a larger role in their choice of partners than many other qualities, specifically the "suitability factor," such as a man's socioeconomic status and the state of his gene pool. More than other women, they were able to overcome the "more than" rule: A man must be older, taller, richer, smarter, better educated, more successful than a woman. They formed relationships based primarily on sexual compatability, and, not surprisingly, loss of desire for the partner was considered the best reason for ending a relationship.

Like many other single women, some of them have had, or are having, affairs with married men. Various studies conclude anywhere from 25 percent to 40 percent of single women have been involved with a married man, with more than one-half to three-fourths of the women studied typically wanting to marry the man. Independent women have little or no interest in marrying their lovers.

"It upsets my friends, both the feminists and the wanna-be wives," writes a thirty-one-year-old executive assistant, "but I am quite happy having an affair with a married man, and I am not so foolish as to be faithful to him. The sex is great, the kind of sex you read about in trashy novels. Sometimes we're so hot for each other we have sex standing up against the door of the hotel room. My hands shake as I'm undoing his belt buckle and shirt buttons. When he runs his finger across my wrist, my nipples stand up.

"Could it possibly be like this if we were married—or if I were constantly thinking about the possibility of marriage with him?"

Another woman writes: "I've been seeing someone else's husband for five years. I know he'll never marry me. No man has ever taken me to the sexual heights like he does. The sex is probably so good because there's no chance of it being a regular thing."

In addition to being generally more willing to date men who can't, or aren't likely, to commit, the independent women less often report becoming enmeshed in unhappy relationships than their sisters who are in search of the one.

"I don't stay in relationships if they aren't good, if the sex isn't good," writes a twenty-eight-year-old administrative assistant from the Midwest. "I have friends who stay with men who treat them badly, and I think they're crazy. One of my best friends is seeing a guy who has never given her so much as a bunch of flowers on her birthday. She pays for everything. He regularly promises to come over for dinner, then doesn't show. She recites this litany of abuse—including, she says, he doesn't like it when she touches herself during intercourse—ending with 'but I love him.'

"No self-respect. She has no self-respect, and I do."

Sexual confidence, which they share with other pleasure claimers, may be partly responsible for their ability to choose partners wisely and to end a relationship which doesn't work for them. Maybe other women put up with bad treatment from men because they aren't confident of their ability to attract a new partner or enjoy the sex once they have attracted him. Like other pleasure claimers, the independent women are able to communicate their sexual needs and to separate sex from the other aspects of a relationship.

In fact, their ability to separate love and sex is so evolved that, as one woman said, they seem "to think sexually like men do."

The Fine Line Between Love and Sex

"In the Fifties, my mother got engaged every time she wanted to have sex with a man," says Laura, a thirty-year-old teacher from the Midwest. "She was engaged three times before she married my father at age twenty. I asked her once if she really intended to marry all those men. She insisted she did. But you'll never convince me! Her behavioral code ruled she must be engaged to have sex. So, she got engaged. My friends fall in love because they think they have to be in love.

"They think I'm depraved. Women are supposed to have made so much progress in the past few decades. How much progress have we made if we don't allow ourselves time to consider before making a commitment to a man? If having sex means putting on blinders, we haven't come very far at all.

"I choose to have sex with a man because I am strongly attracted to him. If the sex between us is good, I'll choose to have sex with him again. But I don't feel obligated to register for china because we're having sex.

"Some of my best lovers have been men I wouldn't consider marrying, for many different reasons. The man I'm seeing now is divorced with two kids. He works too hard. We aren't compatible in many areas. I don't want to be a stepmother to two prepubescents. He is dynamite in bed. This is the first time I've been with a man who was hung like the proverbial horse. It's a new experience. I'm enjoying it."

Separating love and sex is a skill engendered by strong and positive sex attitudes. The independent women don't feel guilty about having needs and desires and acting upon them, and they don't make men responsible for their sexual pleasure or their lives. That doesn't mean they don't value love or want to be part of a loving, caring relationship, but they are realistic enough to admit every sexual relationship doesn't have the potential for becoming a satisfying emotional involvement. They believe there's nothing wrong with sex for the sake of sex—though their average number of partners is no higher the figure for other single women in their age groups. It's their reason for having sex, not the frequency or number of partners, that makes independent women different.

"Ideally, I would like sex to be a love experience every time," writes a thirty-nine-year-old divorced mother of two. "We are not living in an ideal world. And I am a horny woman. I would rather have sex without love than no sex at all. I am honest enough to admit it. By being so honest with myself, I am keeping my options open, not closing them off, every time I get into a less-than-wonderful sexual relationship."

This group of women is more sexually pragmatic than many others, and the common sense approach extends to their use of fantasies.

The Love Fantasy

"My sexual fantasies are of two distinct types," writes a California real estate broker in her thirties. "Some of them are what I would describe as 'hard core.' They are about sex, period. I have fantasies of women with large breasts performing oral sex on me while I perform oral sex on a large man. Or I fantasize that I live in a huge estate where I am constantly serviced sexually by an array of beautiful, muscular, and very horny men. These fantasies are graphic and detailed, down to the drops of sweat sliding off bodies.

"Then there is another kind of fantasy, which I weave around whatever man I'm seeing. I put him in these romantic scenarios. The sex is soft, idyllic. We are making love on a deserted beach in the moonlight or in an ethereal glade with suitably diffused light. I make myself have these fantasies right before I'm going to see my lover or sometimes during foreplay. They loosen me up sexually. But they only work as a form of early foreplay. Otherwise, I think it's silly to romanticize most of these guys, and so, I don't."

Though she doesn't label it as such, the second kind of fantasy she describes is the love fantasy. Like so many other independent women, she is adept at using it to create an erotic mood around a man she does not love—and, equally adept at letting it go when the sexual encounter is over. Perhaps the love fantasy helps her quash the vestiges of sex guilt she may have. Perhaps it helps her adhere to society's standards without paying the price some of her sisters do; it's her own way of loving the one she's with.

Whatever its purpose, the love fantasy is something she deliberately invokes.

"I use fantasies a lot," writes a thirty-one-year-old medical technician. "I summon them when I need them. They are my genie in a bottle, so to speak. My favorite fantasies vary from extremely wild ones, like having intercourse with a large dog while men and women watch and masturbate, to tender and romantic ones, like kissing and caressing my boyfriend on the beach at Malibu. I use the soft ones for setting the mood, for helping me bond erotically to a man when I know I am going to have sex with him soon. The wild ones are strictly masturbatory fantasies, except for occasions when I use them to get me hotter during sex."

The independent woman does summon her fantasies when she needs them. That control over her fantasy life allows her to banish the love scenarios when they have served their purpose.

Sexual Responsibility

Reporting fewer abortions and cases of STDs than the unhappy singles in my survey, she is apparently clearheaded about birth control and disease prevention. Nearly all the single women, and married women who are not monogamous, I surveyed said they were concerned about STDs. But only the independent women reported a high rate of condom usage—almost 70 percent. That, followed by "fewer partners," were their methods of dealing with the higher risk level.

The unhappily single women in my survey, like single women in magazine reader polls, more often said "fewer partners" and "choosing partners more carefully" were their primary ways of avoiding STDs. The latter is an example of dangerously romantic thinking. As much as we would all like to believe "nice" guys are "clean" or STDs don't strike "nice" people, or that love will keep us safe from bacterial harm, the logic won't hold up.

"My friends, who are somewhat sexually judgmental, have had more problems with STDs than I have," writes a thirty-year-old Boston teacher. "I am more open and free about sex than anyone I know, but I'm also careful. To me, the two attitudes go hand in hand.

"So many women say they have trouble asking a man to wear a condom. I don't have any trouble, and I don't ask. I say, 'We have to use this.' It isn't a choice."

Other independent women say they too behave assertively when the issue is disease prevention. "Condoms aren't that bad," writes a Philadelphia journalist. "I make putting them on my partner part of the loveplay; and I perform fellatio on him once the condom is in place. I make it fun. When women say they don't want to use them, I think they're objecting to taking charge of their own sex lives more than they are to the esthetics of using protection. If you carry condoms, you say 'I am in control.'

"And, when they say men don't like them—I know they're objecting to women taking charge of their sex lives."

A woman who uses condoms is in charge of her sex life, and many women are still too afraid to do that.

CHAPTER 16

Wives Who Have Affairs

"The best sex is always with a new lover. I just had that experience again yesterday. My husband's penis is on the small side. My new lover is Puerto Rican and his penis is big. He went down on me, then when we fucked; I felt like I was losing my virginity all over again. The combination of pain, pleasure, the taboo of a white woman with a Puerto Rican, and the fact that he totally adores me (in part because I'm white) resulted in a powerful explosion. I think I came six times, and he actually came twice."

—a twenty-seven-year-old New Yorker

*L*ONG BEFORE Nathaniel Hawthorne wrote *The Scarlet Letter*, the word *adulterous* carried negative connotations for Americans. Moreover, society has judged the adulterous wife more harshly than the adulterous husband.

In the spring of 1990, for example, a divorcing Wisconsin couple became a national news item when he had her prosecuted on criminal charges for adultery. In Wisconsin, as in several other states, including New York, criminal adultery laws are still on the books though they are rarely enforced. (When adultery laws have been enforced in the past ten years, those prosecuted have been women, not men.) The husband, who'd had the foresight to conduct his own extramarital affair in neighboring Illinois, where adultery is not a criminal offense, was championed by a national organization of right-wing women, Concerned Women for America. A spokesperson for Concerned Women, who want to see the existing adultery laws enforced, voiced publicly what many women predictably whisper behind the backs of other women who violate rigid behavioral codes, including, "He only did it once, while she was sleeping around all over town." *She*, however, won their bitter custody battle, despite pleading guilty to the adultery charge and accepting a period of community service.

The moral is obvious: Hell hath no fury like the wrath of a "virtuous" woman—aimed at another woman less virtuous than she.

Supposedly, women have affairs for emotional reasons, while men's motives for seeking sex outside marriage are more often sexual. But with the guardians of a public morality that is based on the double standard surrounding us, women may be ashamed or intimidated to admit a purely carnal motivation for adultery. Both magazine reader polls and psychological research studies have generally supported the belief that women look for love, attention, romance, not sex. In their extensive 1986 survey, *New Woman* magazine concluded women have affairs for "emotional kicks," far more often than sexual ones.

The authors of one study of three hundred white middle-class professionals, median age thirty-six, said in *The Journal of Sex and Marital Therapy* that "traditional sex roles that influence the expressions of sexuality and emotionality in premarital and marital relationships also appear to operate in extramarital relationships."

But some women are different. They aren't looking for romantic balm on the wounds of marital neglect. Like the typical husband having an affair, they claim they love their spouses and insist the affair is not a threat to the marriage. Why are they in it? For the sex.

"I am very happy with my husband," says Katherine, a thirty-four-year-old journalist, who has been married to her second husband for two years. "But sexual variety is as important to me as it is to some men. Between my husbands and my lovers, I've been living with someone since I was eighteen—but never totally monogamously. I don't tell them when I cheat. Why do they have to know?

"Nor do I ask too many questions of them. When my husband and I were dating I told him my philosophy of marriage: To practice anything other than safe sex outside marriage is truly unfair to one's spouse. To have sex for anything other than the pure fun of it is dangerous. No physical risks. No emotional risks.

"I travel a lot in my work. I have what I call 'flings,' not affairs. If something is of short duration and never to be experienced again, it's a fling. They enrich my life with my husband because they keep my sexual energy level high. I want, and need, a lot of sex.

"Two weeks ago I had a fling in Southern California where I was traveling on business. I met the man in the hotel bar, gave him a false name, took him to my room after dinner, and had a wonderful time. He wanted to be tied to the bed, and I obliged him. With my husband, I am not like this. But with strange men, I am often called upon to be the aggressive or dominant partner, and I find it intoxicating. I don't do real kink!"

Katherine isn't typical of wives who cheat. She isn't even representative of the married women in my survey who are having, or have had, affairs. Frankly, some have affairs because they are in marriages maintained for the sake of the children or for financial reasons. But, she isn't a lone cowgirl either.

Who Is She?

The statistics vary with the sources, but the conclusion is inescapable: Infidelity is no longer the men's club it was in America's recent past. In 1953 Kinsey reported in *Sexual Behavior in the Human Female* that 6 to 26 percent of the married women he'd studied had had an extramarital affair. From that time through the mid-Seventies most polls reported similar findings. Then, suddenly, the numbers changed. By 1980, 54 percent of *Cosmopolitan*'s married readers had strayed. Most experts, from Dr.

Joyce Brothers to Masters and Johnson, believe that approximately 50 percent is an accurate figure for both men and women.

Married women comprise 34.2 percent of my survey respondents. Another 32.5 percent are divorced women. Approximately 40 percent of the women in both groups are having or did have extramarital affairs. These women are:

- *Married and have been or are engaged in an extramarital affair.*
- *No longer married, but did have an affair or affairs while married.*

The wives who have affairs fell into two groups: those who felt guilty about their affairs and those who didn't. More than half, 56 percent—women mainly in their twenties or fifties—said they felt guilty. Interestingly, their motives for having an affair were more often emotional than physical. But a sizable number of the wives who have affairs, over 44 percent, did cite motives more sexual than emotional for having affairs, and they reported little or no guilt over their behavior. Women earning higher salaries were more likely to have sex for the sake of sex and to say an affair either enhanced or had no impact on their marriage than was a wife earning less than $25,000 a year.

"If a man can do it, why can't a woman?" Katherine asks. "We've learned how to work without being overly emotional, why can't we learn how to fuck the same way?"

Women Who Feel Guilty for Cheating— And Why They Do It

The wives who report strong feelings of guilt about having affairs and cite primarily emotional motives for doing so may, of course, be focusing on their emotional needs supposedly unmet in their marriages to justify behavior they consider socially unacceptable. Surely for some of these women engaging in "loveless sex" seems as big a "sin" as breaking their marriage vows. Whatever their real reasons, they claim emotional causes for infidelity, including:

BEING EMOTIONALLY NEGLECTED OR STARVED IN THEIR MARITAL RELATIONSHIPS

"I was starved for romantic attention in my marriage," a Midwestern wife writes. "I'd been married ten years; and I wanted flowers, love notes, phone calls. My husband is a good man, a wonderful provider, a good father, but he has no romance in his soul. The affair with a coworker was like spring rain on parched ground.

"We didn't have intercourse for months. The build-up was slow, delicious, romantic. Twice before we actually consummated the relationship we went to a hotel. I took off all my clothes, but he left his pants on. He satisfied me. It ended because I was afraid of getting too involved, but I needed it. I really did."

NOT FEELING SEXUALLY DESIRED BY THEIR HUSBANDS

Either their husbands weren't often interested in having sex with them or made love to them in an abrupt or mechanical fashion. "I needed to prove I could still arouse a man to intense passion," one woman explained. "It had reached the point with my husband where he barely broke a sweat during sex. I felt like a masturbatory instrument, not a desirable woman. Sex with him became dehumanizing for me."

HAVING NO REAL COMMUNICATION WITH THEIR HUSBANDS

Many women say they are driven to have affairs because their husbands no longer "talk" to them. A twenty-seven-year-old Californian writes: "My husband and I don't talk about real things. My lover talks and listens to me. I see him as much for the talk as the sex. One of the best parts about sex is the time spent cuddling and talking afterward. I was hungry for that. My husband and I have quickies and he falls asleep. I have orgasms, but I am not emotionally satisfied."

WANTING TO GET EVEN WITH HIM FOR HAVING AN AFFAIR OF HIS OWN

Revenge is an emotional motive, a means for the spurned woman of reasserting her desirability and getting back at the man who rejected her all at once. "I caught him with another woman, so it's payback time," a thirty-year old writes. "I would never be having an affair if he hadn't done it first. This is not the kind of person I am, the kind of marriage I always dreamed of having. He deserves this, but I still feel uncomfortable with it."

Women who do seek emotional fulfillment outside marriage also often find confusion, pain, and more unhappiness.

"I am torn," a Texas nursing administrator writes. "I'm constantly on a roller coaster, feeling guilty one minute, exhilarated with love the next, sad after that because I can't be with the one I love, then angry at my husband, myself, my lover for the mess we've made. But sometimes I feel very sophisticated about what I am doing. This is crazy. I'll end up losing them both."

Fear of "losing both" was expressed by many guilt-ridden women, who perhaps feel they must somehow pay for their affairs.

Women Who Don't Feel Guilty

The adulterous wives who don't feel guilty, on the other hand, describe different motives for having affairs and seldom mention the fear of losing either husband or lover. They seem to be in control, or believe they are, of their particular situations. Not surprisingly, they are largely women in their thirties and forties, ages when their sexual biology makes them more capable of separating love and sex and claiming pleasure.

Their motives for affairs are primarily sexual, including:

MEETING THEIR OWN FREQUENCY NEEDS, WHICH ARE FAR GREATER THAN THEIR HUSBANDS'
Most of the adulterous wives, guilty or not, say they either are "not getting enough sex" at home or are "not getting enough of the kinds of sex wanted," whereas the guilty group had downplayed the sex motives, listing them as secondary concerns. In a few cases, the women are having no sexual relations with their husbands. Two women in my survey reported marital freezes lasting up to five years (their stories are included in part four).

"I love my husband; and the sex is good, though not as frequent as I would like," a thirty-nine-year-old retail manager writes. "I'm the more voracious partner at this point in our lives, but I'm not going to justify an affair by finding fault with my marriage. I just wanted something else in addition to what I have. Maybe that sounds greedy, but it's true."

"My husband is seven years older than I am," a thirty-eight-year-old writes. "His cycle and mine aren't in sync. He's great in the sack, but I want it more than once a week, so I have a lover."

A twenty-six-year-old Midwestern wife writes: "My husband is in the career building phase of his life. He's young. He should be virile, but he gives his all at the office. My lover is an artist. Isn't that always the way?"

A fifty-nine-year-old New York executive says, "There has been no sex in my marriage for the past year, because of my husband's health and other problems. I consider it a viable marriage for many other reasons. I have handled the situation quite happily. I have affairs, but I am discreet. At this point I feel indiscretion would be a dishonor to my husband, while sex with someone else is not."

Interestingly, the guilty wives often blame that lack of sex on emotional causes, such as "the love has died," while the unguilty wives cite physical reasons, mainly their husband's age, health, or the time-and-energy-draining career obsession.

"My husband and I rarely have sex anymore," writes a thirty-seven-year-old wife of seventeen years, who is troubled by her affair, "because something has died in our relationship. I still care deeply about him, and he about me, but the passion is gone. We have a different kind of love now. I am torn between wanting my marriage to last for security reasons and wanting to be free so I could see my lover more often.

"He is also married, and I think if I were free, he would divorce and marry me. This has not been said between us, but I believe it to be true. I have never experienced anything like the orgasms I have with him."

Several women say they left their husbands in the hopes of

forcing a commitment from their lovers. None, however, were successful, and over half returned to their husbands. The others, who divorced, look back on the affair as the catalyst they needed to get out of an unhappy marriage.

GETTING THE SEXUAL VARIETY THEY CRAVE

Sometimes it's a form of "kink," but more often it's cunnilingus that's missing from marital sex. Many women say they are getting something from their lovers that their husbands can't or won't provide. One woman calls her affairs "necessary supplements to a peanut-butter-and-jelly diet at home." Just as many men say they have affairs because their wives won't perform fellatio, so many of these women say their husbands won't perform cunnilingus, while their lovers will.

"Sex with my husband is boring," writes a thirty-four-year-old from the South who feels entitled to her affair. "He is very conservative. He will not perform oral sex on me at all and doesn't much enjoy having me do it to him.

"This is his idea of sex: Kisses, hugs, followed by 'Are you feeling sleepy?' said with a wink. In bed, he kisses more and plays with my breasts for a few minutes, then plays with my pussy, asks, 'Are you ready yet?' He enters me and within five minutes he's finished. Another five minutes, he's sleeping.

"A few years ago we almost got a divorce over sex. I cried and begged and pleaded for more sex, more variety. He honestly tried, but it isn't in him to be the lover I want him to be. So, I had to choose between giving up the marriage, which I love, and getting sex outside the marriage. I chose to keep my marriage and find my sexual pleasure elsewhere.

"My first lover had a wife who didn't reach orgasm very easily. If I had that problem, I would never have come with my husband! Anyway, my lover was tremendously adept at cunnilingus because that's how he satisfied his own wife. It was heaven! The first time I had an orgasm with him was through cunnilingus.

"My current lover is very good at everything. He is nine years younger than I am and the horniest man I've ever known. We do the stuff I'd only read about in sex magazines and trashy novels. He taught me anal sex, something I thought I'd never like. With him, I do. The first time, getting it inside me hurt like hell. But having it in there was wildly exciting. Each time there is a little difficulty, a little pain, but the excitement is greater than the pain. I have intense orgasms this way.

"I don't think my husband has any suspicions about me. I think he just believes I finally 'settled down' and became exactly the wife he wanted me to be. We're happy together."

Most of the wives who have affairs without guilt say they are involved in these relationships strictly for sex. They have no illusions about what they are doing and where it might lead, while the guilty wives, who often fashion love fantasies around their lovers, often do dream of leaving their husbands and marrying their lovers. And, ironically, the emotional security of marriage seems to make it easier for happily adulterous wives to have sex outside the marriage without risking emotional involvement.

"I don't want an emotional involvement with anyone else," a thirty-six-year-old corporate executive writes. "I have an intensely physical relationship with my lover, and it's exactly what I want from him, all I want from him. Sometimes you don't want to be bothered with the other stuff. Marriage is drama enough! All my life, until now, I've had the emotional strings connected to every sexual relationship. I've never made love before without thinking it's going to lead to something permanent. This is new for me, and I am loving it!"

How Cheating Affects the Marriage

Again, much seems to depend on whether or not the wife feels guilty about having the affair.

The guilty are prone to confessing to relieve their guilt. Other women keep their affairs secret. Guilty women also seem more likely to form emotional attachments to their lovers, thus putting their marriages in jeopardy, and they take bigger risks, often insuring they'll be caught. "I am faithful in this marriage, though I had an affair in my first marriage," writes Peggy, forty-four, and six years into her second marriage. "My first husband wasn't interested in sex much at all. I did everything possible to turn him on. I never lost my figure. Believe me, plenty of other men noticed me even if he didn't!

"But I didn't cheat until we'd been married ten years. I was raised a strict Catholic and it was very hard for me to do. I fell in love with the boy next door. I was thirty, and he was only twenty. We tried to keep it a secret, but we were so much in love, we couldn't. My friends and family were shocked. His mother threatened to kill me when she found out. We kept taking bigger and bigger chances because we were driven to be together.

"Finally my ex-husband caught us in the act. My lover often climbed the tree between our houses, over to our roof, and down into the upstairs bathroom window. I would meet him in the bathroom and we would make love on the floor. It was crazy because my husband and kids were sleeping in the same house. It was only a matter of time until we got caught, and we did.

"After my divorce, I thought he would marry me, but he went away to college instead. Now I can see it was for the best. I'm happier in my second marriage, and I wouldn't cheat. I believe adultery is wrong, understandable sometimes, but still wrong."

Several divorced women say their affairs ended their marriages. In each case, their behavior almost guaranteed they would be caught. One woman had sex with her lover in a bathroom at a party that her husband had also attended. Another had an affair with her husband's brother—and told the men's sister the details.

"Though I didn't realize it at the time, I wanted the affair to end my marriage," one woman writes, and she seems to be speaking for many. "I was so blatant about it. My lover came to my house during the day. My husband, who wore boxer shorts, found a pair of my lover's underwear, bikini briefs, in the corner of the bedroom. I mean, what could I have been thinking?"

The prevailing theory in our society is that an affair cannot be good for a marriage. Yet many women insist their marriages have not been hurt by their outside relationships.

Women who report little or no guilt about their affairs believe the affairs have either had no impact on, or have enriched, their marriages.

"I'm much sexier with my husband now that I have a lover," writes a thirty-three-year-old. "I even go down on him more, because I don't want him to suspect anything." Many women did say their affairs prompted them to "try harder" sexually with their husbands. "Before I started seeing someone else, I was sexually indifferent to my husband," writes a forty-three-year-old Seattle wife. "Now, I am more aroused by him. Maybe it's partly guilt, and I'm going after him more so he won't think I'm going after someone else. I think about sex now more than I did. He loves the new me. I bought several sex books so he won't have to wonder where I'm getting my ideas. He thinks it's great."

A woman in her thirties, who's been married ten years and had "a dozen or so" affairs, writes: "In the past I would say my affairs have had zero impact on my marriage, neither helping nor hurting. But this last one made the marriage better. I have always been at loose ends sexually, never getting enough of what I need from any man, never knowing exactly what it was I needed. This man has taught me so much about myself sexually. I feel both more energized and calmer. It's had a beneficial effect on the marriage all the way around."

It is safe to conclude that fewer married women than married men are able to conduct guiltless "sex for the sake of sex" affairs. We are not socialized to do so, and the recriminations against the errant wife continue to keep all women, if not in our places, at least more afraid of getting out of them than men are. But some women can do it, because they have a highly evolved ability to separate love and sex.

The Ultimate Separators

How do they do it? Not surprisingly, the married women who reported conducting guiltless, or relatively so, affairs seemed to be more independent than other wives and shared several characteristics, including:

• *They are far more pragmatic sexually than the other women.*
• *They believe they are in control of their lives, sexually and otherwise.*

- *They tend to have careers rather than jobs and to consider their own work, personal interests, and time as valuable as their husbands'.*

- *They report high sex drives, few sexual inhibitions, and a willingness to experiment sexually.*

- *They use sexual fantasy to facilitate arousal and/or orgasm during masturbation and intercourse.*

- *They seldom weave love fantasies around their lovers.*

When they do have love fantasies, these women are aware of the pretense. Many say they make their husbands the focus of their fantasies, possibly as a way of keeping the central relationship in their life more vibrantly alive. "I always had romantic fantasies about the men in my life before I was married," writes a thirty-nine-year-old California artist and wife of five years. "When I got married, I knew I had to watch this kind of thinking. It can lead to trouble. I don't romanticize my lovers anymore. If my mind starts drifting in the direction of flowers and candlelight, I switch the channel. I want to stay married. But I don't necessarily want to stay faithful, for my own reasons having nothing to do with any inadequacy on my husband's part."

A forty-year-old Ohio wife and mother writes: "I am able to keep my marriage and my affair separate because I don't let myself dwell romantically on 'the other man.' I banish those thoughts! They are the product of romance-novel thinking anyway."

Another forty-year-old wife, a New York City photographer, says, "When I have these romantic fantasies about my lover, I do an editing job. I cut him out and replace him with my husband. I believe we control our own fantasies. They are useful and helpful, or they are harmful. It all depends on what you make of them."

The ultimate separator cannot be in control of every aspect of her life, even if she believes she is—but she certainly does control one critical area of her emotional life, her fantasies.

PART 5

Women Who Have Lost Pleasure— And How They Regained It

CHAPTER 17

The Saboteurs of Pleasure

"Sex is over for me. Herpes ended it. How could I ever explain this to a man? And, if I did, wouldn't he reject me? Of course, he would!"

—a forty-year-old herpes victim

*B*Y REJECTING HER own sexuality, she thinks she is protecting herself from ever being hurt by a man—by *sex*—again. Advances have been made in the treatment of herpes that mitigate the severity and duration of the symptoms. Furthermore, research scientists working on the two experimental vaccines now being tested are hopeful that one or both may be on the market in three to five years. Herpes, while painful, is not a sentence of lifetime celibacy, though this woman has apparently condemned herself to that fate.

Like other women who have lost pleasure, she equates sex with pain, and she believes she can prevent all future pain by eliminating sex from her life. She has taken pleasure away from herself—or allowed it to be taken from her. For whatever reasons, she has withdrawn sexually. She is negative about men, sex, often about other women who enjoy sex, and especially about herself as a sexual being.

Her sex life is run by the critical and punitive judges inside her head, though she will insist outside forces, the saboteurs, are responsible for her withdrawal from pleasure.

The saboteurs of pleasure include:

- *Sexually transmitted diseases, particularly herpes since it can be treated but not yet cured and therefore carries a lasting stigma.*
- *Rape and other forms of sexual abuse.*
- *Abortion, when it leaves a woman feeling guilty.*
- *Gynecological problems, which prevent natural sexual functioning for extended periods of time.*
- *Repeated sexual disappointment with a partner, particularly when a woman is unable to have an orgasm or her partner is unable to achieve or maintain an erection.*
- *Sexual rejection, especially by a husband.*
- *Overwhelming guilt about past sexual behavior.*

Many women come out of these experiences with their sexuality relatively undamaged. Often with the help of therapists and/or supportive lovers, husbands, and friends, they are able to put what happened in perspective and not inflict additional pain upon themselves. But other women, those who have lost pleasure, can't seem to move beyond their victim status. They equate sex with sin and sickness, deep and crushing disappointment, rejection—and above all with pain.

Who Is She?

While I doubt religious training or family background alone is responsible, women who have lost pleasure do report more religious and other forms of repression in their family backgrounds than other respondents. Many women have lost the ability to enjoy sex following sexual rejection or guilt over past sexual behavior; they may connect sex to early childhood feelings of fear of discovery and memories of punishments when they were caught touching themselves, making out with a boyfriend on the couch, or even saying "dirty" words. These same women wrote about fathers who ignored or abandoned them in childhood, or who castigated them as children for doing the normal things children do, like running through the house naked or asking questions about sex. Some said they felt "distant" emotionally if not physically from their fathers, particularly during puberty and adolescence. Several women said their fathers, and sometimes both parents, were "cold, critical, and rejecting."

Women who have lost pleasure—for whatever reason—are more often firstborn daughters than not. This is not so surprising, since as oldest daughters, they probably internalized more negative sex messages, from many directions, than children born later into their families. They may also have taken responsibility, not only for their own behavior, but for the misconduct of siblings. Psychologists who study the impact of birth order on human development have noted that firstborn daughters tend to be obedient, conscientious women who fear the consequences of rule breaking. They are influenced by the opinions of others, particularly those in positions of authority either in their personal or public lives. They seem to have a lot of faith in the power of goodness to protect them. Their corollary belief, of course, is that if something bad does happen to them, it must be their fault. They blame their own failure of goodness for bringing them down.

A thirty-nine-year-old herpes victim (and firstborn daughter) from the Midwest writes: "It's been nearly five years since I contracted herpes, and I am still shocked and shamed by it. I have not had sex since then. Nor can I imagine ever wanting to have sex with anyone again. Anyway, who would want me if I did? I am spoiled. It's so ironic that this would happen to me. I have always tried to do everything the right way.

"For fifteen years I have been working in a department store in a mall. The rules say employees must use a special mall entrance and have their packages checked even when they are shopping on their days off. Other employees don't do this. They say it is too much trouble to use the entrance way at the end of the mall, and on their days off they should be able to act like any other customer. Well, for fifteen years, I have been using this entrance even when I shop on my day off. If I didn't, I know I would get caught.

"It is important to me to do things the right way. You can imagine how I felt when I discovered a man I'd just started seeing had given me herpes. Over and over again I've asked myself why did I ever have sex with him. I didn't know him that well, and I shouldn't have done it."

Guilt reverberates throughout her letter. She seems to believe a life of celibacy is the punishment she has drawn for having sex with a man she didn't know "well." So many of the women who have lost pleasure share her sense of personal guilt. Others, who have been inorgasmic in their relationships or rejected by their lovers or husbands, say they are unable to attract or hold men, or unable to respond sexually.

Unlike women who work through the traumas of rape or herpes, sexual abuse or physical illness, they continue to blame themselves for their fate. Many victims, male and female, go through an initial period of self-blaming, even if it's nothing more than castigating themselves for being in the wrong place at the wrong time. For the woman who has lost pleasure, the blaming has never stopped.

CHAPTER 18

Sexual Victims

"I have been in an emotionally and sexually comatose state since I was the victim of date rape four years ago. I trusted this man. I thought he was my friend. I thought I knew him. Well, I will never trust another man. I haven't been out on a date since this happened, and I don't have any plans for going out on a date in the foreseeable future. You ask about my sex life. I haven't got one now. I don't even masturbate, because I don't let myself think about sex. I am filling out your questionnaire to let other women know of the dangers sex entails.

—Sandra, a twenty-nine-year-old San Francisco production assistant

*L*IKE MANY OTHER women who participated in my survey, Sandra put her phone number at the bottom of the last page of the questionnaire in response to my request for personal interviews, and I called her. During three phone interviews, each one lasting in excess of two hours, she told me her story, beginning with sexual molestation in early childhood. She thinks what has happened to her is "typical" of the "female sexual experience."

From the age of five until just a few days past her ninth birthday, her father periodically crawled into her bed at night where he taught her "a secret game."

"He told me it had to be our secret between me and him, because Mommy wouldn't understand," she says. "Basically our secret game was masturbating him. He put my little hands around his penis, then put his hands over mine and jacked off. The last few years he had me kiss his penis. By the time he was asking me to take it in my mouth, I was smarter. I gagged myself and threw up on his precious thing. He lost interest in me then.

"Five years ago, a little before the rape, I finally got up the nerve to tell him what he'd done to me; and he denied there was anything wrong in what happened between us. The way he remembered it, he had climbed into my bed 'on occasion' to 'console' me when I was having bad dreams. And, once, he said my hands had accidentally clasped his penis which was protruding from his boxer shorts. I couldn't believe it!

"My mother was listening to this conversation with tears streaming down her face; and he said to me, 'Look what you're doing to your mother!' Never mind what she did to me all those years when she was sleeping in her bed while her husband was violating mine! Finally they both asked me to leave, and I haven't been back. My brother sides with them. He doesn't believe anything ever happened to me. Well, he can't afford to believe it if he wants to stay in their good graces.

"None of them know I've been raped, and if they did know, they would not believe it or they would think it was my fault."

Sandra was raped by a man she'd been seeing for three weeks. They'd had sex together before, but on this occasion, she had said no.

"He was drunk," she says. "I'd had sex with him before when he was drunk; and I didn't like it. Sex was never easy for me. It takes me a long time to come. With this man, drinking didn't slow down his responses very much, but it made him rougher. I said no because I didn't want to be mauled by him. He did it anyway, worse than if I'd just gone along.

"He slapped me across the face, and while I was reeling from that, he threw me across the back of my sofa. It has a low back, which put me in just the position he wanted me in. He pushed up my skirt and pulled down my pantyhose so roughly he tore huge holes in them—and he fucked me first vaginally, then in the ass, so hard I bled. The bastard lasted longer than he ever had with me that night. Or maybe it just felt like he did."

She did not call the police, because she'd read in an article in one of the San Francisco papers that cases of "date rape," then a new phrase in the language, were almost impossible to prosecute.

"I cried off and on all night until I made myself sick," she says. "Then I took a shower, dressed, put on dark glasses, and went to the drug store where I bought Tucks, those little medicated pads, for my asshole. I called my best friend. She came and stayed with me for five days. By then, I was okay.

"I had already decided I was never going to have anything to do with men again."

Some law enforcement authorities estimate that date rape, perhaps the least-reported violent crime, accounts for 80 percent of all rapes. They are careful to stress the word "estimate" because the overwhelming majority of these crimes are not reported, and of those reported, few are actually prosecuted. Privately, prosecutors admit that when the assailant is known to the victim, particularly if she has had sex with him in the past, they are seldom able to overcome the jury's or judge's suspicion she encouraged the rape or, worse, consented to sex, then later changed her mind.

Sadly, whether a woman is raped by her date, her husband, or a stranger, she will find the process of getting legal retribution a long, painful, and frustrating one—if she is able to see her assailant arrested, convicted, and sentenced at all. If she's the victim of sexual harassment in the work place, she may fear that legal action will hurt her career. She's probably right. Surely her disadvantaged legal position contributes to a rape victim's psychological recovery problems. Fortunately many women, whether they prosecute or not, do seek help from professionals at rape counseling centers and other therapists. With that help, they are able to overcome the fear, anger, resentment, and even guilt engendered by rape.

Sandra didn't get help. She is handling this new anger the same way she handled the old anger at her father: by keeping it inside. Her way of surviving is cutting herself off from men and sex. Other sexual victims, women who have lost pleasure, cope in the same self-punishing way by denying themselves the warmth, intimacy, and passion of a sexual relationship.

The best advice anyone can give to a woman who has been victimized by rape is: Get professional help. You wouldn't treat a broken arm yourself, and you shouldn't treat severe psychological trauma that way either. You can get help at no cost in many places. Every major city and most sizeable towns have some kind of rape counseling program. Call your local hospital, women's health center, or mental health agency.

Who Is She?

Some sources put the odds that a woman will be raped as high as one in four, with most studies putting the risk factor at closer to one in ten. Of my survey respondents:

- *Less than 10 percent report being raped.*

- *Less than 5 percent claim to be the victims of incest or other forms of childhood sexual abuse.*

- *Almost 25 percent say they have experienced some level of workplace sexual harassment.*

I did not consider them sexual victims unless: *They have withdrawn sexually because of their negative experiences, which could also include sexually transmitted diseases, abortions, and other traumas.*

Many of the sexual victims in my survey have overcome their negative experiences and claimed pleasure. (See chapter 21 for specific guidance.) But first they had to overcome the victim mentality.

The Victim Mentality

"I've had eight abortions, three cases of STDs, have been raped twice—including my first sexual experience—and suffered workplace sexual harassment on two jobs at two different companies," writes a thirty-one-year-old corporate executive. "Men are shits. Women are victims. Ultimately, men have the power."

This writer has the classic victim's mindset. Her sense of sexual powerlessness dominates the twelve-page letter accompanying her questionnaire in which she describes rapes, harassments, and the sad consequences of not protecting herself against unwanted pregnancy and disease. Like many other sexual victims, she says she shared her experiences to "warn" other women, especially younger ones, of the dangers of sex. Although, strangely, none of the women who've had multiple STDs and abortions include in their warnings: Use birth control and condoms! Their advice is most often: Abstain. Even victims who haven't entirely given up on sexual relationships with men seem not to expect to, or feel entitled to, find joy in them. Like the writer whose first sexual experience was rape, they feel powerless.

Several studies conducted on adult women who were sexually abused as children have found childhood abuse to be a strong predictor of who is more likely to become the victim of date rape. The studies have been controversial because some people fear they will be used to blame the victim of acquaintance rape. It is not my intention in citing the studies—nor, I'm sure, the authors' intention in publishing their results—to suggest that such is the case. In rape, whether acquaintance or stranger rape, the blame rests soley with the rapist, and not with his victim.

The authors of the studies in question, highly respected men and women who specialize in this particular area, include Diana Russell, a California sociologist and writer known for her studies of rape and incest victims. Dr. Russell hesitated to publish her own studies of randomly selected women in which she found that 68 percent of incest survivors were date raped in later life, because she feared the results would be misconstrued and misused to damn the victims further.

She says: "One of the effects of child abuse could be a real difficulty in knowing whom to trust. We don't realize how important it is to a woman's survival not to trust the Ted Bundys of the world."

Some experts believe women who are abused in childhood don't understand they have rights in sexual relationships, including the right to say no. They feel powerless in relation to men and to their own sexuality, and they suffer from low self-esteem. Perhaps they also face threatening sexual situations as adult women in the same way they did as children: passively. Their childhood histories have put them at greater risk than other women in our violent society by instilling this sense of powerlessness in them and in leaving them without the power and self-esteem to choose partners wisely or even to say no.

Possibly, the victim who withdraws sexually understands that, and retreat seems to her the only means of finding safe ground. But women who overcome the traumatic experiences of childhood sex abuse and rape reject the victim mindset.

The Failure to Protect Herself

Some sexual victims suffer from herpes or another STD. They may have had multiple abortions, but they have not been raped nor sexually assaulted. Their stories, juxtaposed with those of rape victims, may not be as gripping, but their pain is as real, and so is their feeling of powerlessness.

"I got chlamydia from my boyfriend probably as soon as I started sleeping with him," writes a thirty-nine-year-old Southern design consultant who had four abortions in her twenties and contracted three different STDs in her thirties. "But I didn't know I had anything. I had no symptoms except a recurring urinary tract infection, which my doctor didn't connect with chlamydia, so he didn't test me for it. After almost a year, he decided I was having too many urinary infections and did the test. I had chlamydia.

"I told my boyfriend he had to be treated so we wouldn't get it again. He agreed, and I thought everything was fine. I didn't want to use condoms with him because I was trying to get pregnant with his baby. He didn't know this, of course. Besides, he didn't want to wear them, and I have never had any luck at persuading men to use them.

"Then I started getting urinary tract infections again. Finally

I got pelvic inflammatory disease, which made me quite sick and in pain. It also left me sterile. Then I found out he was seeing two other women the whole time he was seeing me and is going to marry one of them soon.

"I will never trust another man again. This experience has left me devastated. I haven't had sex with a man since we broke up, almost eighteen months ago."

Victims often trust unwisely. The woman who rejects victim status uses birth control and condoms (until she is in a committed monogamous relationship) and has taken charge of her sex life. She still might end up in a relationship with a man who gives her an STD, but she is reducing the risk of being victimized by her behavior. She also makes better choices than victims, who let sex "happen" to them.

Excuses women gave for not using condoms, even after they'd been treated for one or more STDs or had one or more abortions, include:

"Condoms and diaphragms take the romance and spontaneity out of sex."

"Men don't like to use those things."

"It's the man's responsibility to provide those things. If he doesn't and you do—you look like a slut."

"I don't have sex that often anymore, so I'm never prepared when it does happen."

And the ubiquitous: "I'm too embarrassed to buy them."

I began to hear a subtle silent refrain repeated after each excuse: *I am not in charge here.* Their statements are only a cover for the real reasons some women don't use protective devices. Studies have shown, for example, a direct correlation between the failure to use an effective contraception and negative sexual attitudes. Those attitudes include:

- *Sex is dirty.*
- *Women don't, or shouldn't have, strong sexual needs—and they especially shouldn't express those needs outside a relationship.*

- *Men are responsible for protecting women from the negative consequences of sex.*

Certainly our sexually repressive culture encourages women to behave as victims at least to some degree. Consider these statistics (from the U.S. Government Census Bureau) concerning the results of negative sex attitudes, and the discouraging consequences they have:

- *The United States has the second-highest rate of unplanned pregnancies and the third-highest abortion rate among industrialized nations.*

- *Fifty-one percent of all pregnancies in the United States are unplanned—and 30 percent of all pregnancies end in abortion.*

- *According to Planned Parenthood, less than half of unmarried sexually active women between the ages of twenty and twenty-nine use contraceptives.*

- *And, most shocking of all, according to the Alan Guttmacher Institute, only 16 percent of sexually active American women use condoms.*

Yet, with the exception of AIDS, sexually transmitted diseases are almost as sexist as pregnancy. Their consequences to women, in whom they are largely undetected and/or asymptomatic, are devastating. They can leave a woman sterile, increase her risk of cervical cancer, cause birth defects or other medical problems for her and her baby during pregnancy. America has begun to take AIDS seriously, but a woman's risk of contracting that disease from a man who is not bisexual or an IV drug user is relatively slight, even in unprotected sex. Other STDs, more likely to affect women, also merit our attention and concern.

Women are at great risk of contracting one of at least twenty-five other STDs, the most common infectious diseases in the United States after the common cold and flu, if she has unprotected sex. Four million Americans will contract chlamydia this year. Up to two million will catch the new strain of gonorrhea. Some thirty million Americans already have herpes, with an additional 800,000 new cases reported each year.

While not 100 percent effective, condoms, especially those treated with nonoxodyl 9, are the best means we have of preventing the spread of STDs. (Early detection is important in effective treatment, but few women realize that they must *ask* their doctors to screen them for STDs, which don't show up on the annual Pap smear.) Condoms are far more reliable than a vow of abstinence, which is susceptible to being swept away by a strong romantic urge. Yet, the many sexual victims who wrote to warn other women did not recommend condom use.

They advised sexual retreat instead. Women who have been able to overcome negative sex experiences, however, won't tell you to avoid sex.

The Feelings Behind the Words: Anger and Guilt

Many victims are angry at men. They know they are, and they readily admit their feelings. What they don't recognize is how, in rejecting their own sexuality, they have turned the anger inward upon themselves. Also, few are able to identify the sex guilt experts say lies beneath their behavior.

A thirty-year-old Maryland woman, raised in an Orthodox Jewish home where "sex was something too awful, too filthy for discussion," says, "I rarely have sex anymore, but that's okay with me. Most men don't know how to make love. Their touch is all wrong. It's hard to tell the difference between a lover and a rapist sometimes.

"I was sexually harassed by my first employer when I was twenty-one and working full time, finishing college at night. It was a clerical job. I needed the job. From the first, he demanded sexual favors, which escalated from touching my breasts to me performing oral sex on him. He would call me at home at night and ask me to describe what I was wearing to bed. I think he was masturbating while we talked. He told me if I didn't cooperate he could hire someone else. I was very insecure at the time. Now I know I shouldn't have allowed this to happen to me.

"Two years later I married a man who treated me much the

same way as my employer, like his sexual object, something to which he was entitled. The sex was never very good. After a while, I told him I didn't want to have sex anymore. At first, he agreed. Then he raped me on several occasions, and finally we were divorced.

"He doesn't see sex the way I do. He says I was cold and frigid, that he never raped me. But, he is wrong about the frigid part. I did have good sex with a man once. He was the great love of my life, though we were only together a short time. We spent a weekend in bed. I couldn't get enough of sex with him. He knew how to give a woman an orgasm. I was deliriously happy.

"But he gave me gonorrhea. That's how my 'best ever' sex experience ended. Now I have sex with a man only if we've been dating a while and there seems to be no reasonable way out of it. I guess you could say I'm angry at men. I don't trust them. If you asked me why I bother with dating, I couldn't give you a good answer. I don't that much, but if you never date a man other people suspect you of being a lesbian."

The details of their stories vary, but sexual victims invariably sound the same major themes:

THEY FEEL UNABLE TO CONTROL THEIR SEX LIVES AND THEY'RE VERY ANGRY ABOUT THAT

They don't believe they have the power to refuse sexual demands of a harassing employer, a forceful lover or husband, or even someone they've casually dated. Nor do they assume responsibility for the outcome of sex by using birth control devices and condoms to prevent pregnancy and disease. But, they are very angry at men for not respecting their sexual rights and protecting them from pregnancy and disease. They're also angry at themselves for "letting" bad things happen to them.

THEY BLAME THEMSELVES MORALLY FOR THE NEGATIVE CONSEQUENCES OF SEX

They don't see an unwanted pregnancy or an STD as the predictable result of failure to use mechanical protective devices.

Rather, they see it as evidence of a *moral* failure on their part ("Good girls don't get diseases"). Society reinforces that negative value judgment. If these women saw sexual pleasure as a right, they would be far more likely to take precautions to safeguard themselves.

THEY ARE UNWILLING TO TRUST MEN BECAUSE OF WHAT A MAN OR MEN DID TO THEM IN THE PAST
In cutting themselves off from men sexually—either completely or in large part—they are also deliberately shutting themselves down sexually. By not trusting men, they are admitting total lack of confidence in their own ability to trust wisely, and in their ability to take care of themselves in relationships with men. Repeatedly, they risk again only to be disappointed or hurt by yet another man they trusted despite evidence of his untrustworthiness.

The Ultimate Victim

In the late Eighties, *sex addiction* became the newest child in the over-publicized and over-diagnosed family of so-called "process addiction diseases." Treatment centers and self-help groups, based on the twelve-step program established by Alcoholics Anonymous, sprung up nationwide. But according to a growing number of experts, the "disease" is only the most recent resurrection of American Puritanism.

The sex addict is the ultimate victim, powerless over her erotic desires. (In the Fifties, she was called a nymphomaniac.) She can't say no, and in support groups she is encouraged to see that disability as part of a sickness that cannot be cured. She is taught to control it by remaining celibate until she's in a relationship. The whole concept of sex addiction reinforces a victim's belief in her sexual powerlessness.

And, by insisting upon the link between sex and love and commitment, these programs reinforce sex guilt.

"I've always been an easy lay, and being easy has sometimes led me into affairs I've looked back on with embarrassment," says Charlene, a twenty-six-year-old dietitian who briefly explored a self-help group for sex addicts following a brief but torrid S&M affair. "That one scared me. It got fairly kinky, which made me pull out of it.

"I spent one whole weekend dressed only in a dog collar, leather restraints, and high, high heels. At one point he had me bent backward over the kitchen table, my ankles and wrists fastened to the legs, while he put clothes pins in arcs from under my arms to my nipples. He left me that way, with a gag in my mouth, while he watched television in the living room. After a while he came back and fucked me, and as he fucked me, he removed the clothes pins, one by one.

"It hurt, but God, was it exciting. I was afraid of how far I might let him go after that, so I was on shaky ground about myself when I went to a meeting of Sex and Love Addicts Anonymous. There were ten women and one man in a church basement. People took turns sharing their stories while the rest listened and nodded their heads.

"The stories were not as lascivious as you might expect. One woman had phone sex with a wrong number. The man broke down and sobbed when he said he wanted to masturbate right there and hated himself for it. No matter what your story, the rest of the group would say, 'Yes, you are addicted to sex.' They congratulated each other, and themselves, on achieving sexual piety 'one day at a time.'

"They said they were 'powerless' over sex, and I thought, 'That's ridiculous!' I couldn't wait to get out of there."

If Charlene had been on even shakier ground, she might have stayed in the group. Yet, sex addiction, the dissenting authorities say, is a myth, a punitive myth growing out of our culture's negative attitudes about sex and pleasure. According to Martin Levine and Richard Troiden, authors of the highly regarded paper on "The Myth of Sexual Compulsivity," published in *The Journal of Sex Research*, sex addictions are not "true addictions," but merely "patterns of behavior now stigmatized by our society."

Dr. Marty Klein, author and prominent California sex therapist says "The average person would be considered a sex addict based on answers to the screening test given by support groups. Being promiscuous or even kinky does not make one addicted to sex. The vast majority of sexologists reject such thinking as unscientific and moralistic."

In fact, it is difficult to find a professional not involved in the sex addiction treatment industry who does consider sex addiction a disease and not a social phenomenon. The social climate was ripe for this type of sexual stigmatizing in the late Eighties: People feared AIDS; aging baby-boom women wanted commitment and babies; health became more valued and also equated with abstaining from excesses; the religious right had risen again. All signs pointed to a new philosophy about sex, and in America in the late twentieth century, pop psychology is marketed as philosophy.

This thinking hurts women more than men. We are still the sex most influenced by negative sex messages. It is still difficult for many women to take charge of their own sexuality. We want to conform to society's standards because we think such "good girl" behavior will earn us love and acceptance. If it's hard for us to make our own sexual choices, the concept of sexual addiction only makes it harder.

"Sex addicts" and women who have been robbed of their ability to enjoy sex because of rape, incest, sexual harassment or abuse, even STDs and abortions, do think of themselves as victims. Unfortunately, the victim mentality, especially among women, has run rampant in American society since the early Eighties. The sexual revolution was replaced by the victim revolution, in which everyone seems to claim they are powerless. Sexual victims avoid sex because they feel powerless over men and over their own sexuality. They don't believe they can get what they want sexually—or set their own limits and have them respected. Like other victims, they have given up their power. And only they can take it back.

CHAPTER 19

Sexually Dissatisfied Wives

"Sexual attraction had some importance in my choice of male partners until I passed thirty, when it became of little importance at all. Shortly after my thirty-fourth birthday, I married a man because he also wanted a child. He is a wonderful father and a very good man. We don't have a lot in common, especially sexual chemistry. I have asked myself lately if I regret the marriage, but I don't. What I regret is that I had to become almost forty before my hormones kicked in. I should have felt like this at twenty when I could have had fun with it. Now it is too late."

—a New York lawyer

SHE'S A WOMAN who appears to have it all—career, marriage to a handsome and successful man, motherhood. But, behind the public façade, she is a sexually dissatisfied wife. For many reasons, she plans to stay in the marriage, though she finds it sexually unfulfilling. She isn't comfortable with the idea of having an affair either. Where does that leave her?

"I am trapped," she says.

The phrase is repeated often by women in this category. The trap is a state of sexual frustration to which some women have sentenced themselves because while they believe the sex in their marriage can't be improved they also believe extramarital sex is wrong for them. Their motives for staying married are security-based and include:

"I can't make it financially on my own, at least not in the style to which my children are accustomed."

"I like the perks of marriage, country club membership, the freedom to quit my full-time job and work part-time whenever I want, a big house, trips to Europe. On my own, I would be just another fortysomething former wife living in a small condo with paperboard walls."

"I am emotionally dependent on my husband, on being married."

"I like my husband. I like our life together as a family. It's the sex I don't like."

They stay, they say, for the sake of the children, the house, the lifestyle, the comfort and convenience of companionship—sometimes even in fear of disappointing parents, his and hers, if they left. And, they don't stray, because adultery violates their religious or ethical code or because getting caught would leave them vulnerable to losing everything they cherish.

Who Is She?

The dissatisfied wives are only 19 percent of my married (or formerly married) respondents. They are women who:

- *Are, or were, monogamously married.* In some cases, the divorced women ended the marriages because of the sex, but more often they were left by their husbands for other women.
- *Rate their sex lives as dissatisfactory.*

The majority of the group are late bloomers, with almost half having married after age twenty eight. More than half have been married less than seven years. There seems to be no guarantee that marrying later ensures happiness—or that the seven-year itch won't strike a lot sooner. In fact, several recent studies have shown the onset of marital dissatisfaction is more likely to be the four-year mark, not the seven.

The dissatisfied wife is the woman who didn't need an orgasm a few years further down the path of pleasure denial. Now she is chafing under the erotic restrictions she imposed upon herself when she decided other goals were more important than orgasms. Perhaps she has given up on sex altogether. She's not driven by the need to protect herself from pain as the sexual victim is, but, she is often afraid of something: intimacy or exploring her own sexuality, for example.

Because she puts more responsibility for sex on men, she blames her husband for her dissatisfaction.

"He says he's too tired," writes Ginny, the thirty-four-year-old wife of a corporate vice president ten years her senior. "Or he says my timing is lousy. Or he says I push him too much. He's the male version of the spouse who says, 'Not tonight, dear, I've got a headache.' I could meet him at the door in garter belt, black stockings, and high heels—and he would say, 'What's for dinner?'

"If we have sex once a month, it's a good month. I don't know why I bother. I spend a lot more time thinking about getting it, scheming about getting it, than I actually do getting it. Me and high school boys—we think alike."

In her 1987 book, *Women and Love: A Cultural Revolution in Progress*, Shere Hite drew critical and media fire by declaring the majority of the 4,500 women she interviewed were not happy with men, sexually or any other way. Most experts thought the picture she painted of women and love relationships too dismal. Regrettably, some authorities have used the disagreement over the latest book as reason to discredit her earlier works, *The Hite Report* and *The Hite Report on Men*, which I consider excellent studies, much more on target than the recent one.

I didn't find a high percentage of discontented women. But the wives who are dissatisfied are *very* dissatisfied, and their state of malaise has in most cases persisted too long to be dismissed as a passing phase. They rate their sex lives "not satisfactory" —or worse. Their evaluation of their husbands' lovemaking skills is lower than other married women's. Close to 15 percent report *never* having had an orgasm during lovemaking via any form of stimulation. Nearly half say there have been extended periods during their marriages, ranging from one month to five years, during which no sex at all took place.

They are, however, less likely to masturbate than either happily monogamous wives or women who are having affairs.

"I am not comfortable masturbating," was a frequent response. They almost as often said "I wouldn't feel comfortable having an affair."

Interestingly, fewer than 5 percent have ever been (or are) in sex therapy, although many women claiming they've suggested therapy but their husbands have refused.

What They Say Is Wrong with the Sex

They blame their sexual dissatisfaction on three root problems:

- *Lack of chemistry, which they often defined in ephemeral terms such as "a fluttering in the air between two people."*
- *Their partner's lack of lovemaking skills—and unwillingness to perform certain sex acts, specifically cunnilingus.*
- *Differing levels of desire as expressed in arguments over the timing and frequency of sex.*

Most of them consider their situations irreversible. They do not believe chemistry can ever be revived. Or that unskilled husbands can, or will, learn how to make love. Or that their spouses will ever want the kind of sex they want, when, and how often they do.

His Lack of Skills—Or Willingness to Perform

"How often do I get cunnilingus? Only when I beg," writes a thirty-seven-year-old Cleveland wife of five years. "And I hate to beg. So, that makes it probably every fourth or fifth time we have sex, which would put the number of times I receive cunnilingus each year at—possibly, two. 'Is that satisfactory?' What!

"Nothing about my sex life is satisfactory, thank you."

She had "approximately twenty-five" partners before she married, and in response to the question "How would you change men as lovers?" she replies: "I'd change almost everything about them. Make them more sensitive in the way they touch. Less quickly responsive to touch themselves. More willing to open up emotionally and experiment sexually. I'd give them tits, so they didn't have to covet ours."

Though orgasmic via masturbation, she says, "I rarely masturbate anymore. Ironically, I masturbated more when my sex life was more active."

Nearly two-thirds of the dissatisfied wives said they were "rarely" orgasmic during lovemaking though most were orgasmic via masturbation. Many do understand the need for direct clitoral stimulation during intercourse. They most often complain about the absence of cunnilingus in their husbands' repertoires or his unwillingness to provide manual stimulation or prolonged foreplay. Many also said their husbands expected fellatio on a regular basis—without being willing to perform cunnilingus in return.

"I know sex shouldn't be tit for tat," a twenty-nine-year-old wife of four years writes. "But you begin to think in those terms when you never get what you want and he's always asking for, and usually getting, what he wants. Now, after I perform fellatio two or three times, I say, 'Not until I get mine!' I hate doing this. Having to ask all the time makes me feel resentful."

But, these women didn't blame their partners for being unable to bring them to orgasm via intercourse alone. Many others, however, did cast this heavily weighted stone. Their comments included:

———————

"No one could come with my husband. He's finished in two minutes."

———————

"His touch is all wrong. He's too heavy-handed. I've tried telling him, but he doesn't listen. I read somewhere to tell your husband what you want. It doesn't work!"

———————

"I call him the 'In, Out, Hot Damn! Man.' He doesn't bother to say, 'Thank you.' Why should he? I'm his wife."

"He doesn't understand what I need to reach orgasm. He's still as awkward at foreplay as he was when I married him eight years ago."

"Men are lousy lovers. The only good times in bed I've ever had have been with women. But I'm not really a lesbian, so I'm stuck with men."

These particular criticisms of men indicate a woman's underlying ignorance of her own sexuality as well as an inability to communicate her needs without intimidating her partner. While it may be preferable for intercourse to last longer than a few minutes, it isn't *necessary* for a woman to achieve satisfaction. She can reach orgasm manually and/or orally before or after intercourse. The duration of intercourse isn't the real issue. Her inability to acknowledge and communicate what kind of stimulation she needs *is* the issue.

The dissatisfied wife, and no doubt her husband as well, suffers from the myth of the penis as the ultimate satisfier. When intercourse doesn't produce orgasm, she blames him and his penis. He probably does, too. Both seem to feel her need for additional stimulation indicates something lacking in them.

Differing Levels of Desire

One-third of the dissatisfied wives, who were "frequently" or "nearly always" orgasmic during lovemaking, say the problem is quantity, not quality. Their husbands' low sex drives, not the men's performance skills, are cited as the cause of their dissatisfaction.

Sex therapists say "differing levels of desire" is the source of many marital disagreements about sex, and that in recent years the wife is as likely to be the partner complaining about "not enough sex" as the husband. They advise the dissatisfied partner to masturbate more often and to ask the spouse to pleasure them occasionally when he isn't interested in, or capable of, sustaining an erection or ejaculating himself. Neither is a palatable solution for the dissatisfied wife.

"My husband says he likes sex, but he has a million excuses for why he doesn't want to do it 'right now,' " writes a thirty-five-year-old artist. "He is ten years older than I am, and I understand part of the problem is we're not in sync. His interest in sex has naturally dropped off at just the point mine is naturally picking up. He says it doesn't bother him to masturbate me sometimes, but it bothers me.

"The only other alternative is to masturbate myself, and I don't enjoy doing that either. What is the point of being married if you have to give yourself release? I've never like masturbating anyway."

A forty-four-year-old Maryland wife says, "He knows I don't believe in masturbation, but he still tells me to go do it to myself when I am needy and he is not interested. He says he can't help it he doesn't think about sex as often as I do now.

"But, I do think there is something else behind his disinterest. Sex has become almost a power struggle between us. The one who wants it most, usually me, tries to get the other to capitulate."

She may be right. Withholding isn't something only women do. It is also possible her husband is suffering low libido as a side effect from prescription drugs for any one of several ailments common to middle age men. Whatever the reasons for the erotic imbalance in her marriage, she is dissatisfied—and understandably so.

That Elusive Thing Called "Chemistry"

Almost 70 percent of dissatisfied wives believe chemistry is missing from their marriages. They may have more than a little trouble defining "chemistry," but they're sure it isn't there. In some cases, they say, it never was.

How dissatisfied wives define chemistry gives some insight into their unhappiness. Here are some examples:

"It's the mystical emotional aura surrounding two people."

"The indefinable something letting you know whether your sexual tastes are compatible or not."

"N/A—Not applicable. I've never had it for anyone that I know of."

"The ability of a man and a woman to know at the same time how to please each other in bed."

Contrast those definitions to a few provided by women who are satisfied with their sex lives:

"It's an almost animal physical attraction with elements of love, emotion, intellect. Sometimes it's intense, other times more subdued, like an engine on low."

"Heat between a man and a woman."

"In the beginning it's wanting to rip his clothes off the moment he walks in the door . . . later on, it's remembering you did feel that way once and could again."

When we talk about the chemistry between two people, we're really talking about the sexual desire they feel for each other. The chemistry of desire is both biological and emotional. A different process from arousal, desire can be more easily understood as the underlying attraction that forms the basis for arousal. If the base is missing, sex isn't going to take place as often, because it will be dependent on two people becoming aroused by something or someone other than each other at approximately the same time.

According to researchers and psychiatrists, some people who report they have "no chemistry" with their partners actually suffer a lack of erotic impulses or urges caused by hormonal imbalances, psychological problems—or nonsexual conflicts within the relationship. In the eighties sex therapists began seeing many couples complaining about a new ailment, "lack of desire." Soon it was identified as a syndrome, inhibited desire syndrome, and became the subject of scientific papers and books, both for the professional and lay audience.

Biochemistry does play a role in some cases, *but the most common cause of inhibited desire syndrome is marital conflict*. Loss of desire, a disguised form of anger, is often the power play subconsciously used by one or both partners to control the other. Sometimes the real motives behind the sexual freeze are so well hidden, neither party realizes anger is a factor in the marriage. They may even pride themselves on being a couple who "never" argue.

Following anger, boredom with the partner and the sexual routine, and then depression are cited as leading causes of inhibited desire syndrome. Some partners experience the loss of chemistry as soon as they get to know each other very well, because, according to therapists, they had previously idealized each other. When flawed reality intruded into the romantic universe created around the spouse, desire evaporated. Just as men are more prone to suffer from the Madonna-whore complex, so are women more likely to be the victims of sexual idealism, making princes of ordinary men, then turning them back into men again.

The Attitudes Behind the Disappointments

Most women blame their dissatisfaction on their husbands.

"It's his fault," writes a thirty-one-year-old Southern wife. "I am attractive, willing, and able. He doesn't want to make love very often, and when he does, he doesn't want to take the time to do it right. You know that old saying, 'If it's worth doing at all, it's worth doing right.' "

As a group, they share two basic assumptions about men:

1. HE SHOULD KNOW HOW TO PLEASE ME

Several women included some variation of the phrase "automatically know how to please," as part of her definition of sexual chemistry. Dissatisfied wives are less well-informed about the mechanics of sex and the biosexual differences between men and women and are also less sexually communicative than other wives. They expect him to know what they want and need during lovemaking, and when he doesn't, they're disappointed.

2. YOU CANT TEACH A MAN HOW TO MAKE LOVE

When he doesn't automatically know how to please them, they say "He doesn't know how to make love." This is a frequent complaint, often coming from women who've been married many years. Why didn't they teach him, as many happily monogamous wives have done? Apparently, they feel uncomfortable playing the erotic lead. Less inclined to initiate the sexual encounter or to introduce new ideas into lovemaking than other wives, they are also more critical of their husbands' skills or lack of them.

But, if he doesn't know and they won't teach—where does that leave them?

In addition to their basic assumptions, they are sexual idealists who probably think of themselves as "romantics," a more flattering term. They believe sex should just happen spontaneously. Passions should be ignited by a smoldering glance exchanged by lovers. A hand shouldn't have to be slipped between bodies to trigger the female orgasm. And if it doesn't all happen this way, they believe something is wrong with the sex, not the marriage.

"The marriage is great," writes a forty-five-year-old Chicago wife and political activist who hasn't had sex with her husband in three years. "But, the sex has died. I'm writing to let you know a marriage can thrive without the sexual part, even if, as was our case, the sex in the beginning was quite pleasurable."

Sexless Marriage

The dirty little secret in many American marriages is that no sex has taken place in the marital bed for weeks, months, even years.

Several recent studies have looked at what is not happening in the marital bedrooms of America. In one study, one-third of 365 married couples abstained from sex for an average of eight weeks at a time. According to other research, 20 to 50 percent of couples will stop having sex during some part of the marriage. Some will stop altogether.

Many simply avoid sex, often by unacknowledged mutual consent. The most frequent ploys are not going to bed at the same time and suddenly becoming involved in a book or television show, even a phone conversation, at bedtime.

"My husband and I never talk about sex," writes a thirty-nine-year-old Florida wife and mother who has not had sex with her husband in almost two years. "We arrange it so we aren't going to bed at the same time. He gets up earlier than I do, so he goes to bed by ten-thirty, even on weekends, unless we have plans. And, he can't stand noise or light when he's sleeping, so I stay downstairs to read or watch TV.

"If we have been out together, it is my habit to go to bed first. His excuse is that he's too 'charged up' for sleep, so he stays downstairs until I am asleep. If I'm not asleep, I pretend I am.

"This must sound very silly to you."

Before they stopped having sex, she says, they had "dull, routine, sexual relations in which [they] never got past the fumbling stage." She was rarely orgasmic during lovemaking and now rarely masturbates. Because sex is "not a priority" for them, she adds, doesn't mean the marriage is bad.

"We're very happy. Sometimes I do admit I wonder if we'll ever have sex again. But, I suppose we will when the time, and conditions, are right."

Her protestations of happiness aside, the most common cause of sexless marriage according to the researchers is marital discord. Less than 6 to 10 percent of the couples examined in seven studies cited job stress or tiredness. Unexpressed anger and resentment about nonsexual issues drove most of them to withhold sex as a form of punishment to the spouse or to force a change in some aspect of the other's behavior or personality.

In approximately 10 percent of the cases, spouses abstained

from sex out of fear of repeating past performance failures. Sexual dysfunctions, which the experts estimate do affect about 10 percent of couples, include a woman's inability to have an orgasm or a man's premature ejaculation or difficulty in ejaculating, known as retarded ejaculation. Though dysfunctions are curable—and premature ejaculation, easily so—many couples find not having sex preferable to enduring another performance failure.

"My husband and I have given up on sex," writes an Ohio woman, age thirty-two, who hasn't had sex with her husband in almost a year and rarely masturbates. "We married five years ago after a two week courtship. He is rarely able to ejaculate during sex, which is frustrating for both of us. I don't know how to handle it.

"In the beginning of our marriage, I enjoyed the prolonged lovemaking sessions. But, he was often able to wake up in the morning, roll over on top of me, and after a few minutes of intercourse, ejaculate. This wasn't the most fun for me, to have someone pumping in and out of me for his benefit only at six A.M., but I thought it was fair.

"Eventually even that didn't work. Now, sex is something neither one of us wants to get into."

And, some people, women as well as men, avoid sex because they fear intimacy. Fear of intimacy, marital therapists say, is frequently what motivates two seemingly mismatched people to marry. Subconsciously each finds emotional distance more comfortable than closeness, and so they choose each other as partners. Many such couples lead lives of almost total alienation in a marriage of collusion, in which each fortifies the barriers between them, while blaming the other for whatever they perceive to be wrong.

Dissatisfied wives do blame their husbands for the sorry state of their sex lives, and perhaps the their husbands blame them for not being sexy enough to arouse them. But the situation is not hopeless. If you are committed to the marriage, you can make the sex work again. (Chapter 21, on sexual reawakening, will tell you how women in other situations rediscovered pleasure, and their advice can help—as can that from monogamous wives in Chapter 14.)

Help for the Dissatisfied Wife

"You can turn it around, but you have to take the responsibility upon yourself," writes a forty-four-year-old Maryland wife. "Our sex life was about as boring as it gets two years ago. We could have marketed a video of ourselves making love as a sleep aide for insomniacs. I went around blaming him—behind his back. I was always complaining to my friends about him. One woman gave me a vibrator and a book on masturbation for my birthday. I was embarassed and stuck them in the dresser drawer for a month.

"Then one afternoon I got them out. I began masturbating regularly without telling my husband. Then one night I told him my little secret, which got him very hot. He wanted to use the vibrator on me, and I let him. Things picked up from there. I bought some sex guides. He rented some videos. Life changed for us.

"Somebody just has to have the courage to get over his or her embarassment and do something different."

She's right. You can improve your sex life by:

- *Masturbating more frequently.* Masturbation takes the pressure off sexually, because you aren't waiting for him to "give" you an orgasm. Having more orgasms also makes you feel sexier, increasing the likelihood he'll want more sex with you.

- *Getting rid of old attitudes.* Even a husband of twenty or more years can learn new sexual tricks. Buy some books and videos. Don't present them as instructional material. Rather, tell him you want to learn to be a better lover and need his help in doing that.

- *Being willing to experiment.* A lot of dissatisfied wives aren't willing to satisfy their husbands' desires. Sexual compromise is necessary in ongoing monogamous relationships. If it doesn't cause pain, what's the harm in trying it?

CHAPTER 20

Discarded Women

"Everything in my life turned gray after my husband left. I was totally sexless. I didn't masturbate; I didn't even have sexual dreams. For me, sex with my husband had been on such a high plane. I couldn't think of having sex with anyone else."
— a forty-five-year-old Midwestern advertising executive

*T*HE STEREOTYPICAL IMAGE of the discarded wife is this *hausfrau*, puffy with the accumulated bloat of baked goods, chocolates, tea, and cooking sherry, and blank-eyed from years of watching life pass by on a television screen. Her husband understandably left her for the excitement of a woman whose hips measured less than fortysomething and whose brain still functioned above the level of the walking comatose. In actuality, you'd have difficulty picking the discarded wife from the attractive women in the express checkout lane at the supermarket.

"But people still think something is wrong with you if your husband walks out," says Lynne, thirty-eight, a petite redhead who looks more like Annie Potts in "Designing Women" than a housewife left by a man who could no longer conjure lust, even by fantasizing, when poised over her body. "Old attitudes die hard. Now if you look good, but don't have a job, they say he left because you let your mind go. If you look good and have a job, they say he left because you were no good in bed.

"What woman wants to believe a man could leave a wife who looks good, brings home a paycheck, and has orgasms too?"

Not many women do want to believe that. By extension of logic, it means they could be left someday, too.

"I felt contagious after he left," Lynne says. "All the women in my upper-middle-class neighborhood who were supposedly my friends stopped calling. I was frozen out. A few of their husbands did call. And they said what you've always heard husbands say at a time like this. 'You must be lonely. You still have needs. I could help you out. No one needs to know.' Yech!

"Maybe that's part of the reason I turned off to sex. When he left me, I felt cold, physically chilled for months. I couldn't get warm. I kept turning up the thermostat but it didn't help. Sex was the last thing on my mind. I couldn't get my body temperature up to a comfortable point. How could I think about sex?"

Who Is She?

Discarded wives are only 9 percent of my survey. They are women who:

- *Had been left by their husbands—and describe their divorce in these terms.* The happily divorced women often do not indicate whether they or their husbands initiated the divorce.

- *Are still married to men who are involved in long-term affairs or who repeatedly have affairs.* Unlike other wives of adulterous men, they describe themselves as "devastated" by his conduct.

- *Are involved in sexless marriages, not by unacknowledged mutual consent.* Before the pain of their situation led to a sexual shutdown, the women wanted sexual relations—and in the past have "begged" their husbands to make love to them.

- *Have stopped having sex, even masturbating, because of the rejection.*

Discarded wives feel rejected, so deeply and painfully rejected that they no longer report having or acting upon erotic impulses, either through masturbation or intercourse with their husbands or other men. If ever that overworked phrase, "low sense of self-esteem" applied to a group of women, it's this one. Otherwise, they don't have as much in common with each other as you might expect they do. There really is no composite portrait of a woman men leave.

Especially in the upper-income brackets, discarded wives are less likely to be working than other wives. (Over 60 percent of discarded wives whose husbands earn in excess of $100,000 a year do not work outside the home.) If they do work, they're more likely to regard their work as a job, not a career. But they are no more out of shape, uneducated, or inorgasmic than other women. In fact, the upper-middle-class wife may be in better shape than anyone. They also report having as much interest in sex, before the rejection, as the average respondent, and may, if anything, have tried too hard to please their men, rather than not trying hard enough.

"I would do anything sexually for my husband," writes a forty-two-year-old Californian whose husband left her two years ago for another woman, a coworker. "He can't say he left me for someone who would do things I wouldn't. I performed fellatio whenever he wanted. He liked me to do it while he was driving the car, which scared the hell out of me, but I did. I swallowed. I took it up the ass, though it wasn't my favorite thing. If he wanted to tie me to the shower and fuck me from behind while water was pounding me from the front, I said yes. And, most of the time I thoroughly enjoyed everything.

"I can't remember saying no to him, though I suppose I must have once or a few times in a twenty-year marriage."

The Idealized Man

The one common thread uniting these women, however, in addition to low self-esteem, seems to be their idealization of both their husbands and the sexual relationship. Before his fall from grace, he was everything to them. They considered his needs more important than theirs and built their lives around his life. The sex they shared was passionate and almost holy.

"You can't imagine how I felt about my husband if you've never known this kind of pure love and passion for a man," writes a fifty-year-old Midwestern marketing director. "There was no one else but him for me. I was a virgin bride at twenty-one, product of a small-town, repressive, religious background. It wasn't that I didn't have sexual instincts before I met him. I repressed them, because I was scared to fool around.

"But, I knew such passion with him as most women never experience. I couldn't believe he would look at another woman, since I could never have looked at another man. I thought what we had was perfect until I found out he was seeing another woman.

"When I confronted him, he cried. He said he would stop, but I didn't hear him. I literally didn't hear him. It was several years later when I was driving alone in the car that I remembered him begging me to forgive him and not to leave him. I was deaf, dumb, and blind when I found out what he had done. I couldn't hear a thing he said after, 'Yes, I've been having an affair.' "

Like other discarded wives, she didn't know how to feel about her husband when he could no longer occupy the pedestal upon which she'd placed him. Presumably, pedestal-building is something that men do and women don't. However, I found these women did build pedestals. Their husbands were larger than life—until they violated the marriage vows.

These wives are, or in some cases *were*, as one woman says in describing herself, "extremely unrealistic and romantic about men and sex."

What Happened and How

"He was building this new life, and I didn't know it," writes Carrie, a forty-year-old Houston "upper-middle-class homeless person," who, two years after a bitter divorce, is staying with friends and still trying to put her life back together. "I was making gourmet dinners, and he was hiding his assets. I was collecting fabric swatches to redecorate the bedroom, and he was looking at condos with his lover. When he had everything in place and all he had to do was pack his clothes and tell his lawyer to move ahead—that's when he told me he was in love with somebody else and he wanted a divorce so he could marry her.

"Later, I learned from other women I met through a support group that this is a common pattern among men of means. They make up their minds to leave, arrange all the details, *then* tell their wives. I was devastated when he left. I felt like I had no warning.

"Until the end, we were still having sex, granted, not as often as in the past. But I had no idea anything was wrong. I was always there for him sexually. He couldn't have had any complaints in that department."

Carrie's description of how her marriage ended was similar to the stories many women told, stories that could be divided roughly into three parts:

The blissful unknowing. Detecting no signs of unhappiness in their spouses, they describe the time before his rejection of them as "good," or "wonderful," even "perfect." The more financially comfortable the wife, the less she seemed to realize what was happening behind her back.

The husband's announcement. It was nearly always met initially with the stunned silence of disbelief, giving way to tears and recriminations, and finally a shocked acceptance.

The frozen aftermath. Once the wife accepted his rejection, she became "frozen" with grief, anger, and total loss of sexual desire.

Those responses are shared by discarded wives whose husbands haven't left. Though the details of their lives are different from those of the women who are divorced, the patterns are similar. Whether men leave in the physical sense or only leave emotionally and sexually as they retreat into extramarital affairs, they seem often to negotiate the leave-taking without alerting their wives until the abandonment is virtually completed. Then, faced with a reality they cannot avoid, the women react in the same way, beginning with stunned silence and ending all too often in sexual retreat. They take on the responsibility for their husband's loss of interest in them.

"He said it was my fault he cheated, and I accepted the blame for fifteen years," writes a fifty-three-year-old who only recently left her philandering husband. "I didn't question. I thought he was so desirable. It had to be me. I had to be the one who wasn't worth being faithful to."

"We don't have sex anymore," writes a fifty-four-year-old Chicago grandmother. "We haven't had sex in three years, because my husband doesn't want me anymore. After we'd not had sex for several months in spite of my begging for it, he finally told me why.

"He said he can't get aroused by an older body. He said my sagging breasts and ass leave him limp. No, he really said, 'impotent.' He said I have made him impotent, and the sound of the word was like a knife in my chest. I shut down sexually from the moment he said it. The sight of my own body now repulses me.

"It took me almost another year to ask the obvious question. When I finally did ask if he has sex with other women, he changed the subject. He said I should know he will never answer the question.

"I haven't even masturbated since the day he told me I made him impotent. For many years we had the most wonderful sexual relationship a woman could ever want. I desired him with my whole being. I worshiped the man. Now it is gone, and sex is over for me too."

And from a forty-four-year-old woman whose husband has been involved in an affair with a neighbor for five years: "I had no idea this was going on until last year. I'm such a fool, I thought we were the perfect couple. Another neighbor told me, and when I asked him, expecting him to deny it, he said it was the truth. He doesn't want a divorce, probably because she doesn't want to marry him.

"We haven't had sex since the night he told me. Occasionally he makes a halfhearted effort, but I turn him away. I haven't had a sexual thought since that afternoon before our talk. I feel like someone remembering how it was before the bomb was dropped and the world changed irrevocably forever."

The Sexual Shutdown

"I don't even masturbate anymore" is the phrase that flags the discarded women's questionnaires. It's an expression of self-denial separating them from other divorced women who have never considered themselves discarded wives, regardless of whether they or their husbands initiated the divorce. If they are married to impotent or adulterous men, it sets them apart from other women in similar situations who haven't cut off sexual feelings because of what their husbands are, or are not, doing.

"I am in an asexual period," writes a forty-five-year-old Philadelphia writer whose husband told her a year ago, after several months of impotence, that he was only able to have an erection with another woman. "My body is the erotic wasteland. Nothing happens inside me in the sexual sense. It's eerie.

"Before this happened, I was telling people the forties are going to be my sexiest years. I thought everything was so good between us. And I was looking forward to growing old with him and continuing to have sex into our nineties."

Like other women she says she is not repressing sexual thoughts—she doesn't have them.

Kathleen, a St. Louis executive in her fifties, says, "After my husband left me for another woman, I turned off sexually—to the point where I didn't have a sexual thought for seven years. I had such tremendous passion for that man—and suddenly all erotic feeling was gone, dried up inside me. For seven years, I was as asexual as you can possibly be.

"I felt physically cold for a long time after he left. I couldn't get warm. I remember lying on the floor when the sunshine was streaming through a window, trying to get warm. Nothing worked. Each winter I would be so cold, I thought I couldn't stand it.

"I never thought about sex during those years. I didn't even get jokes about sex. People would have to tell me—my kids would have to tell me—it's a joke about sex. Don't you get it?

"No, I didn't get it."

The shutdown is that complete. But, in some women it isn't a permanent state.

The Spark

"After seven years, something happened to me," Kathleen continues. "It wasn't big or dramatic. I was working closely with a client on a project. We had files and charts and drawings spread out on a conference table. While pointing something out to me, he accidentally brushed my hand.

"My flesh tingled from his touch. I wasn't attracted to him, but his touch reignited me sexually. I felt as if he'd switched my pilot light back· on, and suddenly I was running at this low humming speed. I wasn't dead anymore. Then, I began to notice men again, in the sexual way.

"Within months, I was involved with someone. It was a passionate affair. He eventually left me too, but when he did, I didn't go into another asexual phase. No, I got what I call the 'Fuck the World' syndrome. I wanted to have a lot of men. I was fairly promiscuous for a while after the second one."

Most of the women who came out of their asexual periods describe similar moments when they literally felt the spark being reignited deep inside themselves.

"I hadn't masturbated or thought about having sex with a man for almost two years after my husband left," writes a Denver woman in her thirties. "Then one day a friend's husband put his arm across my shoulder when he was walking me out to my car after dinner at their house. It was a friendly gesture, devoid of sexual content, and I didn't take it to mean anything more. But the weight of his arm on my shoulder made something kick back on inside me.

"I masturbated that night. It took me twenty-five minutes to reach an orgasm, and when I did, I cried my heart out. Then, I was okay again."

Most women report the spark happened by the accidental touch of an acquaintance or stranger or the affectionate gesture of a friend, but a few say it was generated by sudden or unexpected physical contact with their husband or ex-husband.

"I was dead to sex for a year after he left," writes a Boston teacher. "One day when he was picking up the kids, he put his hand on my arm and told me I looked tired. It was meant as tenderness, but it felt sexual. His hand on my skin made me feel lust again. I knew it couldn't be for him, so I began to look around."

A few women report the spark was exchanged with another woman, which sometimes led them to lesbian experimentation.

"I had not considered myself lesbian or bi until two years after my husband left," writes a thirty-eight-year-old Southerner who now has sexual relations with both men and women. "One hot lazy afternoon in the country I was sitting under a tree with a friend. Our kids were playing nearby. She was talking excitedly about something, and at one point, she took my hand. That was it. My whole body began to boil. When my face turned red, she dropped my hand in confusion.

"Two weeks later I was in another woman's bed for the first time in my life."

However it happened and wherever it led, the spark caused these women to masturbate and then to reach out sexually, to men or sometimes women. It brought them back to sexual life.

CHAPTER 21

Overcoming Rejection

"It began with rage. I'd been divorced two years before I got mad about what he'd put me through. I was numb, dead sexually—and then I got mad at him. The kids told me he and his new wife kept the bedroom door locked and made 'funny noises' in their room. I imagined him having sex with her in exquisite detail, and I was furious. Within a week I had bedded a stranger to get even with him. I kept that up for a while before I began to get healthy again. But, in a funny way, I think the anger saved me. If I hadn't gotten so mad at him, I might have remained sexually dead."
—a thirty-eight-year-old television producer

*F*OR THIS WOMAN, the spark igniting her was not the casual touch of another person: It was her own anger spewing flashes of heat and light like a Fourth of July sparkler, scorching her skin and making the sexual nerve endings come alive again. Hers is not an unusual experience. Many women report a sexual re-awakening taking place only after they finally got angry. Often the anger is not directed at the husband or ex-husband, but at themselves for allowing his rejection to shut them down.

"After I found out my husband had been sleeping with his sister-in-law for something like eleven years, I went around in a protective fog, feeling nothing, especially arousal, for nearly a year," writes a Cleveland management consultant. "I wasn't mad. I wasn't jealous. I was just stunned, cowed into this horrible state of accepting my own undesirability.

"He's always been able to do this to me to some extent. With-holding sex had been his primary means of controlling me. It is the most hideous form of control, because it leaves the other person doubting her ability to arouse. There is no more flat-out rejection than sexual rejection.

"When I found out about the two of them, the rejection was complete. I couldn't function sexually. I couldn't think sexual thoughts.

"I'll tell you what finally snapped me out of it. I got mad at myself for being so nice to him, so accommodating to his schedule and his personal needs while he was unconcerned that I had turned to stone. I got so mad, I told him I wanted a divorce. I wasn't thinking about sex at the time, about becoming sexually active again.

"No. I just knew I couldn't stay with someone who didn't want me anymore. I hated myself for sleeping in the same bed with him at night. When I took steps to end the marriage, I began to feel better. But I didn't feel sexual again until a few months after the divorce.

"I was chaperoning a class field trip for the boys' school. In the bus I sat next to one of the fathers, also a chaperone. He was one of those animated talkers who reaches out to touch your hand or arm when he makes a point. By the end of the trip, I was feeling horny. That night I masturbated for the first time since I found out about my husband's affair."

Anger, perhaps the most difficult emotion for women to ex-press, has led many women to make the positive, healthy changes they needed to make before they could become sexual again.

After the Spark

Whether the spark is generated by anger or the electricity of a sudden, unexpected touch, it reawakens the sexual sleeper as surely as did the Prince's kiss placed softly on the bright red lips of Snow White. But, unlike the fairy tale heroine, this re-awakened woman isn't dewy-eyed and trembling, waiting for a prince to make it all happen for her. This time around she's smarter.

In the traditional myth of romantic love, a woman believes she must plan her life around the man who sexually attracts her—particularly if she is very responsive to him. The myth victimizes many women, but none so much as the women who lose pleasure when they are rejected by "the one," the very one who was supposed to love her for the rest of her life. Some women are so totally devastated by the loss they never become sexual again. Those who do reawaken say they view sex in a different way, as an integral part of their lives, not as a mysterious power wielded by men.

"I no longer let sex determine my decisions about how I will live my life," explains a forty-two-year-old Texas waitress and "unpublished short story writer" whose husband's desertion left her devoid of sexual feeling for five years. "I married him when I was seventeen. The lust I felt for him was something else. It had the power of holy writ in my life. I would have followed him anywhere, done anything he asked, because I believed desire was God's way of telling you to do just that. I never looked at another man.

"When he left, I felt like I didn't exist anymore. I wondered why I wasn't dead."

Her sexual reawakening began when a regular customer hugged her. The "simple hug" reminded her she was a sexual being and led to a "new openness to the sexual vibrations" in men around her. The first post-divorce relationship, however, was full of surprises, and a revelation for her.

"For the first time in my life, at age thirty-nine, I was having sex with a man and not thinking, 'This is the love of my life,' " she says. "It blew my mind to discover I could have great sex with a man—and not have to plan my life around him.

"And the sex *was* great. He did things my husband would never do. I had my first oral orgasm with him. When he said, 'I want to eat you out,' I didn't know what he was talking about, but I said yes so he wouldn't think I was that naive. When he began to tongue my clitoris, I went wild.

"But I never kidded myself we were a match made in heaven anywhere outside the bedroom. This represented real growth for me. I only wish I had figured things out sooner than I did."

She was an early bloomer, who masturbated at age ten and was orgasmic with her husband even before they had intercourse. Yet she still allowed the romantic myth to limit her sexually for thirty-nine years.

Who Is She?

In my survey, reawakened women are more likely to come from upper-income brackets than the middle or working classes. Perhaps their socioeconomic status allowed many of these women to hang on to a romantic myth others rejected as they gained more experience in the world. Financial dependence can keep women in a childlike state where the validity of fairy tales doesn't have to be seriously questioned. Also, being outside the work force may make it easier for them to avoid noticing that other men are arousing—if they want to avoid making the observation.

Reawakened women are 7 percent of the survey respondents. They are women who:

- *Had lost the desire for sexual pleasure following devastating rejection by a husband or live-in lover for at least a year.*
- *Had been able to regain that pleasure.*

Most were over thirty-nine when the spark reignited them sexually, in part suggesting the reawakening may be aided by sexual biology. After thirty-five, the ratio of testosterone, responsible for sex drive in both sexes, to female hormones increases with a woman's body, increasing her drive. Perhaps sexual biology both creates a more favorable climate for the spark to catch fire and encourages the development of new liberal attitudes. But many women who were financially dependent also credit the increased sense of self-esteem generated by holding a job with influencing them sexually. Whatever the reasons, they say they no longer think the way they did back in the days of blissful ignorance before a husband's announcement changed their lives.

Her New Attitude

SEX IS GOOD

As wives, they had believed sex is good only *if* . . . and the qualifiers were primarily "if you're truly in love" and "if you're married." In retrospect, they realize they were often highly judgmental of other women who didn't live by their rigid moral code. Some were even active in conservative women's groups such as Right to Life and the Concerned Women for America.

"I clucked my tongue over many a wanton woman back in my Puritan privileged past," writes a forty-five-year-old Midwesterner who "didn't lift a finger" during seventeen years of marriage to a wealthy lawyer and now runs a garden supply outlet. "Everything was so black and white then. I was such a romantic idealist, incapable of imagining how a woman could have sex without being madly in love, or of how she could possibly want to abort a child, because weren't they all conceived in almost holy passion?

"Have I changed! When my husband dumped me for his legal partner—who was, by the way, five years his senior and so much for the myth of the younger woman!—I was like the Princess being tossed off her pile of feather mattresses onto a stone floor. And I thought the presence of an occasional tiny pea under my mattresses represented hardship! What a shock. It numbed me sexually for a year and a half.

"When I woke up in the real world, I finally learned that sex is something we need. *I* need sex. It doesn't always come in a package with wedding bell trimmings. It isn't always a sacrament."

I DESERVE SEXUAL PLEASURE

As rejected wives, they thought they were unworthy of pleasure. Even before, as wives, many of them felt guilty about taking their own pleasure. Abandonment reinforced their sex guilt and underscored their negative views of themselves. Because their husbands no longer desired them, they didn't feel desirable.

"I never felt entitled to enjoy sex until last year," writes a newly reawakened woman, age forty-one. "That's not to say I didn't enjoy sex during my marriage. I did! I was intensely attracted to him, even at the end, when he was telling me he didn't want me anymore. But I never got past thinking pleasure was something he gave me. And if he gave it, he could, and did, take it away.

"I had no intrinsic right to feel good 'down there,' as my mother would say, if she ever said such a thing at all. Going through the pain of being left and starting over on my own changed me. If I could survive that, I am a valuable person too. Now I stick up for what's mine.

"I deserve a good sex life."

SEX NEED NOT COME WITH STRINGS ATTACHED

This is a major attitude change. Imagine Cinderella discovering the Prince wasn't the only one who could tickle her foot. Well, these women are just that shocked to discover sex can be wildly, joyously fulfilling, even when it's clearly "leading" nowhere. While most still believe sex within a committed, intimate relationship may be the most desirable and fulfilling, they are now realistic enough to know every sexual relationship doesn't fit the criteria. The choice isn't between all and nothing. They don't need to pretend they are choosing all when their sex drives demand something rather than nothing. They need not make every man they find arousing into the one.

"I never thought I'd answer the question, 'Should sex be only an expression of love?' with a resounding 'NO!' " writes a thirty-eight-year-old reawakened woman, who discovered sex again four years after a divorce that left her sexually flattened. "While I was still married I would have told you, quite smugly too, that sex without love would be unbearably empty.

"After I found out, after ten years of marriage, that my husband began cheating on me on our honeymoon, my life changed—now finally for the better. I am not smug anymore. I understand a lot more about human needs and emotions and how a man and a woman can come together to give each other erotic comfort without there being any plan for happily ever after."

Many women described their new thinking as a "loss of romantic idealism"—something they regarded as a positive loss, like losing the training wheels on a bicycle.

No More Fairy Tales

"My kids gave up Santa Claus years before I let go of Sleeping Beauty," says a California journalist, a forty-six-year-old reawakened woman. "Looking back, I don't know why it took me so long, but there's nothing I can do about it now. My husband was my first lover, and I never cheated on him, never was tempted to.

"We didn't have sex for the last two years of our marriage. I remember the last time. It was three days before I discovered he was having an affair with a coworker. After I found out, I lost all interest in sex for a long time. I was devastated. Sex had so much meaning for me I couldn't comprehend how he could do this to us.

"I know it sounds incredibly naive, but I couldn't imagine him ever being with another woman. I kept thinking it was a bad dream, from which I supposed I expected to awaken with his kiss. Yes, I was living in an alternate reality for quite some time.

"If I could snap out of it, any woman can. And the good news is that sex is better, life is better, when you have both feet on the ground. I idealized my husband, my marriage, the sex. I was a fool."

There is a difference between enjoying the aura of romance in one's life and living a life strictly bound by the script of a romantic fairy tale. Romance is an ambiance we can knowingly create around a sexual encounter, while romantic idealism is a code of behavior we are meant to outgrow well before our thirtieth birthday. Reawakened women finally understand the difference.

"I could never again believe a sex partner was the ideal man who holds the only key to my erotic being," writes a forty-year-old children's book illustrator. "My husband's leaving shattered my illusions. But, unlike Humpty Dumpty, I went back together stronger, wiser, and eventually, after a long dead spell, sexier than ever before."

Many women write about how much more they enjoyed sex after they surrendered their romantic idealism. Men, they say, became real people, not distant, powerful icons, when no longer cast in the restricted role of ideal hero. And, not surprisingly, more than half report discovering this new sexual attitude in the arms of a thoroughly "unsuitable" man.

The Good Lover

Few stories of sexual reawakening end with the rediscovery— or, in some cases, the *discovery*—of masturbation. Once the spark has ignited a passionate side thought long dead, the reawakened woman either actively seeks, or is open to, a sexual relationship with a man or another woman or both. Choosing the right partner for erotic reentry is, if not critical to her future sexuality, certainly important. The overwhelming majority of these women do report finding a good lover when they needed him. Or her. Eighteen percent turned to another woman first.

"My first partner when I came back to life sexually was a woman," writes a Midwesterner. "It was also my first and only bisexual experience. It began with mutual masturbation one afternoon when we'd had too many glasses of wine. Afterward, she confessed she was bi.

"The next time it started with an embrace. We were fully clothed and soon the 'friendly hug' turned into a passionate embrace, with each of us placing a leg between the other's thighs. Suddenly she was on her knees, pulling down my panties, tonguing my clit. She knew exactly where to go and what to do with her tongue, her fingers.

"She made me feel alive again."

A New York chiropractor wrote: "My first experience after I became sexual again was with a window washer. Yes, don't laugh—a window washer! He did the windows in my office building, of course. One day he was dangling outside my window holding a sign asking for my phone number. I wrote it out for him, and he called.

"I didn't tell my friends, but I saw him for several months. He was fantastic in bed, very attentive to my needs and enthusiastic about my body. I never felt so sexy, so sexually cherished in my life.

"He taught me things about my body. When he performed cunnilingus on me, he often inserted a finger in my anus. I never even knew I had sexual feelings there."

Their stories have several things in common, including:

- *For the first time in their lives, they chose lovers for sexual, not suitability, reasons.*

- *For the most part, they kept the liaisons secret from friends, who they feared would have pounced on the "unsuitable" factor and discouraged them from seeing their lovers.*

- *They were most strongly drawn to people who wanted them, a reversal from their erotic pursuit of a disinterested husband.*

- *Cunnilingus played a bigger role in their sex lives after the spark than it had during their marriages.*

They described their lovers as warm, tender, caring, passionate, and often, sexually skilled—qualities they said were missing in their husbands, at least toward the end.

"I've learned to value different qualities in men," writes a thirty-nine-year-old Texan. "I've stopped looking for the flash and sizzle, the big wallet, and the impressive job title. The irony is there are still plenty of good men out there, even for women in my age group, but they get overlooked because they don't have the power jobs or drive the power cars.

"The man I'm seeing now teaches in a public high school. I admire him enormously, and he is a genius at oral sex.

"Good men aren't so hard to find. Rich men are."

PART 6

Reclaiming
Pleasure

CHAPTER 22

The If-Busters

"I am having the best sex of my life with a passionate Latino who is twelve years younger than I am. I don't care what anybody says. Ten years ago I would have cared and thus missed out on this wonderful experience. With age comes greater wisdom—and greater horniness."

—a forty-two-year-old physical therapist

AND, ALAS, FEWER opportunities.

Few women who have claimed pleasure, or especially *reclaimed* pleasure, did so in their twenties. The woman who is finally in charge of her sex life is probably at least in her thirties. She may have overcome some negative experience to become sexually responsive, skilled, and confident, and is no longer influenced by what other people think she should do in her own bed. She is truly in her prime.

But prime time for women in a culture that worships youth and equates sex appeal with young, pouty mouths and upturned, perky breasts isn't without its drawbacks. The sexual dilemmas facing women over thirty-five have been thoroughly documented since the baby boom generation crested the hill at thirty about fifteen years ago. Suddenly many women were asking the same questions. How can she handle her ripening sexuality without threatening a partner whose own libido is subsiding? Or how can she compete against younger women in the sexual market-

219

place to find a new partner? The scarcity of partners—particularly of the "suitable" kind who meet the requirements of age, occupation, net worth, and social class—begins in early middle age, often before thirty-five, just as women begin to experience anxiety about their looks.

Whether she has claimed or reclaimed pleasure, the woman at thirty-five and beyond is faced with another set of hurdles to overcome. They loom like huge wax birthday candles bent across what was only moments ago a clear path. Sometimes even the most confident woman hesitates before leaping them.

"The hardest part for me in becoming sexually active again following my divorce was taking off my clothes," writes a forty-year-old photographer. "I am keenly aware of where my body fails—or should I make that *falls*?—to meet the standards it once met. I took some advice I read in *Cosmo* and bought wonderful lingerie, tap pants and camisoles, teddys, garter belts and stockings, which I left on during sex. It helped my confidence tremendously."

But, some younger women face the moment of unveiling with the same trepidation because they are overweight or have small breasts or heavy thighs or all of the above. And, if the forty-year-old white woman thinks finding a suitable partner isn't easy, she should talk to the successful young black woman or the lesbian woman of any age. Our bodies—their ages, sexual orientations, sizes, shapes, and colors—do limit our choices, at least to some extent.

The woman who has busted the "ifs" and broken the "rules" knows all this, but she also knows her way around many of the restrictions. She understands her real needs, and she is a lot smarter about choosing partners who can meet them than she was in her sexual ingenue period. Like the photographer who indulged in an orgy of lingerie shopping before her first post-divorce tryst, she knows how to make it easier for herself, and she does. Other women's sexual performance concerns are seldom hers.

"I know I'm a good lover," writes a thirty-three-year-old Seattle office manager. "When you aren't worried about whether or not you can come or whether or not you'll do the right things for your man or what the neighbors will think, you can make much better sexual choices for yourself. You relax and take care of yourself—not only by having orgasms, but by using condoms and setting the pace and tone of the relationship to meet your requirements."

The woman fully in charge of her own sex life shares these traits (previously listed as those of pleasure claimers):

- *Sexual confidence, in her ability to be orgasmic as well as to attract and please a partner.*
- *Positive, nonpunitive, nonjudgmental attitudes about sex.*
- *Willingness to take responsibility for her own pleasure—and her own protection against unwanted pregnancy and disease.*
- *Ability to communicate sexually.*
- *Ability to separate sex from everything else.*

And, in addition, she:

- *Decides when, where, and with whom she will have sex—primarily based on her own needs and desires, but not the need to please.* She's open to a wider range of possibilities in her selection of sexual partners—and sometimes sexual practices—than she ever has been. For many women, this new freedom includes being comfortable with saying no to sex for the first time in their lives.
- *No longer needs even minimal approval of her sexual lifestyle from anyone else.* She doesn't consult with friends on the wisdom of her partner choices or spend long hours on the phone getting them to validate her romantic rationalizations about men. Social prohibitions against lesbianism or bisexuality, interracial sex, or sex with younger men do not keep her from setting her own erotic course. While she doesn't need to flaunt her behavior, she doesn't feel shamed into hiding it either.
- *Has a positive attitude about sex and aging.* She doesn't think sex will end with menopause. While she realizes her body at forty isn't as taut as it was at twenty, she also knows how much

more skilled and responsive she is now than she was then. She values her own sexual evolution.

- *Has outgrown the romantic illusions that often restricted her sexually.* Adept at creating and using romantic fantasy to aide sexual arousal and orgasm, she is equally skilled at putting the fantasy aside when the sex is over. She has found real men to be better than the larger-than-life cardboard characters she may have once created in her mind. Best of all, she's discovered sex is more exciting and fulfilling when it takes place between adults, rather than between an aging ingenue and a fantasy Prince.

"I think of myself as a sexual survivor," writes a forty-five-year-old Boston meeting planner. "I've overcome most of the challenges to my sexuality that a repressed society and a female body can throw in the way: Italian Catholic childhood; workplace sexual harassment beginning when I was sixteen and working in the neighborhood bakery where the owner pinched fannies; marrying as a virgin; four full-term pregnancies and two miscarriages; being dumped for a woman my age, but half my size.

"Now, I'm in my second marriage, to a wonderful Jewish man, ten years younger than I am. The sex, my dears, is the best I've ever had. I know Marla Maples supposedly said that about Donald Trump. But she hasn't lived long enough to know what she's talking about, and I have."

Even women who haven't lost pleasure will reach the point where they feel in some danger of having it snatched away by an aging body or a society in which people still have trouble imagining that older women do have sex. If-busting, then, is for all of us. Only in fairy tales does the sleeping virgin awaken to the best sexual experience of her life.

In real life, overweight Italian mothers of four grown children find such joy with younger Jewish men.

CHAPTER *23*

Sexual Explorers

"My kids are horrified. They say he isn't my intellectual equal. What, they ask, do you talk to a plumber about? I'm sorry they're embarrassed Mom's dating a plumber, but I can't live my life to suit them. He is kind, thoughtful, considerate, and he makes me laugh, even in bed. I've never had so much fun in my life. I've never been so sexually turned on either. Partly it's him; partly it's me. I excite myself these days."

—a forty-eight-year-old New York attorney

THE SEXUAL EXPLORER has broken the rules governing sexual behavior. She may have multiple sex partners, engage in sexual variations, have a bisexual or lesbian lifestyle, or choose her lovers from outside the socially approved circle of suitable men. Sometimes motivated by panic—"This is my last chance for a fling before my body goes"—or sometimes by the euphoria accompanying the realization she's truly free of the internal negative voice at last, she may break the rules in a dramatic way, like the white Florida woman in her forties who wrote about an affair with a black graduate student in his early twenties. Sometimes the sexual explorer is very young, a wildflower motivated by her own lusts, but more often she is over thirty.

"To explore your own sexuality to the limits, in all its aspects, takes courage," writes a forty-six-year-old Northeastern professor. "I did not have that kind of courage until I was forty, when

I was able to break free of the conventional restraints keeping me in place.

"I have long desired to explore my submissive side, something which I was not able to do in the conventional relationships I've had. Shortly after my fortieth birthday I responded to a personal ad in a city magazine placed by a 'Dominant Man' who promised to fulfill my 'hidden fantasies.' In a series of carefully orchestrated encounters, filled more with drama than with pain, we did just that.

"Nothing has thrilled me in quite the same way as being blindfolded, gagged, and bound, suspended from a bar by my wrists, anticipating the lash. I have played those scenes over and over again in my mind and masturbated to them.

"He helped me claim my submissive side and not to be ashamed of it any more than I am of the dominant side who enjoys being on top."

For other women, the exploration may be of a dominant side they'd previously feared to unleash or of bisexual desires they had suppressed. But for many, perhaps most, women, conditioned as we are to link sex with love and marriage, breaking the rules means having sex with a partner you wouldn't want to marry. Approximately 67 percent of my survey respondents would have sex with a man they wouldn't consider marrying—the big exception being among late bloomers, only 20 percent of whom would have sex with such a man. But they may be only kidding themselves about their marital intentions.

"I've been divorced for ten years and have had several relationships in those years," writes a forty-year-old Philadelphia insurance claims adjustor. "But I maintained a certain mental pretense with all of them. I told myself I could and might marry them. Even though I had no real desire to marry again, I needed to tell myself I could and might and would—because I knew I *should*.

"I woke up next to my new lover, who is only twenty-seven, last Saturday and it dawned on me. I have no intentions of marrying this kid—or he, me. I'm not pretending anymore! A few years ago I wouldn't have been able to enjoy myself with him because it would have put me in a difficult spot in my own head: I couldn't have fooled myself about my intentions, but I wasn't ready to accept that, yes, I do have sex for the sake of having sex.

"I don't know if it's my freer attitude or his age, but the sex is good this time. And I've never had trouble with the sex. The first night we made love, he surprised me with his agility and his lovemaking skill. He was all over the bed like a little monkey. I outweigh him by probably twenty pounds, but who cares?

"He was kneeling on the bed before me, performing cunnilingus, when suddenly he switched his body around and dangled his penis over my mouth in exactly the right place without missing a lick. Such luxury to open your mouth and suck without having to consider the logistics. Rarely does 69 work as well as it did that night!"

Some sexual explorers do marry their unsuitable men—but marriage is not a goal they hope to achieve through sex.

Who Is She?

Sexual Explorers are 26.8 percent of the survey group. They are women who:

- *Are involved with men five or more years younger than they are;*
- *Or with men of a different race* (seventeen percent of survey respondents have been involved with a man of a different race);
- *Or with men from a different socioeconomic class;*
- *Or with women.* While only 7 percent of survey respondents identify themselves as bisexual and another 6 percent as lesbian, nearly one-third of the total group report having had at least one sexual experience with another woman.
- *Regularly engage in sexual variations, including anal sex, bondage, and S&M activities.*

"I've always been wilder than my women friends," writes a forty-five-year-old Chicago artist who is living with a man twenty years younger than she. "I wanted to try everything, at least once, and I'm lucky to have been young before the AIDS scare changed sex. For the past ten years, I've only been involved with younger men, at least ten years younger. I don't seek them out. They come to me.

"I don't know why I don't attract men my age and older. Maybe it's because they sense I'm too much for them sexually. Younger men are wilder, because of their age—and also I suspect because they aren't looking at someone my age as a potential wife and certainly not mother of their kids. So, anything goes. They aren't imposing a sexual conservatism on me that would be befitting the wife and the mother.

"I like sex to run the gamut from sometimes tender to sometimes rough. When I'm in the mood, I like to have my wrists tied behind my back and be turned over my lover's knee for a brisk spanking. Each slap grinds my cunt against his thighs and excites me terribly. Then, he places me on the bed, on my knees, my ass up in the air and fucks me doggy style.

"I can't explain how good it feels to be totally submissive. My orgasm is in his control, since my hands are tied, and I need him to stroke my clit while he fucks me.

"Other times we make love like two teenage virgins, all fluttery kisses and touches like angels' wings."

In addition to possessing the traits of all pleasure claimers, sexual explorers share these common attitudes:

- *Consider sexual attraction the most important element in a relationship.* When they say age, race, or class are "not important," they mean it. Sex is important.

- *Are not bound by prevailing social standards on acceptable sexual behavior.*

- *Are not focused on marriage, but haven't ruled it out in the future.* The majority, over 80 percent, say they could marry a man of a different race or class or a much younger man. But, marriage and sex are clearly two separate pursuits.

- *Are comfortable making the first move.* Many women of a "certain age" believe men's eyes skip over them unless they do something active to get attention. They are more likely to be direct than coy. "It's not enough to bat your eyes after forty," one woman wrote. "You need to smile broadly, make your way across the room, offer your hand, introduce yourself, and say, 'I've been admiring you from afar.' "

• *Have a strong sense of their own identity.* They are not dependent on men to define, support, or validate them.

Interracial Sex

I interviewed three white women and two black women who were *only* interested in partners of the opposite race, one white woman who would *only* have sex with Hispanic men, and an Asian woman who restricted herself to white men *only*. Not surprisingly, they didn't have the characteristics of true sexual explorers—or of pleasure claimers in general—and are more inclined to romanticize and idealize their partners, and fantasize and rationalize their relationships, than are the other women I interviewed, and are certainly much more inclined to do so than other women their age.

A sexual explorer involved with a man of different race didn't choose him *because* of his race. Of my total survey, 80.4 percent are white, 12.1 percent black, 7 percent Hispanic, and 2.5 percent other, largely Asian. Only 17 percent are, or have been, sexually involved with a man of a different race, and nearly all who are or have been in such relationships live in large metropolitan areas on either coast, where the likelihood of social interaction between races may be somewhat greater.

"I've been seeing a white man for the past year," writes Jonelle, a thirty-nine-year-old black entrepreneur from the Northeast. "We met at a small business conference and hit it off immediately. The sexual attraction was instant, almost explosive. Over the years, I have dated an occasional white man and always felt I was letting down my brothers by doing so. I don't worry about it anymore. I'm about more than being black.

"I'm his first black woman. He was married to a white woman and lived with a Mexican woman for two years when he was working in Mexico City. I think he's one of the few people in this world who truly isn't racist in any way.

"I love the way our bodies look together, the play of skin tones as we embrace. I love to watch him eat me out, his long, skinny white nose pushed against my pubic bone. But, I don't think 'Lordy, I'm with a white man!' every time we make love. It's just him and me."

And, a thirty-eight-year-old white woman from a small Midwestern town writes: "My lover is a black man, the first for me, though I've had an affair with a Hispanic. We met in the stacks of the public library. After bumping into each other over thrillers a few times, he suggested coffee. I was attracted to him, so I said yes.

"We had sex on the first date. It just happened naturally. From the moment he put his hand on my thigh, I knew we were going to click. I can always tell by how a man's hands feel on my body if we're going to connect or not.

"Race has nothing to do with it, either way, for us. We click. Who cares about race when you do?"

The Younger Man

The sexual relationship between the older woman and younger man has received as much media hype in the last decade as the trend toward late motherhood. In reality, the average woman finds it difficult to conceive after age thirty-five and to attract a much younger man. But, the sexual explorer's appeal cuts across age, race, and class lines.

"Younger men are drawn to me," writes Jayne, a forty-two-year-old New York illustrator. "But men have always been attracted to me. Often they choose me over women who are younger and prettier.

"Why? I'm sexy. I'm good in bed. I like men. I'm very relaxed about sex, which attracts younger men. They have been with young women who get so uptight about sex or link it to marriage and commitment, or who need ages to reach orgasm. I am an erotic breathing spell for them."

Jayne believes any man can be taught to be a good lover—and younger men are no more, and perhaps less, in need of lessons than older men.

"You have to show every man what you like, because every woman is different. He'll start to do what he did with his last partner, which may not be what you want him to do at all. Younger men are more open to suggestion and guidance. Their egos aren't as caught up in knowing exactly how to please you, first try.

"By the same token, I want a man to tell me how he likes to have fellatio performed before I do it. You wouldn't believe how aroused a man can get in describing what he wants. I take his penis in my hand, say, 'Tell me how you like it,' and slowly lower my mouth."

While the situation may not be as bad as we once thought it was when women were told we had a better chance of being attacked by a terrorist than receiving a marriage proposal at forty, there *is* a shortage of available men for single women over thirty-five. That is, a shortage exists if women insist upon limiting themselves to men their own age or older. United States government population statistics do show more single men than women in the twentysomething generation.

Sexual explorers are more likely to beat the odds and find a partner, either for sex or marriage or both, than the average woman.

Class Differences

We like to pretend there are no social classes in America, but if this were so, would a lawyer's children be embarrassed by her relationship with a plumber? A few years ago I wrote a story for *Cosmopolitan* magazine about women who marry "down," meaning they marry a man who is younger or poorer, less educated or in some way considered their social inferior. I still get calls from talk show producers wanting the phone numbers of the people quoted as potential guests for their programs on nontraditional marriage. If it seems the same college professor wife

and plumber husband—and, why is it so often a plumber?—
have been on more than one show, they have, leading me to
believe it isn't easy to find examples of nontraditional marriages.
But nontraditional affairs abound.

"I've often been involved with men who earn less than I,
because I make an obscene amount of money," writes a forty-
year-old West Coast executive. "Until recently, they were always
creative types—writers, artists, photographers, cinematogra-
phers. It's okay for men like that to earn less. They may not
have big salaries, but they have social cachet.

"Now, however, I am seeing someone who doesn't have a big
salary, though he earns more than the average writer. He has,
however, no social cachet. Construction workers are the butt of
jokes in my world, and that's what he is. In his spare time, he
moonlights at the gym as an instructor, which is where I met
him. He was covering the low-impact aerobics class for a girl
who had the flu. I was charmed by both his ass and his embarrassment in leading the class.

"I'd been going through a sexual dry spell, and I was horny.
I introduced myself to him after class and asked him for a date,
just like that. He was so nonplused, he accepted. Later he told
me he almost canceled because he expected me to be a bitch.

"We get along great, especially sexually. He was more into
straight sex than I like, but I've loosened him up. I'm teaching
him games. Last week he let me tie him spread-eagled to the bed
and tease him orally until he was nuts begging me to let him
come. I like to play sexual power games where the point is in
delaying orgasm until one's need for release is intolerable."

Another woman, coincidentally also a California executive in
her forties, says: "I'm having the sexual time of my life with a
blue-collar worker. He spends a lot of time in the water, so he's
tan and lithe, in much better shape than I am. In this relationship,
I am the one who slavishly admires the body of the other. I love
his penis so much I would write poems to it if I had the time.
I've never felt this way about a penis before.

"But I'm a realist. Aside from making love, drinking wine,
and watching the sun set over the ocean, we don't have much
in common. I would never marry him."

Women and Women

Many women deny their bisexual urges until they are over thirty-five, when perhaps they have the confidence to cope with being so different from the social norm. It's also true that lesbian women often marry, have children, and divorce before they realize they are only sexually drawn to other women. In some ways, it is easier for gay women to exist in a homophobic society than gay men. For example, two women sharing an apartment don't attract the critical attention two male roommates do. But lesbians, like heterosexual women, are still more likely to internalize negative sexual messages than men are, so that privately accepting oneself as a lesbian can be difficult.

"I am thirty-eight years old and until a year ago sex was never a big part of my life," writes an Atlanta teacher. "I'd assumed I was a heterosexual with a low sex drive. My grandmother was a certified Southern belle. How could I be a lesbian? I'd been married for two years and had a lifetime total of nine affairs. The sex was never any good, but I thought I hadn't found the right man. I was always eager to have sex with a new man because I wanted him to like me, to accept me as his woman.

"Last year I suddenly realized I was a lesbian, and everything in my world changed. Another woman seduced me. She did it so adroitly I didn't know what was happening until her mouth was covering mine and my heart began beating faster than any man had ever made it beat. She brought me to orgasm the first time by dry humping, both of us fully clothed and stretched out on the floor.

"After that I was well and truly interested in sex. I also realized I'd been depressed for years, no doubt the side effect of suppressing my natural desires. Depressed people aren't sexy. I am sexy as hell now."

A bisexual woman from St. Louis describes her sexual awakening: "My husband had begged me to participate in a threesome for so long I agreed. I talked my best friend into it. He might as well not have been there. When she put her mouth on my pussy, I was gone, and she was equally delighted by me. He and I are divorced now, but she and I still get together regularly.

"I also see men. I really enjoy both sexes. I guess I owe the selfish bastard a debt of gratitude for helping me find myself."

Was She Always So Free?

Rarely. With the exception of some wildflowers, a sexual explorer is a woman who has taken some time to move beyond claiming pleasure to own her sexuality completely. She may have overcome sexual disappointments, ranging from the minor gynecological and cosmetic problems associated with aging to the devastation of rejection by a spouse or long-term lover.

You can't chart your own erotic course in a repressive society unless you are supremely confident. The majority of women don't break the rules, or, if they do, they break them in quiet or fairly acceptable ways, like married women who have discreet extramarital affairs. A few take the reverse approach and outrageously flaunt their rule-breaking to get attention. The sexual explorer moves from a position of confidence and inner strength, and she doesn't need to be noticed or validated.

She also knows something other women don't. Women often blame men in general, or the specific men in their lives for keeping them down, sexually and otherwise, but the truth more often is: We do it to ourselves.

Joanne Woodward said, in talking about India Bridge, the sexually (and otherwise) repressed character she played in the movie, *Mr. and Mrs. Bridge*, adapted from the Evan Connell novels about a marriage during the Forties and Fifties, "She's dominated, not by him [Mr. Bridge], but by the society that tells her she has to be dominated by him. She believed she had to do things in a certain way. . . ."

Women still believe they have to do things in a certain way, though the definition of "certain" has changed somewhat over the years. Other women continue to hold tremendous sway in our lives as the arbiters of definition. We exhort each other to conform to rigid behavioral standards, thus turning more power over to men than they would think to request or often even want to have. Truly, we give away our power throughout much of our lives. It isn't wrested from us.

The sexual explorer knows that, and she doesn't give her power away, not to the men in her life nor the ubiquitous "they" who say what is acceptable and what is not.

CHAPTER 24

Surviving the Droughts

"How has aging changed my sex life? Only in that there are fewer partners now than in the past. What would I change about men as lovers? I'd make them easier to find!"

— a thirty-eight-year-old Washington lobbyist

RARE IS THE single woman who hasn't experienced a sexual dry spell for one reason or another. Revirginizers may choose celibacy, but they have the option of changing their minds and also have a man in their lives who is begging them to do so. Somehow that lessens the negative psychological impact a dry spell can have on one's ego. Women in their late thirties and early forties often find the first real drought as shocking as a dive into icy water, but not nearly as bracing. Women fifty and beyond say, "You get accustomed to it, but you never learn to love it." Even married women experience the sexual drought. The challenge is surviving with one's sexual self-esteem intact.

For many women, the realization they're actually going through a drought dawns gradually.

"When I was younger, men gave me appreciative glances no matter what I was wearing, including jeans or sweats," writes a forty-five-year-old divorced Philadelphian. "In the past five years I've noticed I don't get noticed unless I'm dressed up, preferably in a skirt above the knee, dark stockings, and high heels. I still look good in clothes, but the point is I have to be in the right clothes to get male attention.

"I've also recently concluded, to my chagrin, that I'm no longer in the first line of attack at large parties either. You know what I mean. Men head for the most attractive women first—with the exception of the drop-dead-beautiful broads, who usually get ignored because they're so intimidating, but how many of them exist outside the movies and TV anyway?—then fan out to the second line from there. I am in the second line now. At least I hope it's the second line. I'm sure it doesn't go past three.

"Several weeks ago I came home from a large cocktail reception *without* a single business card from a man interested in getting together for a drink or dinner. That's never happened to me before. I remember the days when I came home with a half dozen cards and tossed them into the trash. How wasteful I was! This time, I had cards from five or six interesting women who wanted to get together for a drink. Everywhere I go there are great women, but where are the men?

"I'm forced to admit I haven't had a sex partner in over a year because I am not attracting men the way I once did. I've been telling myself, and friends, I was being 'choosy.' The truth is really no one has asked."

What Constitutes a Drought?

For some women, six weeks constitutes a very long dry spell. Others barely notice sex is missing from their lives until their birth control pill prescription has long expired. It's less a measurable unit of time than an attitude expressing how one feels about the time lapse.

Therefore, the answer to the survey question, "How often do you have sex?" was less telling than it's follow-up: "Is that satisfactory?"

- *Almost one-third of all respondents wanted more sex than they were having*, even if they were having sex at a rate equal to or greater than statistical averages for women of their age and marital status.

- *More than 80 percent of the women who hadn't had sex in periods ranging from two months to several years—about 11 percent of the total—were dissatisfied with this lack of sexual activity in their lives.* Many women scrawled: "NO! Not satisfactory at all!" and often underlined their words.

For anyone but a revirginizer or a woman mired in gyneco-logical problems a sexual drought is not often a self-imposed period of denial in the face of partner options. As we get older, such a drought is also less often a result of being choosy. Rather it is a result of not being chosen, which even happens to rule breakers sometimes.

"I haven't had a sex partner in the past year," writes a fifty-year-old New Yorker. "I'm not happy about that at all. I miss having sex. I miss being held afterward. Human beings weren't meant to live without physical contact.

"Throughout my forties, I maintained a relationship with a younger married man, which sustained me during the increas-ingly longer dating lulls I experienced. He and his wife have moved to Europe, so he is out of my life for all practical purposes. I am at the age now where sex is harder and harder to come by, and I resent that.

"It makes me sad, but I am surviving. I masturbate. I keep myself in good shape, and I keep my eyes open."

Her survival strategy is the game plan of a woman who has a good attitude about sex and her own desirability, one who un-derstands that surviving the drought is primarily a matter of attitude and masturbation.

The Wrong Attitude

"I don't feel attractive physically anymore," writes a forty-nine-year-old divorced secretary from the Midwest who has not had a sexual relationship in four years. "I am not fat and am reasonably fit thanks to a program of walking and bicycling. But I have the body of a fit woman in her forties, which does not compare to the body of a fit woman in her twenties or thirties. I can't afford plastic surgery to be like Cher.

"I don't feel attractive. It turns me off, and I'm sure it turns men off too. Why should they give me a second look? It's over for me."

A small, but bitterly vocal, minority of survey respondents express similar views about the effect of aging on their ability to attract and arouse men. They believe sex is over at forty for all but women involved in loving marriages or long-term relationships. Their attitude seems to be: No man could find an older woman desirable unless he is blinded by love or is a creature of habit. A sexual drought reinforces their negative attitudes about sex and aging.

But, the drought can have the same effect on younger women, too.

"I've always been the woman who didn't have a date for the important events, from high school on," writes a thirty-five-year-old St. Louis nurse. "I didn't even have a date for my own Sweet Sixteen party, which killed my mother, who's a tiny little thing, a beauty even today. She died of embarrassment for me.

"I love sex, but I don't get the opportunity to have it often enough. I've had two long-term relationships with long dry spells between them. I don't feel really alive unless I am sexually involved with a man. So, most of my life is spent not feeling really alive."

At this point, you can fill in the clichés you'd like to shout, after the fashion of a sexual cheerleader, into her ears. If you feel sexy, you are sexy. You get back what you put out. You have to be excited to excite someone. If she believed them, perhaps the droughts would be shorter and certainly they would be less painful. If she could understand the statistics are not in her favor, perhaps she wouldn't blame herself for the long dry spells between partners. But, there would be still be droughts.

Knowing how to handle droughts is one of a woman's most important erotic skills.

The Right Attitude

"How can you face involuntary celibacy without getting down on yourself?" writes a fifty-year-old California retail manager. "I don't really believe I am nothing without a man, but sometimes, after I've been without one for a long time, I do question if I'm not less than the something—something hot!—I once thought I was.

"How do you stay sexy if you aren't having sex?"

"Sexy" is an attitude. Women who have it also have:

FACED THE FACTS

There is no way for most single women, particularly over the age of thirty-five, to avoid having an occasional sexual drought. Women who handle them well accept the inevitability of their occurrence—and don't blame themselves.

"I recognize the odds aren't with me anymore," writes a forty-year-old management consultant from Ohio. "To paraphrase Mick Jagger, time is no longer on my side. My sex life isn't over, but it's not the erotic equivalent of an all-night party either. I am often sleeping alone when I wish it were not so. But, there's nothing wrong with me!

"I'm a good lover. It may take me longer to hook up with a man than it did ten years ago, but when I do, he's still hooked."

OPENED THEIR MINDS AND HEARTS TO DIFFERENT MEN

You should perhaps consider men you may have overlooked in the past, but without feeling either desperate or too quick to "settle." Being less picky is good if it means putting aside superficial criteria in favor of a better set of values. A truly free woman doesn't feel desperate to make a connection with *any* man just because he's available.

"Five years ago, when I was at the height of my physical attraction power, I put an ad in [a city magazine] saying I wanted to meet men—but only those making over $100,000 a year," writes a thirty-eight-year-old editor. "I got a half-dozen replies. I think all but two exaggerated their incomes and assets. They were all arrogant, but then so was I.

"The one I settled on bilked me out of $10,000 in six months' time. I finally wised up and left him. He was probably going to leave me anyway since I was broke by that point.

"Now men don't flock to me the way they once did, but the men I do get to know are nicer. Maybe my values have changed as the wrinkles have popped out around my eyes and my waistline has expanded. Really, I think things are better now. And, I haven't had to settle for a loser by any means. No, I was deliberately seeking out the losers five years ago. Now I am meeting the quiet winners, who are rich in all the right qualities, no matter how much money they earn."

FILLED THEIR LIVES WITH PEOPLE AND ACTIVITIES

Yes, it's the standard women's magazine advice for getting through a seemingly endless string of lonely nights, but it's good advice.

HAVE LEARNED TO PUT THE "DOWN TIME" TO GOOD PERSONAL USE

Again, good women's magazine advice. Women who feel confident about their sexuality and their ability to attract partners don't spend their dry spells agonizing over how and where they'll meet the next man. They don't scour the weekend sections of the newspapers in search of activities that might put them in contact with single men. Rather, they follow their own passions, not the scent of male musk. They devote more time and energy to themselves—to learning French or improving their muscle tone or reading the novels they didn't get around to reading when a man was in their beds. As one fifty-eight-year-old woman put it, they consider the time "a gift, not a penance."

The Masturbation Factor

And, above all, they masturbate.

All but 10 percent of the women who report dissatisfaction at the lack of sex partners masturbate at least once a week. The minority who don't are the most depressed about their situation and the least optimistic about it changing in the future. They seem to believe "sexy" is a feeling generated from the outside by male attention rather than from within. The other 90 percent know better.

"I am not happy about the absence of a partner in my life now," writes a forty-year-old Chicago executive. "But when no one is loving me, I am still loving myself. I would rather make love to myself than go to bed with someone who didn't attract me that much just so I could say I didn't sleep alone last night.

"Masturbation is good. I fantasize all kinds of wild things I wouldn't do, like having sex in a limo or a taxi, being in an orgy, having sex with Bryan Brown on the set during the pledge break for "Masterpiece Theatre." I think we would do it doggy fashion because my breasts look great when they hang free since I've had implants. When I masturbate, I let my mind go totally free."

A fifty-year-old divorced government administrator says, "A woman's finger is her best friend after age forty. Forget the diamonds. Really, if you don't take off the rings first, you might get scratched anyway."

Beginning with Masters and Johnson, sex researchers have been telling us for years that masturbation is the key to remaining sexually alive during the droughts. "Use it or lose it" is more than an amusing slogan for senior citizen's bumper stickers. It's the truth. Women who are not sexually active—and masturbation is a form of sexual activity—will lose vaginal elasticity and the ability to lubricate as they age.

"If I didn't masturbate, I think I'd be desperate," writes Carolyn, a forty-five-year-old journalist. "I'd be so horny I'd jump the doormen in my building. It would be embarrassing. I don't want to think of what I might do if I couldn't get sexual release somehow.

"Actually I've had some of my strongest orgasms masturbating. It always has a place in my life, even when I'm with a man.

"The focus of my masturbatory fantasies now is on anal sex, something I haven't done much, but find wildly exciting when all conditions are right. In my fantasies, I am having an affair with a man who is a little rough. Sometimes he spanks me. He loves to take me anally.

"I imagine myself positioned for entrance, on my knees leaning forward on my elbows. He inserts his fingers in my anus, lubricating me with KY jelly, preparing his way, and my cunt is on fire, erotic dread in the pit of my belly. I want it. I fear it.

"He never enters me the way the *Joy of Sex* book says, slowly and only going glans deep. No. He positions himself so that his large cock is pressed against my tiny anal opening, grasps my hips with both hands—and thrusts. Hard. Repeatedly. He feels like a thick piece of hot iron ramming relentlessly inside me, and I want it, fear it, love it, hate it. The orgasm is fantastic.

"Listen, in real life this would hurt like hell."

Fantasy isn't real life, but used as an aide to masturbation (or arousal and orgasm during lovemaking), it makes real life better, especially during the sexual droughts.

CHAPTER 25

Second-Chance Women

"After my first marriage, I knew I wasn't going to do it again unless the sex was great. 'He would have to be a very good lover,' I told everyone. And, he is. On a scale of one to ten, the first was a one-half. The second is a nine."

—a thirty-nine-year-old New Jersey writer

JANE, A WASHINGTON WRITER, is married to her third husband. The first marriage ended in divorce, the second in the death of her husband following a long battle with cancer. I didn't know numbers one and two, but Wesley, the third, is as good as it gets. An independent woman, Jane professes not to know why she has married three times while so many women lament their inability to marry once. My guess is: She likes being married, likes men, and is very good in bed.

The remarried women in my survey, who were willing to talk about how and why, fall into two groups:

- *Second-chance women*, the majority, who like men, marriage, and sex and express confidence in their erotic skills.

- *Second-time losers*, the minority, less than 20 percent, who claim they are as unhappy this time around as they were the first time, don't seem to like their own men, marriages, and sex lives.

Sex seems to be even more important in second marriages than first. Perhaps that's because it was one of the problems with husband number one—and also perhaps because second wives are older (as we've seen, women do reach orgasm more easily after age thirty and particularly after thirty-five for both psychological and physical reasons).

"My second marriage is so much better than the first, sexually and otherwise," writes a thirty-eight-year-old Florida secretary. "The first time I was nineteen and pregnant, which I got to be without ever having had an orgasm! Terrible start, wouldn't you say?

"We were both ignorant about sex. Five years, two kids, and no orgasms later, I was on my own. I would have become enmeshed in another no-orgasm marriage—I was desperately lonely and constantly broke—but my mother, bless her heart, intervened.

"She said, 'Ginny Sue, don't marry another man unless you have that special feeling down there from being with him.' I didn't know what she was talking about. She couldn't say the word 'orgasm,' but eventually I figured out what she was saying. I'd been with two men without ever feeling strongly attracted to either one of them. I didn't marry either guy. Daddy helped me financially for a few years. Then I met my husband.

"It was worth the wait! He turned on the switch inside me the first night we met. He picked up my hand and held it and I thought, 'Jesus, what is this zzzzing!

"I love kissing, and he kisses my neck, back, forehead, my ass, everywhere. My ex wasn't much of a kisser. He kind of sucked on my lips until they hurt or he rammed his tongue into my mouth. But kissing is all my husband has to do most times, and I'm ready. He also taught me how to have an orgasm during intercourse by using one of our hands or in the sideways position by having a thigh pressing against my clit.

"I am crazy mad in love with this man!"

Who Is She?

Second-chance women are 12.5 percent of my survey, and are women who:

- *Were remarried.*
- *Report a high level of sexual satisfaction with the marriage.*

According to the National Center for Health Statistics, over 40 percent of marriages are remarriages, meaning one or both partners has been previously married. Half of men who divorce will remarry within three years and half of women who divorce will remarry within three and one-half years. The second marriage isn't any more likely to last than the first, but the odds for success increase if you make it past the four-year mark. Just as you suspected, the statistics prove men do marry even younger women the second time around, when the average age difference between bride and groom is double what it was in the first marriage. The odds of remarrying do favor the younger divorced woman.

Several studies, including a national survey conducted by the University of Wisconsin, have found that approximately 40 percent of women who divorced in their thirties will not remarry, nor will 70 percent of the women who divorce at forty or beyond.

The numbers would seem to indicate that older women are not desirable as brides, but it is often the women who reject the role. Many older women do not want to be married again. Though they may form long-term monogamous relationships, they elect not to marry their partners. Over half the divorced women in my survey are involved in such relationships, some as live-ins, others not, and they report being satisfied with the arrangement.

Sociologist Andrew Cherlin, Ph.D., made the case in his book, *Marriage, Divorce, Remarriage*, that women with less education, younger children, and lower-paying jobs remarry more quickly than other women do because they are dependent on a husband's income for basic family survival. The majority of the women in my study who were the least satisfied with their second marriages did remarry at a younger age and apparently from economic necessity. The unhappily remarrieds were more likely to consider their work jobs, not careers, and to have less education and earn less money than the happily remarrieds, the second-chance women.

But, happily monogamous women, those partners in long-lasting marriages, are also more likely to have jobs, if they work at all, than careers. Why should financial dependency make for happiness in a first marriage while the reverse seems to be true in a second? Perhaps children are part of the explanation. The financial demands of parenting must weigh heavier on men who are the stepfathers, rather than the fathers, of those children. The mother's inability to care for them independently puts extra pressure on him and the marriage.

Whatever the underlying reasons, financial dependence, too often a motivating factor for remarriage, appears to work against the woman.

But What About the Sex?

Not surprisingly, women who rate their second marriages as generally dissatisfying aren't pleased with the sex. Second-chance women, however, report the sex is much better the second time around. The majority are, in fact, almost euphoric about the difference.

"I wouldn't have married again if the sex weren't great between us," writes a forty-year-old Chicago executive who, like the majority of second-chance women says good sex, not his salary, influenced her choice of a mate. "It was never good with my first husband. I believe many women marry the first time, as I did, for reasons of emotional and financial security. We were brought up to believe you fell in love with a good-looking man who could take care of you—and the sex would follow. It doesn't necessarily. I don't blame myself or him for the first divorce. It doesn't make me a failure. We weren't lucky together, that's all.

"This time I chose wisely. The sex is fantastic. We are very inventive and playful with each other. If I'm in a sexy mood, I can have my first orgasm during the foreplay from the friction of our bodies rubbing together. He excites me enormously. And he's quite skilled. He's found places with his tongue I didn't know I had."

Why is the sex better for second-chance women?

THEY ARE PLEASURE CLAIMERS

Many experienced a sexual reawakening that led them to leave a marriage where their sexual needs weren't being met. They don't idealize their mates or romanticize marriage as they might have done the first time around. Many of them did not claim pleasure, however, until after they were divorced.

THEIR NEEDS FOR SEXUAL FREQUENCY AND VARIETY ARE MORE LIKELY TO BE MET IN THIS MARRIAGE THAN THEY WERE IN PAST SEXUAL RELATIONSHIPS

Women who are sexually dissatisfied with their marriages report not getting enough sex or enough of the kinds of sex they want. These do seem to be the two key sexual issues in most marriages and long-term relationships.

SEX IS MORE IMPORTANT TO THEM THAN IT IS TO THE UNHAPPY SECOND WIVES

Eighty percent say sex was an important consideration in their decision to remarry, whereas less than 30 percent of the unhappy wives say it was a consideration. And, over 60 percent of second-chance women say sex was a contributing factor in the divorce.

"I married at nineteen," writes a fifty-year-old Boston journalist. "I knew nothing. Neither did he. It was a disaster because he was never able to overcome his repressed Catholic upbringing. I got out, because I wanted more, and I found it in my second husband's bed."

THEY HAD OTHER SEXUAL RELATIONSHIPS BETWEEN MARRIAGES

Many of the unhappy second wives had rebounded from one marriage to another. Second-chance women explored their sexuality and developed sexual confidence as single women, waiting an average of four years to remarry.

"I almost married the first man I slept with after my divorce," writes a thirty-six-year-old Minneapolis accountant. "It would have been another mistake because I hadn't yet learned you don't have to marry a man just because you're having sex with him. Five years later I married this man because the sex is wonderful, because I adore him—not because it was the right thing to do under the circumstances."

THEY ARE ABLE TO KEEP DIFFERENCES ABOUT CHILDREN— HIS, HERS, AND SOMETIMES THEIRS—OUT OF THE BEDROOM
Admittedly, their greater incomes give them more power in the marriages. Also, their children are more often older than those of the unhappy wives. Some second-chance women say they postponed marriage until their children were out of the nest, because they wanted to avoid the conflicts clashing loyalties produce.

"I always knew I wanted to marry again eventually," writes a forty-six-year-old investment banker from the Northeast. "I like being married, but I remained single for seven years after my divorce because I wanted to devote myself to my work and my kids. I knew I couldn't handle the kind of three-way pull that happens in second marriages when you are divided between the kids, the work, and the husband—and the husband and kids are going at each other every time you turn around. I've watched some of my friends try to keep all the balls in the air at the same time. It takes more energy than I have ever had! These are the people who truly don't have time for sex.

"I met a wonderful man in my younger daughter's junior year of high school. We had everything—great sex, shared values and interests—and I took a chance on losing him when I asked him to wait another year for marriage. But he did. We're very happy together."

The Monogamy Question
Are spouses who weren't faithful in their first marriages likely to be so in their second?

Second-chance women do report a higher rate of fidelity.

While 50 percent of them had affairs in their first marriages, only 20 percent have had or are having affairs this time. And fewer than that, less than 10 percent, believe their husbands have had sex outside the marriage.

"In my first marriage I had affairs because they put a spark into a listless, lustless love life," writes a thirty-seven-year-old Cleveland entrepreneur. "Whether adultery is morally wrong or not depends on each person's individual conscience. I never felt it was morally wrong—and still don't. In this marriage, however, it isn't necessary.

"The sparks are there. I still occasionally find other men attractive, which I think is natural, but I don't act on the attractions. I love my marriage. The sex is great. Why mess up a good thing?"

And a California artist writes, "In my first marriage I had affairs to get even. He was constantly cheating on me, so I cheated back. It began to seem ridiculous after six years, so I got out.

"To me fidelity is important, though I wouldn't walk out if I discovered my husband had an indiscretion or two. To me, a lot depends on whether we're talking about ongoing affairs or one-night stands. If it's something that lasts, it gets in the way. He travels a lot, and I wonder sometimes if he ever has sex with anyone on the road. I hope he doesn't, and if he does, I hope he's being careful. But I wouldn't leave him over something like that.

"My first husband and I had messy affairs, one right after another. We were trying to tell each other something without talking. This is not how marriage should be. Marriage is supposed to represent a special commitment two people make to each other."

They may be more monogamous this time around, but an overwhelming majority, over 75 percent, of second-chance women believe adultery is acceptable and understandable when the marital sex isn't satisfying.

"Absolutely, it's understandable for anyone to cheat when the sex in the marriage isn't good!" writes a Miami boutique owner on her third, and "this time happily sexual," marriage. "There are many good reasons to stay in a marriage when sex is bad—but no good reason to live in virtual celibacy.

"My first husband was thirty years older than I, and I was only seventeen when we got married. I married him for a home. His idea of sex was a quickie once a week. After a year or two I began to play around.

"He divorced me. Husband number two was twenty years older, also no good in bed, but fortunately he sent me to school so I could support myself. Ten years later when I married for the third, and final time to a man ten years younger than I am, I made a good choice, based on sexual compatibility, not a need for a home."

Second-chance women, like happily monogamous women, enjoy being married, and for them, they say, marriage is the relationship most conducive to sexual fulfillment.

Conclusion: Your Sexual Turning Point?

"When I was thirty I spent a wild night in bed with a man I hardly knew. It was passionate, tender, exciting beyond anything I'd ever experienced—and, I didn't expect it to lead anywhere. That was a real turning point for me, admitting I'd never see him again. I left my hotel room the next morning feeling incredibly sophisticated because I had finally done what men do easily, I'd separated love and sex. After that, I enjoyed sex more, and I was a lot more careful about who I loved."

—a fifty-year-old psychologist

IF WE CHARTED our sexual histories on graph paper, every woman's line would take a different course. While many individual milestones represent common experiences—first orgasm, loss of virginity, and menopause come easily to mind—even they can occur at wildly divergent points on each woman's personal map. Though hers is the bloom to which we relentlessly compare ourselves, we are not all perfect buds, tightly closed until adolescence is nearly over, then opening slowly under the loving touch of the right man, continuing to open predictably to full bloom throughout our thirties and fading gently in late middle age.

In other words, there is no standard female sexual history line ascending slowly up the chart to a peak then descending slowly back down, though that is the guide by which most of us measure the correctness of our experiences and responses. In real life, some lines shoot straight up while others appear flat for years after the so-called budding; some have numerous ups and downs while others remain at a high, or a low, for long stretches. But, in every woman's sexual life, there are milestones beyond the obvious biological ones: The key experiences that, in retrospect, she can recognize as turning points that changed her behavior or her feelings about sex and love.

Our sexual evolution is also affected by social trends and the prevailing myths of our times, by religious teaching and family upbringing, and by negative experiences such as child molestation, rape, abortion, and STDs, even by the childhood memory of having a hand jerked away from our genitals and roughly slapped. A woman's own biochemical development and her initial experiences with a partner have an impact on how she will evolve sexually. Sometimes, in fact, having the right partner at a crucial stage of development can be the determining factor in whether or not a woman will claim pleasure at that point.

Though a man can be a help, we can't blame men when we fail to achieve sexual fulfillment. Too often, we don't tell them what we want and need sexually, and then we blame them for not giving it to us. Too often we give our power away to men, then blame them for misusing it. Pleasure claimers don't expect men to give them pleasure and they don't give their power away—and they make the best partner choices.

I am reluctant to draw conclusions about female sexual evolution in general based on a survey of women who, in addition to indicating more than an average degree of openness about sex by their willingness to participate, also have higher levels of income and education (a great number of respondents are journalists, editors, television executives, and are in advertising or public relations) than a random sampling of women would have. Despite this particular bias, the survey results are reinforced by many similar studies conducted by sexologists, sociologists, psychologists, and other professionals. And, the experiences of these women—regardless of occupation or education—are relevant to those of other women.

Still, rather than draw conclusions, I will make the following observations:

THE TIGHT BUD THEORY OF FEMALE SEXUALITY DOESN'T APPLY TO ALL, OR EVEN TO MOST, WOMEN

Perfect buds composed only 23.3 percent of my survey respondents. Trying to fit all women into the same sexual evolutionary pattern is like trying to put everyone in a size six. It doesn't work. But, one's pattern of *discovering* pleasure does seem to be connected to sexual satisfaction in later life.

Perfect buds, for example, have a high level of sexual satisfaction, particularly in marriage, and are more likely than any other group to be happily monogamous wives. Perhaps that is true because they have a sense of "correctness" about their sexual development, which gives them the self-confidence to express their sexual needs and helps them make good choices in marital partners.

Early bloomers also report high levels of sexual satisfaction, though they are more likely to be happily single than happily married, more often sexual explorers than any other group except wildflowers. Perhaps their strong independent streaks are encouraged by the belief they aren't quite "normal" in their sexual development.

Wildflowers often alternate between flaunting their unconventional sexual behavior and punishing themselves for it. Perhaps their pattern reflects an internal war between their passion and their desire to fit the mold of traditional female sexuality. Wildflowers in later years, however, do report high levels of sexual satisfaction, and are, after age thirty-five, more pragmatic about partner choices, often making good late or second marriages.

Late bloomers generally report the lowest sexual satisfaction levels of all groups at all ages. They also are the least sexually pragmatic, clinging to love fantasies years after other women have recognized them for the romantic illusions they are. Perhaps this group of women most deeply internalized the negative sex messages they received in childhood. When late bloomers do overcome the obstacles in their paths, however, they bloom *brilliantly*. Some of the most moving and erotic sexual ephiphany and reawakening stories came from late bloomers.

WOMEN ARE RESPONSIBLE FOR SENDING MORE NEGATIVE SEX MESSAGES TO OTHER WOMEN THAN MEN ARE

If you've ever been socially excluded from a group of females because your sexual behavior was different from their *professed* behavior, you know the truth of the *Ladies Home Journal*'s motto: *Never underestimate the power of a woman*. The relentless enforcing of group standards starts in junior high school, and it never really ends. The right-wing Christian wife and mother and the left-wing feminist have something in common: They are judgmental and censorious of other women who don't behave according to their own sexual standards. Mom told you to hold out for marriage and your girlfriends are still advising, "Don't have sex too soon or you'll lose the man." Who needs enemies when we have sisters like these?

MORE WOMEN ARE CAPABLE OF SEX WITHOUT LOVE THAN WE REALIZE

The majority of women who admit they can and do separate love and sex also say they pay lip service to the prevailing mores. They tell their friends sex without love is "empty and meaningless," the modern woman's *mea culpa*. And, the more sexually active women say they lie about the extent of their sexual activity, often even to best friends.

The ability to separate sex and love improves the sex lives of women in monogamous marriages and long-term involvements, too. Women who don't withhold sex as punishment or use it as a reward have better sex lives—and better relationships.

THE WOMAN-AS-VICTIM MINDSET THAT PERMEATES OUR SOCIETY ALSO AFFECTS WOMEN'S SEXUALITY

From the women's movement, which has focused almost solely on the negative consequences of heterosexual sex, to the glut of support groups for the loved ones of addicts, composed mostly of women, come messages reinforcing female vulnerability and powerlessness in the world. With few positive sexual images of women in front of us, it's no wonder so many women view sex as another thing men control. We have few female sexual role models, and the ones we do, like Madonna, an independent woman who revels in all aspects of female sexuality, are often ignored or condemned by feminists. Madonna has shown us that a strong woman can choose to play the submissive role, as well as the dominant, in sex games.

LOVE FANTASIES GET IN THE WAY, NOT ONLY IN CLAIMING PLEASURE, BUT IN MAKING GOOD PARTNER CHOICES

The women most caught up in their romantic fantasies also experience the most difficulty in reaching orgasm and in connecting with good men. By idealizing and romanticizing sex, they don't take the steps necessary to ensure good sex, such as touching themselves during intercourse, telling a man what kind of stimulation they need, and taking adequate steps to protect themselves against unwanted pregnancy and disease. By idealizing and fantasizing men, they create fairy-tale heroes out of ordinary men, and blinding themselves to the truths about the men in their lives. They also guarantee they'll be disappointed in the reality of a relationship, which can never match their fantasies.

WOMEN WHO CLAIM SEXUAL PLEASURE HAVE BETTER RELATIONSHIPS WITH MEN

Claiming pleasure is something you do for yourself, not for a man, though it's a happy side effect that most men respond positively to women who are sexually confident and responsive, women who don't put the burden of sex exclusively on them, women who aren't mired in sexual dissatisfaction and anger.

A forty-three-year-old Chicago late bloomer wrote to say that claiming pleasure "softened" her outlook on men:

"I didn't have an orgasm until I was thirty, and they didn't come easily or regularly for me until I was thirty-five and began masturbating. I don't know why I waited so long—good Catholic girl, I suppose—but I did. After I discovered the delights of my own body, I changed. When I was not orgasmic, I went around hating men yet trying to 'get' one, to catch him as my own. I was vague about what I wanted him for, marriage or just to be a regular date? I knew I should have one, and I was angry at them for not choosing me. I was one of those women always bitching about 'men!'

"About six months after I had been masturbating, I caught sight of myself in a mirror when I was going down an escalator in a department store. I was shocked to see a sexy, relaxed woman looking back at me. I smiled at myself and I began smiling at men. I didn't hate them anymore. I wasn't trying to 'get' one anymore. Some of them made me feel soft and warm inside. I forgave them their little flaws because the touch of their skin against mine was so good.

"I have met a wonderful man, and the sex is wonderful, too. I'm still too much the good Catholic girl to describe it for you."

If it hasn't happened to you yet, it *can*.

A note scribbled across the top of a questionnaire from a fifty-five-year-old woman said, "Call me if you need words of encouragement for older women or advice to the young ones! Off to see my man. Have late in life discovered the joy of oral sex, the giving and receiving of it. Love it, love it, love it!!!!"

Bibliography

GENERAL BACKGROUND INFORMATION
AND STATISTICAL DATA

Hite, Shere, *The Hite Report: A Nationwide Study of Female Sexuality*. New York: Dell, 1976.

Kinsey, Alfred, *Sexual Behavior in the Human Female*. W. B. Saunders Co., 1953.

"Kinsey Revisited, Part I: Comparisons of the Sexual Socialization and Sexual Behavior of White Women Over Thirty-three Years," *Archives of Sexual Behavior*, Vol. 17, No. 3 (1988).

"Kinsey Revisited, Part II: Comparisons of the Sexual Socialization and Sexual Behavior of Black Women Over Thirty-three Years," *Archives of Sexual Behavior*, Vol. 17, No. 4 (1988).

Masters, William H., M.D., and Virginia Johnson, *Human Sexual Inadequacy*. Boston: Little Brown, 1970.

Masters, William H., M.D., and Virginia Johnson, *Human Sexual Response*. Boston: Little Brown, 1966.

GENERAL BACKGROUND STUDIES ON WOMEN, SEX
ATTITUDES, AND SEX FANTASIES

"An Analysis of Experimenter Effects on Responses to a Sex Questionnaire," *Archives of Sexual Behavior*, Vol. 17, No. 3 (1988).

"Perceptions of Responsibility and Irresponsible Models of Sexuality: A Correlational Study," *The Journal of Sex Research*, Vol. 23, No. 1 (Feb. 1987), pp. 70–84.

"The Pinney Sexual Satisfaction Inventory," *The Journal of Sex Research*, Vol. 23, No. 2 (May 1987), pp. 233–251.

"Premarital Sexual Behavior and Attitudes Toward Marriage and Divorce Among Young Women as a Function of Their Mothers' Marital Status," *Journal of Marriage and the Family*, No. 48 (Nov. 1986), pp. 757–765.

"Proceptive and Rejective Strategies of U.S. and Canadian College Women," *The Journal of Sex Research*, Vol. 23, No. 4 (Nov. 1987), pp. 455–480.

"The Relationship of Age, Sex Guilt, and Sexual Experience with Female Sexual Fantasies," *The Journal of Sex Research*, Vol. 24, No. 2 (1988), pp. 250–256.

"Sexual Fantasies and Sexual Satisfaction: An Empirical Analysis of Erotic Thought," *The Journal of Sex Research*, Vol. 22, No. 2 (May 1986), pp. 184–205.

"A Survey Instrument for Assessing the Cognitive Association of Sex, Love, and Marriage," *The Journal of Sex Research*, Vol. 22, No. 2 (May 1986), pp. 206–220.

"Volunteer Bias in the Psychophysiological Study of Female Sexuality," *The Journal of Sex Research*, Vol. 22, No. 1 (Feb. 1986), pp. 35–51.

"Women's Attitudes Toward and Experience With Sexually Explicit Materials," *The Journal of Sex Research*, Vol. 24, No. 3 (1988), pp. 161–169.

PART ONE: WHO ARE YOU?

"The Sexually Experienced Woman: Multiple Sex Partners and Sexual Satisfaction," *The Journal of Sex Research*, Vol. 24, No. 3 (April 1988), pp. 141–154.

"Sexual Motivation," *The Journal of Sex Research*, Vol. 23, No. 4 (Nov. 1987), pp. 110–119.

PART TWO: PLEASURES DENIED

"Dating Couples' Disagreements Over the Desired Level of Sexual Intimacy," *The Journal of Sex Research*, Vol. 24, No. 1 (Feb. 1988), pp. 15–29.

"Desired and Experienced Levels of Premarital Affection and Sexual Intercourse During Dating," *The Journal of Sex Research*, Vol. 23, No. 1 (Feb. 1987), pp. 23–33.

"The Dimensionality of Perspectives on Premarital Sex: A Comparison of Guttman and INDSCAL Dimensionality," *The Journal of Sex Research*, Vol. 22, No. 1 (Feb. 1986), pp. 94–107.

"Extrapremarital Intercourse: Attitudes Toward A Neglected Sexual Behavior," *The Journal of Sex Research*, Vol. 24, No. 1 (Jan. 1988), pp. 291–299.

"An Initial Investigation Into a Continuum of Premarital Sexual Pressure," *The Journal of Sex Research*, Vol. 25, No. 2 (May 1988), pp. 255–256.

"Patterns of Premarital Cohabitation Among Never-Married Women in the United States," *Journal of Marriage and the Family*, Vol. 49, No. 3 (Aug. 1987), pp. 483–497.

"Sexual Behavior of Cohabitors: A Comparison of Three Independent Samples," *The Journal of Sex Research*, Vol. 22, No. 4 (Nov. 1986), pp. 492–513.

PART THREE: ORGASMS

Barbach, Lonnie, *For Yourself: The Fulfillment of Female Sexuality* (New York: Doubleday, 1975).

"Female Orgasmic Experience: A Subjective Study," *Archives of Sexual Behavior*, Vol. 13, No. 2 (1984), pp. 155–174.

"Female Orgasm via Penile Stimulation: A Criterion of Adequate Sexual Functioning?" *Journal of Sex and Marital Therapy*, Vol. 12, No. 1 (Spring 1986), pp. 60–64.

"The 'G Spot' and 'Female Ejaculation': A Current Appraisal," *Journal of Sex and Marital Therapy*, Vol. 12, No. 3 (Fall 1986), pp. 79–91.

Meshorer, Marc, and Judith Meshorer, *Ultimate Pleasures: The Secrets of Easily Orgasmic Women*. New York: St. Martin's Press, 1986.

"Orgasm in Women in the Laboratory: Quantitative Studies on Duration, Intensity, Latency, and Vaginal Blood Flow," *Archives of Sexual Behavior*, Vol. 14, No. 5 (1985), pp. 439–448.

"Pattern of Female Sexual Arousal During Sleep and Waking: Vaginal Thermo-Conductance Studies," *Archives of Sexual Behavior*, Vol. 12, No. 2 (1983), pp. 97–122.

PART FOUR: PLEASURE CLAIMERS

"Effects of Sex Guilt, Repression, Sexual 'Arousability' and Sexual Experience on Female Sexual Arousal During Erotica and Fantasy," *Journal of Personality and Social Psychology*, Vol. 49, No. 1 (1985), pp. 177–187.

"Sex Role Orientation and Intimacy Status in Men and Women," *Sex Roles*, Vol. 11, No. 5/6 (1984), pp. 112–121.

"Social Desirability in the Bedroom: Role of Approval Motivation in Sexual Relationships," *Sex Roles*, Vol. 11, No. 3/4 (1984), pp. 303–313.

PART FIVE: WOMEN WHO HAVE LOST PLEASURE

"Endocrine and Metabolic Changes of Menopause," *Medical Aspects of Human Sexuality*, Vol. 22, No. 1 (Feb. 1988), pp. 74–81.

"Gynecology and Sexuality in Middle-aged Women," *Women and Health*, Vol. 13 (1987–88), pp. 67–80.

Appendix: The Questionnaire

I AM WORKING on a book about the sex lives of American women; and I need you to help by answering some questions.

My name is Susan Crain Bakos. I write frequently on sex and relationships for *Cosmopolitan*, *Woman*, *New Woman*, and other magazines. In addition, I have been a contributing editor and advice columnist for *Penthouse Forum* magazine and am the author of *Dear Superlady of Sex: Men Talk About Their Hidden Desires, Secret Fears, and Number-One Sex Need*, to be published by St. Martin's Press in October 1991. The results of this questionnaire will be included in a book on women and sex, also to be published by St. Martin's in 1992. Your input will be invaluable. (Use the backs of sheets for your answers if necessary.) I want as many responses as possible from women of all ages and every part of the country. Please copy the questionnaire and pass it along to friends. Include your name and phone number if you would like to be interviewed at length by phone. Thank you for your help!

The Questionnaire

BACKGROUND INFORMATION:

Age _____ Where do you live? _____

Marital (and/or Cohabiting) history _____

Religious affiliation _____ Race _____

Income (personal and/or family) _____

Job _____

Number of pregnancies ending in: live birth _____

miscarriage _____ abortion _____

Number of sexual partners _____

Educational background _____

Have you ever been a victim of rape? _____

Incest? _____

Other childhood sexual abuse? _____

Workplace sexual harassment? _____ Wife abuse? _____

Please explain on back, if you are able to do so.

PRIMARY EXPERIENCES:

At what age did you first masturbate? _____

Do you masturbate now? _____ How often? _____

Do you reach orgasm via masturbation? _____

At what age did you learn about sex? _____

And how? _____

_____

_____

What was your family's prevailing attitude toward sex? _____

_____

_____

At what age did you lose your virginity? _____

Experience your first orgasm? _____ With a partner or via masturbation? _____

_____

Tell me about that first experience. _____

_____

_____

Are you bisexual or have you had a lesbian experience? _____

_____

Are you sexually active now? _____

With a partner or via masturbation or both? _____

How often do you have sex? _____

Is that satisfactory? _____

ATTRACTION:

What is sexual chemistry? _____

How do you know if you have it? _____

What attracts you to a man? _____

_____

What inspires you to have sex with a man? _____

_____

Would you say your motives are more often physical or emotional?

_____

_____

How large a role does sex play in your choice of a male partner?

_____

_____

FOREPLAY:

What constitutes sufficient foreplay for you? _____
_____
_____
_____

Do you usually get that from your partner(s)? _____
If not, why not? _____

INTERCOURSE:

How long does it last? _____
Is that satisfactory? _____
Do you achieve orgasm this way? _____
Is one position more pleasureable for you, and if so, which?
_____
_____

Does your lovemaking include a variety of positions? _____
Who usually initiates sex? _____
Approximately how often do you initiate, if he usually does?
_____

What do you like best about intercourse? _____
_____

ORAL SEX:

How often does your partner(s) perform cunnilingus? _____
Is that satisfactory? _____
Are you orgasmic this way? _____
How often do you perform fellatio? _____
Does he reach orgasm this way? _____
Do you enjoy performing fellatio? _____

SEXUAL VARIATIONS:

Do you participate in anal sex? How often? _____

_____

Are you orgasmic this way? _____

Do you participate in other sexual variations, including spanking, bondage, S&M? If so, please describe _____

_____

Do you use a vibrator or other sex toy? _____

Watch X-rated videos? _____

Please describe your favorite or most prevalent sexual fantasies.

_____

_____

_____

_____

Are you orgasmic via fantasy? _____

Have you ever had an orgasm from dreaming? _____

NEGATIVE CONSEQUENCES OF SEX:

Have you ever had a Sexually Transmitted Disease (STD)?

_____

If so, please describe. _____

_____

Are you concerned about STDs? _____

How does that concern impact upon your sexual behavior?

_____

Fewer partners? _____

Choose partners more carefully? _____

Abstain from sex? _____

Use condoms? _____ Other? _____

What form of contraception do you use? _____

Do you use it regularly? _____

If an abortion, STD, rape, or other experience has had a negative impact on your sexuality, please describe. _____

_____

_____

SINGLE WOMEN:

Are you currently involved with someone? _____

If not, have you had trouble finding sex partners in the past year?

_____

_____

Have you ended a relationship because he wouldn't commit?

_____

Do you want a committed relationship? _____

How soon do you go to bed with a new man? _____

Is sex generally satisfactory for you? _____

If not, why not? _____

COHABITATING WOMEN:

Do you want to get married? _____ Does he? _____

Is the sex satisfactory? _____

If not, why not? _____

Is this a monogamous relationship? _____

Has he ever forced sex upon you or physically hurt you? _____

_____

MARRIED WOMEN:

Have either of you had an affair? _____

If you did, why? _____

_____

How has an affair affected the marriage? _____

_____

Are you satisfied with marital sex? _____

If not, why not? _____

What do you do to keep sex exciting? _____

_____

Have you ever been in sex therapy? _____

SECOND MARRIAGES:

How does this marriage compare, sexually, to the first? _____

_____

PERFORMANCE FACTORS:

Have you ever had difficulty achieving orgasm? _____

_____

Are you multiply orgasmic? _____

Has your partner ever experienced impotence, premature ejaculation, retarded ejaculation, or other problem? _____

_____

How have you handled it? _____

ATTITUDES:

Do you think sex is wrong if you're not in love? _____

Or not married? _____ Or not engaged? _____

Is adultery wrong? _____

Acceptable or understandable under certain circumstances?

_____

Such as? _____

Is sex on a first date okay? _____

Have you ever had sex on a first date? _____

Do you risk losing a man by having sex too soon? _____

_____

Should sex only be an expression of love? _____

Or can you enjoy sex for physical pleasure alone? _____

Could you have sex with someone you didn't consider commit-

ment material? _____

A much younger man? _____

A man of a different race? _____

A less educated or less affluent man? _____

Could you marry one of these men? _____

Do you think women lose interest in sex at a certain age? _____

_____

What age? _____

What do you think men want from sex? _____

_____

_____

What would you change about men as lovers? _____

_____

Do feelings about your body affect sexual desire? _____

_____

Do you have sex during menstruation? _____

Has a hysterectomy, menopause, or other gynecological problem or surgery affected your sexuality, and how? _____
_____
_____

How has aging changed your sex life? _____
_____

How would you describe a "best ever" sexual experience? ____
_____
_____
_____
_____
_____

ADDITIONAL COMMENTS?

NONFICTION PERENNIALS
FROM ST. MARTIN'S PAPERBACKS

25 THINGS YOU CAN DO TO BEAT THE RECESSION OF THE 1990s
Alan Weintraub and Pamela Weintraub
_____ 92646-4 $3.95 U.S./$4.95 Can.

THE PEOPLE'S PHARMACY
Joe Graedon
_____ 91762-7 $5.95 U.S.   _____ 91763-5 $6.95 Can.

HOW TO STAY LOVERS WHILE RAISING YOUR CHILDREN
Anne Mayer
_____ 92715-0 $4.99 U.S./$5.99 Can.

76 WAYS TO GET ORGANIZED FOR CHRISTMAS
Bonnie McCullough & Bev Cooper
_____ 91253-6 $2.95 U.S.   _____ 91254-4 $3.95 Can.

YOU CAN SAVE THE ANIMALS: 50 Things to Do Right Now
Dr. Michael W. Fox and Pamela Weintraub
_____ 92521-2 $3.95 U.S./$4.95 Can.

COOKING? DIETING? HERE'S HELP!